INTERPRETING THE BIBLE

Introduction to Biblical Hermeneuutics

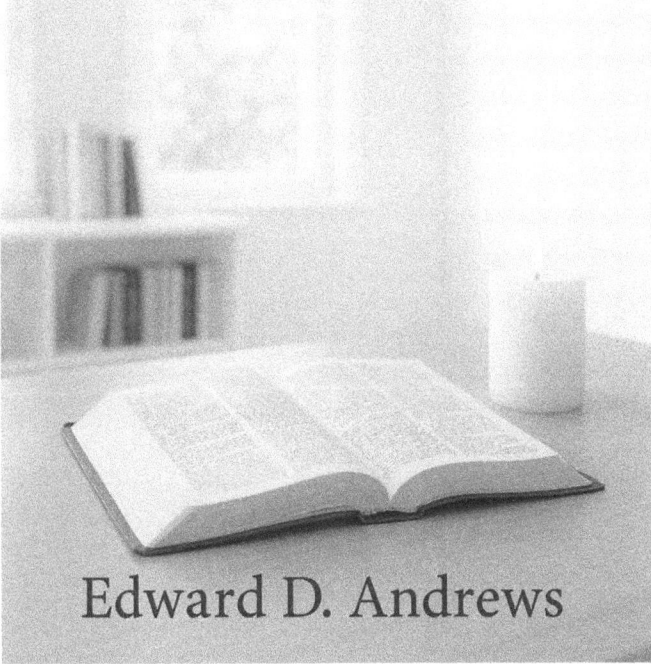

Edward D. Andrews

INTERPRETING THE BIBLE

Introduction to Biblical Hermeneutics

UPDATED EDITION

Edward D. Andrews

Christian Publishing House

Cambridge, Ohio

CHRISTIAN
PUBLISHING
HOUSE

FOUNDED 2005

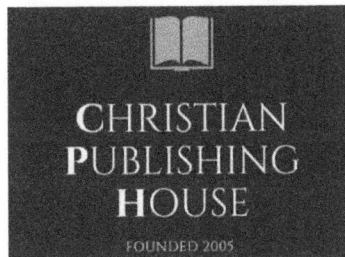

INTERPRETING THE BIBLE Introduction to Biblical Hermeneutics by Edward D. Andrews

ISBN-10: 1945757078

ISBN-13: 978-1945757075

Table of Contents

Edward D. Andrews

Preface

The Bible is the inspired, inerrant, and all-sufficient Word of God. It is Jehovah's revelation to mankind, given through human authors who were "carried along by the Holy Spirit" (2 Peter 1:21). Because it is God's Word, it demands careful handling. The responsibility of the church is not to impose human ideas onto Scripture but to discover, with reverence, the meaning that God's Spirit-inspired authors intended to communicate to their original audiences. This is the task of hermeneutics.

This book was written to equip believers with the tools to interpret Scripture faithfully. Our approach is grounded firmly in the historical-grammatical method, which seeks to understand the Bible in its historical setting, literary form, and grammatical detail. We reject allegorizing, typology invented by later interpreters, and all forms of speculation that separate the text from its inspired meaning. Only the biblical authors, under the Spirit's direction, had the right to employ allegory or typology. Our role is not to reinvent their methods but to submit to their meaning.

Throughout these chapters, the reader will find careful attention to genre, context, and authorial intent. We examine how to read narrative, poetry, prophecy, wisdom, parables, hyperbole, epistles, and idioms—not as disconnected writings, but as parts of the unified revelation of God. Each section follows a deliberate rhythm: clear exposition, application for the church today, and safeguards against misinterpretation. At the end of every chapter, *Review Questions* provide reinforcement, while *Exercises in Interpretation* (beginning in Chapter 5) guide the reader in applying principles to actual passages of Scripture.

This book is not designed for the academy alone, though it is rooted in rigorous scholarship. It is written for pastors who proclaim the Word, teachers who instruct the church, and every believer who longs to handle the Scriptures rightly (2 Timothy 2:15). Our prayer is that it will help readers develop both skill and reverence, knowing that interpretation is not merely an intellectual exercise but an act of obedience to the God who speaks.

We also write with urgency. In every generation, the church is threatened by distortion of the truth—whether by careless handling, human tradition, or worldly philosophies. Sound interpretation is one of the great safeguards Jehovah has given His people. When believers rightly understand the Word, they are strengthened in faith, guarded from error, and equipped for every good work (2 Timothy 3:16–17).

We commend this volume to those who desire to hear the voice of God clearly in the pages of Scripture. May it stir a greater love for the Word, a deeper commitment to truth, and a renewed resolve to proclaim Christ faithfully until He comes.

Edward D. Andrews

Author of over 220 book and Chief Translator of the Updated American Standard Version (UASV)

Edward D. Andrews

INTRODUCTION

The Bible stands alone among all writings in human history. It is not merely a collection of ancient religious documents or a treasury of moral reflections, but the very Word of the living God, "breathed out by God and profitable for teaching, for reproof, for correction, and for training in righteousness" (2 Timothy 3:16). For this reason, how we interpret Scripture is of eternal consequence. A right interpretation leads to truth, clarity, and faithful obedience; a wrong interpretation leads to distortion, error, and spiritual ruin.

From the beginning, Jehovah has entrusted His Word to His people with the expectation that they would understand it and live by it. When Ezra and the Levites read from the Law and explained its meaning, "they gave the sense, so that the people understood the reading" (Nehemiah 8:8). When the apostle Paul charged Timothy to "rightly handle the word of truth" (2 Timothy 2:15), he made plain that interpretation requires diligence and reverence. The same responsibility falls on the church today.

Yet interpretation is not without its dangers. Through the centuries, many have twisted the Scriptures to suit their opinions. Some have imposed allegories and hidden meanings never intended by the inspired authors. Others have sought mystical impressions or "inner voices" that bypass the text itself. Still others have treated the Bible as a mere historical artifact, stripping it of its divine authority. Each of these errors results from neglecting the fundamental truth that meaning is determined by the inspired author in his historical, cultural, and literary context, and that the task of the interpreter is to uncover and submit to that meaning.

This book is written to equip believers with the tools to interpret the Bible faithfully. Our method throughout is the historical-grammatical approach. This means we study the words of Scripture in their grammatical form, within their historical and cultural background, and in the literary structure in which the Spirit inspired them. We ask: *What did the author intend to communicate to his original audience?* That

8

meaning is singular, fixed, and authoritative. From that foundation, we draw out applications for doctrine, worship, and life.

Each chapter of this book addresses a different genre or form of biblical literature. We begin with foundational matters—what hermeneutics is, why it is necessary, and how terms such as *meaning, implication, significance,* and *context* shape interpretation. We then move through genres—narrative, covenant law, poetry, psalms, proverbs, prophecy, idioms, parables, hyperbole, and epistles. In each case, the goal is not to impose meaning but to recover what the inspired author communicated.

The structure of each chapter follows a consistent rhythm: a clear exposition of principles, illustrations from Scripture, clarification for modern application, and a section on why the matter is vital for the life of the church. To reinforce learning, every chapter concludes with *Review Questions,* and beginning in Chapter 5, *Exercises in Interpretation* allow readers to practice applying the principles to actual biblical texts.

This book is intended for a wide audience. Pastors will find it a reliable aid in preaching. Teachers will find it a guide for leading others in Scripture. Believers at every level of maturity will find it a companion in daily study. The Bible was not given to scholars alone but to the people of God, and every Christian is called to study it with diligence and faith.

The times in which we live demand clarity. Confusion about Scripture abounds, and the church is often pressured to adapt the Bible to fit cultural expectations. Yet God's Word is eternal and unchanging. The task before us is not to reshape the Scriptures but to be reshaped by them. By learning to interpret rightly, we protect ourselves from error, strengthen the church, and magnify the glory of Christ.

It is our prayer that this book will help believers approach the Scriptures with reverence, skill, and joy. May it stir up confidence in the sufficiency of God's Word, sharpen discernment in interpretation, and cultivate obedience to its truth. Above all, may it lead readers to know Christ more fully, for He is the center of all God's revelation and the hope of all who believe.

Edward D. Andrews

Part 1 The General Rules of Interpretation

CHAPTER 1 An Introduction to Hermeneutics

The Nature and Necessity of Biblical Interpretation

The study of hermeneutics—the discipline of interpreting Scripture—is not a matter reserved only for theologians or scholars; it is essential for every Christian who seeks to understand and apply the Word of God accurately. While the term itself may sound academic, its meaning is straightforward and deeply practical. At its core, hermeneutics refers to the principles and methods by which one explains, translates, or interprets what has been written. When applied to the Bible, hermeneutics becomes the God-ordained pathway through which the believer discerns the Author's intent and submits to His revealed truth.

The Meaning of Hermeneutics

The English word "hermeneutics" is derived from a family of Greek words built on *hermēneuō*, meaning "to interpret" or "to translate." This concept appears throughout the New Testament, not only in direct discussions of interpretation but also in the practice of explaining spiritual truths. For example, when the Ethiopian official was reading Isaiah, he confessed that he could not understand the passage without someone to guide him (Acts 8:30–31). Philip then explained the Scripture, showing that the prophecy pointed to Jesus Christ. This account illustrates the very essence of hermeneutics: taking the inspired Word and unfolding its meaning so that the hearer grasps what God has communicated.

In another instance, the apostle Paul emphasizes the importance of intelligible interpretation in the gathered assembly: "Unless you speak intelligible words with your tongue, how will what is spoken be understood? For you will be speaking into the air" (1 Corinthians 14:9). Later in the same chapter, he insists that if someone speaks in another language, there must be an interpreter so that the church may be built up (1 Corinthians 14:28). These examples underscore that interpretation—whether of Scripture or speech—serves the purpose of clarity, understanding, and edification.

The Necessity of Interpretation

The necessity of hermeneutics arises from the very nature of Scripture. The Bible is God's inspired Word (2 Timothy 3:16), but it was communicated through human languages—Hebrew, Aramaic, and Greek—across different cultures, contexts, and centuries. For modern readers, this creates barriers of language, history, and worldview that must be bridged. Hermeneutics provides the means to cross these barriers without distorting the text or imposing foreign ideas upon it.

The apostle Peter warned that Scripture is not a matter of "one's own interpretation" (2 Peter 1:20–21). This does not mean believers are forbidden to interpret, but rather that interpretation must align with the Spirit's inspired intent, not human imagination. Since "men spoke from God as they were carried along by the Holy Spirit," the interpreter's task is to uncover that original meaning, not invent new ones. Without sound principles of interpretation, Scripture can be twisted to suit human preferences—a danger already evident in the early church, as Paul cautioned against those who distorted God's Word (2 Corinthians 4:2).

The Goal of Biblical Hermeneutics

Hermeneutics is not merely about acquiring knowledge or mastering a method; it is about rightly handling the Word of truth. Paul urged Timothy, "Do your best to present yourself to God as one approved, a worker who has no need to be ashamed, rightly handling the word of truth" (2 Timothy 2:15). The phrase "rightly handling" (*orthotomounta* in Greek) carries the idea of cutting straight, as one would in laying a path. The faithful interpreter cuts a straight line through Scripture—avoiding distortions, detours, or careless handling—so that the meaning flows clearly and directly from the inspired text.

The goal of hermeneutics, therefore, is twofold:

1. To understand the meaning God intended when He inspired His Word.

2. To apply that meaning faithfully in doctrine, worship, and daily living.

The Practical Relevance for Believers

Some imagine that interpretation belongs only in seminaries or academic circles, yet the Bible itself demonstrates that every believer must engage in hermeneutics. Consider how Ezra and the Levites, after the return from exile, read the Law to the people: "They read from the book, from the Law of God, clearly, and they gave the sense, so that the people understood the reading" (Nehemiah 8:8). Here we see the pattern of true interpretation: the Word is read, explained, and understood, producing obedience in the lives of God's people. Hermeneutics is therefore not optional—it is the pathway to understanding, faith, and transformation.

Author, Text, And Reader: How Meaning Is Fixed and Understanding Grows

Hermeneutics requires precision about the parts that make communication possible. Biblical interpretation does not float in abstraction; it is anchored in a real Author who wills to communicate, a real written Text that encodes that meaning in shareable symbols, and real Readers who are responsible to grasp and obey what the Author willed to say. Remove any one of these and interpretation collapses. Because Scripture is the Spirit-inspired Word authored through chosen men, this triad is not optional; it is Jehovah's ordained pathway for knowledge and obedience.

The Communication Triad in Scripture

Biblical revelation repeatedly displays the full communication chain—sender, message, receiver—so that no one mistakes what is happening when Scripture speaks.

Authorial Purpose Is Explicit. Luke announces why he wrote: "it seemed good... to write an orderly account... that you may have certainty concerning the things you have been taught" (Luke 1:1–4). Luke's purpose fixes the trajectory: he wills to produce certainty through a carefully arranged narrative. John states likewise: "these are written so that you may believe that Jesus is the Christ, the Son of God, and that believing you may have life in His name" (John 20:31). Authorial intent is not hidden behind the text; it stands in front of it, governing how the text is to be read.

The Text Is the Authorized Medium. Jeremiah dictated; Baruch wrote; the king heard; and Jehovah commanded that the words be read to the people again (Jer. 36:1–8, 27–32). Meaning is not housed in a mystic experience detached from writing; it is bound to the written column of words that can be recopied and reread.

Readers Are Responsible Receivers. The Bereans are commended because they received the message "with all eagerness, examining the Scriptures daily" (Acts 17:11). Scripture expects readers to engage the text carefully and consistently.

Jehovah Binds Meaning to Words. "Seek and read from the book of Jehovah" (Isa. 34:16); "The unfolding of Your words gives light" (Ps. 119:130). Jehovah has chosen words—not private impressions—to convey His will.

The triad is therefore not negotiable: the Author wills a determinate meaning, the Text encodes and preserves it, and Readers are obligated to understand and obey that meaning.

Where Meaning Comes From: The Case For Authorial Intention

Meaning is what the author willed to communicate by the words he chose in their context. This is not academic hair-splitting; it is the only position that honors how the Bible itself speaks.

Scripture Presents Itself As Intentional Communication. The biblical writers repeatedly state their purpose. Moses wrote and commanded public reading so Israel "may hear and learn to fear Jehovah" (Deut. 31:9–13). Ezra's life was ordered "to study the Law of Jehovah, and to do it and to teach" (Ezra 7:10). Paul wrote letters and expected them to be read, circulated, and understood (Col. 4:16). These are conscious acts of will that bind meaning to what was written.

Jehovah Ties Efficacy To His Purposed Meaning. His Word "shall accomplish that which I purpose, and shall succeed in the thing for which I sent it" (Isa. 55:11). Purpose precedes and governs accomplishment. To sever the text from the author's purpose is to contradict Jehovah's own assertion.

Jesus Holds Readers Accountable To The Intended Sense. When disputants misread Scripture, He does not congratulate their creativity; He rebukes them: "You are mistaken, because you know neither the Scriptures nor the power of God" (Matt. 22:29). Responsibility falls on readers to discover what the Author meant, not to invent meanings.

The Apostolic Warning Assumes A Fixed Authorial Meaning. Some distort Scripture "to their own destruction" (2 Pet. 3:16). You cannot twist a text unless it has a determinate meaning that you are distorting.

Thus, the interpreter's fundamental task is to recover, from the text itself in its historical and literary context, the meaning the human writer willed to communicate. Only when that is understood can faithful application proceed.

Text-Centered Autonomy: Gains Acknowledged, Boundaries Drawn

A text-focused approach rightly reminds us to read the words actually present, to notice structure, literary features, and the final, canonical form. Close reading is indispensable. Yet treating the text as semantically autonomous—cut loose from its author—is a fatal move for biblical interpretation.

Texts Are Vehicles, Not Originators, Of Meaning. Letters, vowel points, and syntactic arrangements are inanimate marks. They convey meaning; they do not originate it. Meaning is a property of persons. Scripture models this repeatedly: "The Spirit of Jehovah spoke by me, and His word was on my tongue" (2 Sam. 23:2). The words bear meaning because a Speaker willed to speak.

Scriptural Purpose Statements Forbid Autonomy. When John announces "these are written so that you may believe" (John 20:31), he does not leave us free to treat his Gospel as an aesthetic object to be admired without reference to authorial aim. His purpose limits legitimate readings and excludes others.

Canonical Intertext Does Not Undermine But Clarifies Authorial Sense. When one inspired writer sheds light on another, it is not to replace the original author's meaning but to expose and confirm it within the canon's unity. Isaiah's proclamations, for instance, illuminate Gospel events precisely because both share Jehovah's unified saving purpose, not because texts evolve meanings independent of their authors.

Autonomy of the text sounds sophisticated but replaces the Author's will with a mute artifact. It produces either skepticism about knowing what Scripture means or an interpretive elitism that smuggles in foreign agendas under the guise of "what the text does."

Reader-Centered Relativism: Contributions Noted, Errors Exposed

Reader-centered methods make several useful observations: readers bring preunderstandings, communities influence interpretation, and engagement matters. Scripture itself calls for active, thoughtful reading (Rev. 1:3; 1 Tim. 4:13). But when the reader is enthroned as the determiner of meaning, the authority of Scripture is surrendered.

Preunderstanding Is Real—But It Is Not Sovereign. "The heart is deceitful above all things" (Jer. 17:9). Because readers are fallen, their preferences cannot govern meaning. Scripture corrects readers; readers do not correct Scripture.

Reader Response Cannot Produce Multiple True Meanings. Proverbs opens by declaring that its sayings are given "to know wisdom and instruction... to understand words of insight" (Prov. 1:1–6). The goal is understanding what was given, not manufacturing equally valid alternatives. If every reading is equally valid, rebuke for error (Matt. 22:29) becomes nonsensical.

Communal Consensus Is Helpful But Not Decisive. Congregational reading and qualified teachers are appointed by Christ for the church's good (Eph. 4:11–12; Heb. 13:7). Yet communities can err (Hos. 4:6). The standard is not group preference but the Author's intended meaning encoded in Scripture.

Reader-centered relativism confuses **application**, which rightly varies across cases, with **meaning**, which is fixed. It elevates personal resonance over apostolic intention, turning revelation into a mirror for the self rather than a window into the Author's world.

The Role of the Text: Shareable Symbols, Stable Sense, Contextual Control

Because Jehovah wills to be understood, He ordained that His Word be inscripturated in the ordinary languages of real audiences. That design principle yields several non-negotiables.

17

Shareability Of Language. Biblical authors write in words, idioms, and grammar their audiences share. Kings were to copy the law and read it "all the days of his life" (Deut. 17:18–19). The words must be intelligible to the people for them to "hear" and "learn." When Scripture speaks of Jehovah, covenant, sacrifice, repentance, faith, righteousness, and resurrection, it does so within the semantic ranges of Hebrew, Aramaic, and Greek as used by real people in real settings. Interpreters must therefore study vocabulary and syntax as the original audiences would have used and understood them.

Context Determines Specific Sense. Words possess ranges of meaning, but sentences and paragraphs constrain which sense is in play. "The fear of Jehovah is the beginning of knowledge" (Prov. 1:7) does not speak of terror but of reverent submission because the wisdom context demands it. The immediate sentence, the paragraph, the book's structure, and the entire canon each tighten the circle until only one sense remains that accords with the author's purpose.

Genre Governs Expectations. Poetry compresses and parallels; narrative recounts; law commands; prophecy announces and calls; wisdom instructs in patterns of life; apocalyptic unveils. Psalmic parallelism (e.g., Ps. 19:7–9) intensifies or complements ideas rather than multiplying meanings. To read a parable as if it were courtroom historiography or a proverb as if it were an unconditional legal statute is to violate the author's chosen form.

Literary Features Serve Meaning. Chiasm, inclusio, repeated motifs, and discourse markers are not ornaments; they are communicative strategies. Mark's fast-paced "immediately" drives narrative urgency; John's "signs" structure belief; Matthew's fulfillment formulae tie events to prophetic expectation. These are not self-interpreting symbols; they are the author's tools for guiding the reader to the intended sense.

Clarity Is Promised—Not Exhaustive Ease. "The law of Jehovah is perfect... making wise the simple" (Ps. 19:7). Scripture is clear in its message of salvation and godliness, though some matters require hard work (2 Pet. 3:16 acknowledges difficulty, not indeterminacy). Difficulty invites diligent study, not surrender to subjectivism.

The text is therefore a stable, shareable medium that reliably carries the author's meaning to readers who will do the honest labor of grammatical-historical exegesis.

The Role Of The Reader: Humble Posture, Responsible Method, Obedient Practice

Readers matter—not as creators of meaning but as servants of understanding. Scripture outlines the reader's responsibilities.

Adopt The Right Posture. Reverence and humility are foundational. "Open my eyes, that I may behold wondrous things out of Your law" (Ps. 119:18). This is not an appeal for private revelation beyond Scripture; it is an appeal for teachability before the written Word. The same psalm instructs, "Your word is a lamp to my feet and a light to my path" (Ps. 119:105). The light is the Word itself.

Practice Diligent, Canon-Conscious Reading. Public and private reading is commanded and blessed (1 Tim. 4:13; Rev. 1:3). Colossians directs the circulation of letters (Col. 4:16), modeling the value of comparing Scripture with Scripture. Romans affirms that what was "written in former days was written for our instruction" (Rom. 15:4), inviting us to read the whole canon as coherent revelation.

Use Sound Method.

Observation. Note terms, connectors, pronouns, verb tenses, quotations, and structure.

Word Studies With Discipline. Establish the lexical range from appropriate lexicons, then choose the contextual sense. Avoid illegitimate totality transfer (reading all possible meanings into one occurrence) and etymologizing (deriving meaning from word-parts rather than usage).

Syntax And Discourse. Clause relationships, purpose/result markers, contrasts, inclusio, and thematic development often decide the meaning.

Historical Setting. Identify author, audience, date, geography, customs, and presenting problem using reliable background sources.

Genre-Sensitive Reading. Poetry uses imagery and parallelism; wisdom gives general maxims; narrative shows by events; prophecy announces divine verdicts and promises; parables teach through comparison; epistles argue by proposition and support.

Canonical Context. Later revelation never contradicts earlier; it clarifies and fulfills it. John 5:39 affirms that Scripture bears unified witness to Christ; that unity safeguards against readings that isolate a verse from the redemptive plan.

Embrace The Hermeneutical Spiral (From Parts To Whole And Back). We read words in sentences, sentences in paragraphs, paragraphs in books, and books within the canon. As our understanding of the whole sharpens, it refines our grasp of the parts, which in turn further clarifies the whole. This is not relativism; it is the normal way understanding matures under the constraint of the text.

Obey The Meaning You Have Understood. Scripture is given to be kept, not merely parsed. "Blessed is the one who reads aloud the words… and those who hear, and who keep what is written" (Rev. 1:3). James calls us to be doers of the Word (Jas. 1:22–25). Understanding that does not lead to obedience is self-deception.

Readers, then, are neither passive nor sovereign. They are active servants whose minds and wills are bound to the Author's meaning as carried by the text.

One Meaning, Many Faithful Implications

Meaning is singular; implications are many. The author wills a specific sense in his context, but that sense often carries principled implications into situations not explicitly named in the text.

A Clear Example Of Principle And Implications. The eighth commandment forbids stealing (Exod. 20:15). The meaning is fixed: taking what is not yours is forbidden. Yet the implications extend naturally to modern forms of theft never envisioned in the ancient setting—identity theft, digital piracy, fraudulent accounting, and plagiarism. These are not new meanings; they are natural applications of the same authorially willed principle.

Jesus Models Authoritative Unfolding Of Implications. When our Lord confronts legalistic reductions of God's commands, He exposes their principled reach rather than altering their meaning (cf. Matt. 23:23–28). He insists on the heart-level obedience those commands always required. This is not allegory or creativity; it is faithful implication.

Guardrails For Implications.

1. The implication must genuinely arise from the author's meaning and purpose, not from cultural preference.

2. It must cohere with the rest of Scripture. Jehovah does not contradict Himself.

3. It must be framed at the right level of generality. Overly narrow implications multiply rules; overly vague ones dissolve concrete obedience.

Recognizing the difference between **meaning** and **implication** protects the church from both interpretive anarchy and wooden literalism. It allows Scripture's fixed sense to speak wisely to changing circumstances.

Addressing Common Objections to Authorial Intention

Objection 1: "We cannot access the author's mind."

We are not asked to reproduce the writer's private experiences. We are called to understand what he publicly willed to communicate in the words he wrote. Luke, John, Moses, and Paul place their meaning in the public domain by committing it to writing and often stating their purpose. Readers are responsible for that accessible, textual meaning.

Objection 2: "Ancient authors are too distant for modern readers."

Cultural distance is real, not decisive. The image-bearing humanity we share bridges much. The Bible expects cross-generational understanding: "what was written in former days was written for our instruction" (Rom. 15:4). Moreover, Scripture's clarity and the ordinary tools of language study enable faithful understanding across time.

Objection 3: "Literature should be read differently— meanings multiply."

Scripture never grants permission to detach literature from authorial will. Poets and narrators title their works, frame prologues, and signal purposes precisely to steer readers. The Psalms and the Prophets announce what they intend to proclaim. Treating biblical literature as if it floats free of intention denies how authors actually write and how Jehovah binds His Word to His purpose (Isa. 55:11).

Objection 4: "Communities should decide what readings are valuable."

The church's teachers are gifts for equipping (Eph. 4:11–12), and the gathered church is a vital context for reading. Yet community consensus is not the standard of truth. When communities stray, Scripture stands in judgment over them (Mal. 2:7–9). The only safe authority is the Author's meaning in the written Word.

Practical Commitments For Interpreters Who Honor Authorial Meaning

Pledge To Seek The Author's Willed Sense. Begin every passage by asking, "What did this writer intend to communicate to his original audience here?"

Submit Method To Purpose. Let purpose statements and structural signals govern your reading.

Read In Canonical Company. Use Scripture to interpret Scripture responsibly, allowing later and earlier revelation to illuminate, not overwrite.

Work At Grammar And History. Words in sentences, sentences in paragraphs, paragraphs in books, books in the canon—anchored in real times and places.

Distinguish Meaning From Implications. Apply principled sense broadly without inventing new meanings.

Cultivate Humble Courage. Humility before the text; courage to reject fashionable readings that dethrone the Author.

Aim At Obedience. Knowledge divorced from obedience is rebellion. Keep what is written (Rev. 1:3).

Case Study: Author, Text, Reader In Action (Without Reusing Your Verses)

Consider the healing of the paralytic lowered through the roof (Mark 2:1–12).

Authorial Aim. Mark's opening (1:1) and the pericope's climax ("the Son of Man has authority on earth to forgive sins") reveal the intent: to display Jesus' divine authority to forgive.

Textual Features. The narrative tension (forgiveness pronounced before healing), the scribes' inner reasoning, Jesus' public demonstration, and the crowd's response all direct the reader to the theological point.

Reader's Role. A responsible reader resists reducing the account to architectural trivia or mere moralism about persistence. Those elements may be present as subject matter, but Mark willed to magnify Christ's authority. Application then flows—assurance of forgiveness rests in Him, and the church proclaims that authority today. This honors one meaning while acknowledging many implications.

This simple exercise shows the triad working as designed: the Author fixes meaning, the Text conveys it, and the Reader, constrained by the Text, understands and obeys.

Why This Matters: Authority, Unity, And Life

Authority. If the author does not determine meaning, then the reader does—and Scripture's authority yields to human preference. The only way to preserve **sola Scriptura** in practice is to bind ourselves to the meaning the biblical authors willed to communicate.

Unity. Authorial intention anchors the unity of Scripture across genres and centuries because Jehovah's purpose is one (John 5:39). The canon is not a collage of competing readerly constructions; it is a cohesive revelation from the God Who speaks.

Life. "Your words were found, and I ate them, and Your words became to me a joy and the delight of my heart" (Jer. 15:16). Joy comes not from inventing meanings but from receiving Jehovah's intended truth and walking in it.

Summary List For Classroom And Pulpit Use (Not A Conclusion)

- Meaning = the author's willed sense encoded in the text.
- The text is shareable, stable, and context-governed.
- Readers are responsible, active servants—neither passive nor sovereign.
- One meaning; many faithful implications; no competing meanings.
- Genre, syntax, and historical setting are required tools, not optional curiosities.
- Scripture interprets Scripture within the unity of Jehovah's purpose.
- The aim is understanding that results in obedience and proclamation.

Review Questions – Chapter 1: An Introduction to Hermeneutics

1. What is the meaning of the term *hermeneutics*, and how is it rooted in the biblical concept of "interpreting" or "translating"?

2. Why is hermeneutics necessary for every believer, not just for scholars or theologians?

3. How does Acts 8:30–31 (Philip and the Ethiopian official) illustrate the role of interpretation in understanding Scripture?

4. What barriers make hermeneutics necessary for modern readers of the Bible?

5. How does 2 Peter 1:20–21 safeguard interpretation against "private" or imaginative readings of Scripture?

6. According to 2 Timothy 2:15, what is the responsibility of the interpreter in handling God's Word?

7. What is the ultimate goal of biblical hermeneutics, both in understanding and in application?

8. How does Nehemiah 8:8 demonstrate the proper pattern of reading, explaining, and applying the Word of God?

9. Why is it dangerous to think of interpretation as optional or reserved only for academic study?

10. In what ways does faithful interpretation shape not only doctrine but also worship and daily Christian living?

CHAPTER 2 Terminology for Interpretation

Defining Meaning in Biblical Interpretation: The Author's Willed Sense

When we speak of "meaning" in the realm of biblical interpretation, we are not dealing with an abstract, shifting, or subjective notion, but with a fixed reality anchored in the intention of the inspired author as conveyed in the text. Meaning is the lifeblood of hermeneutics. Without clarity about what meaning is and where it resides, interpretation becomes a playground for speculation and personal preference rather than a discipline of submission to Jehovah's revealed Word. The church must therefore affirm with unwavering conviction that meaning is singular, authorially determined, textually encoded, and binding on all readers.

Meaning Defined: The Author's Willed Communication

Meaning is precisely what the human writer, under the guidance of the Holy Spirit, intended to communicate to his original audience through the words, grammar, and literary structures he employed. It is not the inner experiences of the author, nor is it the emotional impressions of the reader, nor some evolving sense created by later communities. Meaning is the product of intentionality—the author's deliberate act of communication carried out in written form.

Moses did not write the Torah so that Israel might imagine a multitude of possible meanings. He wrote so that Israel might "hear and learn to fear Jehovah your God" (Deut. 31:12). Luke did not compose his Gospel so that readers could construct their own interpretations; he wrote so that Theophilus and others "may have

26

certainty concerning the things you have been taught" (Luke 1:4). Paul did not pen his epistles to invite endless reinterpretations; he wrote with specific doctrinal, ethical, and pastoral aims, commanding that his letters be read publicly in the churches (Col. 4:16).

This consistent pattern across Scripture establishes a simple but profound truth: the inspired writers willed to communicate particular messages, and those willed communications constitute the meaning of the text.

Meaning Is Singular, Not Plural

Every biblical passage has one meaning, though it may carry multiple legitimate implications and applications. That singular meaning is fixed by the author's intention in the original historical and literary context. When Paul writes in Romans 5:1, "Therefore, since we have been justified by faith, we have peace with God through our Lord Jesus Christ," the meaning is not open to personal reconstruction. It is a declarative statement of the reality of justification by faith. From that fixed meaning, believers may draw various implications—assurance in suffering, confidence in evangelism, motivation for holiness—but none of these implications alters or replaces the one authorial meaning.

To speak of multiple "meanings" is to deny the clarity and authority of Scripture. As Peter warns, the untaught and unstable distort Scripture "to their own destruction" (2 Pet. 3:16). Such distortion presupposes that there is a correct, singular meaning that can be twisted. If every reading were equally valid, distortion would be impossible.

Meaning Resides in the Text, Not Beyond It

Meaning is not an ethereal concept floating in the author's mind apart from words. Nor is it a hidden code requiring mystical revelation. Meaning is tied to the very words of the text in their grammatical and historical setting. "The unfolding of Your words gives light; it imparts understanding to the simple" (Ps. 119:130). Jehovah has bound His meaning to words that can be read, studied, translated, and understood.

This is why the inspired writers took pains to write clearly and in the languages of their audiences—Hebrew, Aramaic, and Greek. Meaning is not found in secret impressions but in the intelligible text itself. The interpreter's task is to analyze the words, syntax, literary features, and historical background in order to recover the meaning that the author inscribed.

The Dangers of Redefining Meaning

Throughout the history of biblical scholarship, alternative conceptions of meaning have arisen that undermine the authority of Scripture. Three errors are particularly destructive:

1. **Textual Autonomy** – This view claims that once a text is written, it detaches from its author and generates meanings on its own. This denies that words are vehicles of authorial intention and turns the Bible into a mute artifact open to endless reconfiguration.

2. **Reader-Centered Relativism** – This approach enthrones the reader's experience as the source of meaning. Under this philosophy, the Bible means whatever it means to me. But Jeremiah 17:9 reminds us that "the heart is deceitful above all things." Readers must be corrected by Scripture, not creators of its meaning.

3. **Community-Centered Consensus** – This error locates meaning in the agreement of an interpretive community. While teachers and congregations are vital, they are not sovereign over meaning. Communities can fall into error (Hos. 4:6), but Jehovah's Word stands forever (Isa. 40:8).

Each of these approaches substitutes human authority for divine revelation. They make meaning a human construct rather than the divine Author's intent encoded through human writers.

Application of Meaning: From Understanding to Obedience

Understanding meaning is never an end in itself. Meaning willed by the author carries with it authority because the biblical authors spoke from God (2 Pet. 1:21). To uncover the meaning without obeying it is to fall into self-deception (Jas. 1:22–25). Proper hermeneutics therefore moves from comprehension of the singular meaning to faithful application in doctrine, worship, and daily life.

For example, when Paul commands, "Flee from sexual immorality" (1 Cor. 6:18), the meaning is clear: believers must avoid sexual sin. That singular meaning generates implications for many contexts the Corinthians never envisioned—pornography, casual dating, or internet exploitation. But all those implications are governed by the original meaning. Christians must not add meanings but must extend the one meaning faithfully into new situations.

Why Meaning Matters

If meaning is not fixed in the author's intention, the authority of Scripture collapses. The Bible then becomes a mirror for human imagination rather than a window into Jehovah's revelation. Sola Scriptura in practice depends entirely on affirming that Scripture has a determinate meaning that binds all readers in every age.

Jesus Himself presupposed this when He rebuked the Sadducees: "You are wrong, because you know neither the Scriptures nor the power of God" (Matt. 22:29). Their error was not a failure to resonate personally with the text but a failure to grasp the meaning intended by God through the human author.

Therefore, the interpreter's most solemn responsibility is to seek, by diligent grammatical-historical exegesis, the meaning the inspired author willed to communicate. Only then can we stand approved before God, "rightly handling the word of truth" (2 Tim. 2:15).

Defining Implications in Biblical Interpretation: Faithful Extensions of Meaning

When we have clearly established that meaning in biblical interpretation is fixed in the author's willed intent, expressed in the inspired text, the next vital concept is implications. Many confuse implications with additional meanings, but the two are not the same. Meaning is singular, precise, and bound to the historical and literary context of the author. Implications are the legitimate, necessary, and natural extensions of that one meaning into broader contexts not directly named in the passage.

The Nature of Implications

Implications are truths or applications that legitimately arise from the author's willed meaning. They do not invent new ideas or expand meaning beyond its contextual boundary, but they unfold what is already present in seed form. Because biblical writers often state principles with timeless relevance, implications extend those principles into situations unforeseen by the original audience.

For example, the eighth commandment—"You shall not steal" (Exod. 20:15)—has one meaning: the prohibition of taking what does not belong to you. That meaning was immediately relevant to Israel's covenant life. Yet from this fixed meaning flow many implications that extend to later contexts—embezzlement, plagiarism, digital piracy, identity theft, and fraudulent accounting. None of these modern situations was directly envisioned in the ancient setting, but they all fall legitimately within the scope of the author's meaning.

Implications Distinguished From Meaning

The difference between meaning and implication must be maintained to preserve the authority of Scripture. Meaning is singular, the author's willed communication. Implications are multiple, applications that naturally flow from that meaning. To confuse the two is to risk one of two errors:

1. **Multiplying Meanings** – treating every implication as if it were a new meaning, thereby creating a false pluralism.

2. **Wooden Literalism** – refusing to draw principled implications, thereby limiting the Word of God to its first-century or ancient Near Eastern horizon without recognizing its enduring relevance.

Sound exegesis avoids both extremes by keeping meaning fixed while drawing faithful implications.

Scriptural Evidence for Implications

The Bible itself models the movement from meaning to implications.

Jesus, in the Sermon on the Mount, exposes the heart-level implications of the Law. "You have heard that it was said to those of old, 'You shall not murder'… But I say to you that everyone who is angry with his brother will be liable to judgment" (Matt. 5:21–22). He is not adding new meanings to the commandment; He is drawing out its true implications regarding hatred, contempt, and verbal abuse.

Likewise, Paul in 1 Corinthians 9:9–10 cites the law about not muzzling an ox while it treads grain (Deut. 25:4). The meaning in its agricultural setting is literal—farmers must allow their animals to eat while working. But Paul draws the implication: the principle of just compensation applies to human laborers, particularly gospel workers. This is not allegory or speculation; it is the faithful application of the original principle into a broader context.

Guardrails for Drawing Implications

Because implications extend meaning, they must always be disciplined by the following principles:

- **They Must Arise from the Author's Meaning.** Implications cannot be invented from imagination; they must be traceable to the author's willed communication.

- **They Must Harmonize with the Whole of Scripture.** Jehovah does not contradict Himself. Implications that create doctrinal tension with other passages are invalid.

- **They Must Remain at the Right Level of Generality.** Too narrow an implication fragments the text into endless regulations; too vague an implication dissolves its force. Faithful implications are principled, not arbitrary.

Practical Examples of Implications

The biblical command, "Flee from sexual immorality" (1 Cor. 6:18), means that believers must avoid illicit sexual activity. Implications naturally extend this to contexts such as pornography, cohabitation outside marriage, homosexual behavior, or digital exploitation. These implications are not new meanings; they are contemporary applications of the same principle.

The teaching, "Do not be unequally yoked with unbelievers" (2 Cor. 6:14), has one meaning: Christians must not enter binding partnerships that compromise faith. The implications extend to marriage, business ventures, or spiritual alliances where loyalty to Christ would be jeopardized.

In every case, the difference is preserved: the meaning is one, but the implications are many.

Why Implications Are Essential

Without implications, the Bible would appear to be locked in the past, relevant only to ancient customs and settings. But because Jehovah inspired timeless principles through His chosen authors, the Word speaks powerfully into every generation. Implications safeguard the enduring authority of Scripture while protecting against the distortion of adding multiple meanings.

When Jesus declared that Scripture "cannot be broken" (John 10:35), He affirmed both its fixed meaning and its enduring implications. To honor Scripture faithfully, interpreters must uncover meaning by grammatical-historical exegesis and then unfold its implications for life, doctrine, and practice in every age.

Defining Significance in Biblical Interpretation: The Reader's Response to Meaning

After clarifying *meaning* as the author's willed sense and *implications* as the principled extensions of that meaning, we now turn to *significance*. Significance is not a new meaning, nor is it an implication flowing directly from the text. Instead, significance refers to the personal and corporate importance of a text's meaning for the interpreter, the church, or society. Meaning is fixed; implications are principled extensions; significance is the lived recognition of how that meaning applies to us.

The Nature of Significance

Significance is the relationship between the fixed meaning of the text and the individual or community that encounters it. It answers the question: *What difference does this text make for me, for us, here and now?* Whereas meaning is objective, significance is subjective. It varies across times, cultures, and situations, because individuals and communities stand in different relations to the one meaning.

For example, the statement "You shall not steal" (Exod. 20:15) always means the same thing: the prohibition of taking what belongs to another. The implications extend into varied forms of theft. But its *significance* will differ for a child tempted to cheat on an exam, a corporate executive facing accounting fraud, or a church community battling corruption. The meaning is fixed; the implications are principled; but the significance shifts according to one's relationship to that truth.

Scriptural Evidence for Significance

Scripture itself highlights the distinction between meaning and significance.

In Acts 2:36, Peter declares: "Let all the house of Israel therefore know for certain that God has made Him both Lord and Christ, this

Jesus whom you crucified." The meaning of the statement is unchanging: Jesus, whom Israel crucified, is both Lord and Messiah. But the *significance* for the hearers was immediate and piercing: "When they heard this they were cut to the heart" (Acts 2:37). The same meaning carries significance for unbelievers today, though it will strike them differently based on their relationship to Christ.

Hebrews 3:7–8 cites Psalm 95:7–8, urging: "Today, if you hear His voice, do not harden your hearts." The meaning of Psalm 95 remains stable: Israel is warned against hardness of heart. But its *significance* for first-century Christians under pressure was urgent, calling them to perseverance in faith. Its significance continues for modern believers, challenging them not to resist God's Word in their unique circumstances.

Guarding the Boundary Between Meaning and Significance

It is essential to guard against confusing significance with meaning. To say a text "means something different to me" is a misuse of language. The meaning does not change. What changes is the *significance*—the way that meaning intersects with my life.

Blurring this boundary leads to interpretive chaos, where Scripture becomes whatever it "signifies" to each individual. This reduces the Bible from divine revelation to personal impression. Instead, conservative exegesis insists:

- The **meaning** is always what the inspired author intended.

- The **implications** are principled extensions of that meaning into unmentioned contexts.

- The **significance** is the varied weight, importance, or impact that meaning carries for readers across times and circumstances.

Practical Examples of Significance

Paul's statement in 2 Timothy 4:2, "Preach the word; be ready in season and out of season," always means the same thing: ministers are to proclaim Scripture faithfully at all times. The implications include being prepared in preaching, teaching, counseling, and evangelism. The significance, however, differs. For Timothy, it meant pastoral urgency in Ephesus. For a persecuted house church, it may mean courage under threat. For a modern preacher, it may mean diligence despite apathy in the congregation. The meaning is one, but the significance multiplies according to the audience's condition.

Similarly, Jesus' Great Commission (Matt. 28:19–20) has one meaning: His disciples are commanded to make disciples of all nations. The implications extend to cross-cultural missions, evangelism, and teaching obedience. The significance varies for each believer: for one, a call to full-time missionary service; for another, a responsibility to share Christ at work or in the home. The meaning does not change, but the significance differs according to circumstance.

Why Significance Matters

Recognizing significance protects the interpreter from two dangers. First, it prevents reducing the Bible to a relic of the past, locked in ancient meaning with no present force. Second, it prevents inventing new meanings under the guise of personal relevance. By distinguishing meaning from significance, we preserve both the stability of the text and its living power.

The Bible is not a dead word. "The word of God is living and active" (Heb. 4:12). Its meaning is fixed, but its significance reverberates in every heart, culture, and age. Faithful interpretation ensures that significance flows from meaning, not apart from it, leading to conviction, transformation, and obedience.

Defining Subject Matter in Biblical Interpretation: The Content Distinct from Meaning

When studying biblical interpretation, it is essential to distinguish *subject matter* from *meaning*. Subject matter refers to the content, or the "stuff," that a passage talks about. It is the material referenced in the text—people, places, events, doctrines, practices, and realities. However, subject matter by itself is not the same as meaning. Meaning is what the inspired author intended to communicate about the subject matter through the selection, arrangement, and wording of the text.

Failing to distinguish between subject matter and meaning can easily lead to misinterpretation. The subject matter is raw content; the meaning is the author's communicative act concerning that content.

Subject Matter Defined

Subject matter is the topic or material under discussion in a passage, apart from the author's use of it. It is the difference between what is being talked about and what is being *said* about it.

For example, in 1 Corinthians 15:12–20, the subject matter is the resurrection of the dead and specifically Christ's resurrection. But the meaning is Paul's argument that if Christ has not been raised, Christian preaching and faith are useless, and believers are still in their sins. The subject matter is resurrection; the meaning is Paul's defense of the reality and necessity of Christ's resurrection.

Distinguishing Subject Matter From Meaning

This distinction is critical for exegesis.

- **Subject Matter Without Meaning:** If one simply notes that Paul discusses "resurrection," that does not yet establish what he *meant* to communicate about it.

- **Meaning Without Subject Matter:** If one tries to interpret meaning while ignoring the content, the interpretation becomes abstract and detached from the text's concrete realities.

- **Proper Interpretation:** Faithful interpretation keeps both in view—recognizing the subject matter and discerning the meaning the author conveyed about it.

Thus, subject matter is necessary but insufficient for interpretation. The interpreter must always move from recognizing subject matter to discerning the meaning encoded in the text.

Scriptural Illustrations of Subject Matter

The Gospel accounts provide clear examples of this distinction.

- In Luke 10:25–37, the subject matter is a parable about a man attacked by robbers and aided by a Samaritan. The meaning, however, is Jesus' teaching that love of neighbor transcends ethnic and religious boundaries, exposing the lawyer's narrow view of righteousness.

- In Genesis 22:1–19, the subject matter is Abraham's near-sacrifice of Isaac. The meaning is Abraham's obedience of faith and Jehovah's provision of a substitute sacrifice. The event itself is the subject matter; the theological point drawn by the inspired author is the meaning.

Dangers of Confusing Subject Matter with Meaning

Many interpretive errors arise when readers collapse subject matter into meaning.

- **Mere Historical Curiosity:** Some treat Scripture as a collection of interesting subject matter—ancient laws, genealogies, or stories—without discerning what the author communicated about them. This reduces the Bible to a historical archive rather than divine revelation.

- **Reader-Centered Missteps:** Others latch onto subject matter that resonates with them but impose their own meaning on it. For example, focusing on "shepherds" in Psalm 23 and then attaching personal associations while ignoring the author's meaning about Jehovah's covenant care.

- **Critical Misuses:** Certain schools of liberal scholarship analyze subject matter (social customs, political movements, cultural backdrops) without acknowledging the inspired meaning conveyed through the author's composition.

In all these cases, the authority of Scripture is undermined because the interpreter stops short of the author's willed communication.

The Role of Subject Matter in Exegesis

Though subject matter is not meaning, it is still essential in the interpretive process. The interpreter must accurately identify the content a passage addresses, since meaning is always about something. For instance:

- The subject matter of Exodus 20:13 is human killing. The meaning is the divine prohibition against murder, distinguishing it from lawful acts of war or judicial execution.

- The subject matter of John 3:16 is God, His Son, the world, belief, and eternal life. The meaning is God's love expressed in giving His unique Son, so that those who believe will not perish but have everlasting life.

Without subject matter, the meaning cannot be grounded in the realities the author was addressing. Subject matter provides the raw material, but only meaning supplies the author's interpretive message about that material.

Why the Distinction Matters

The Bible is not simply a record of subject matter; it is Jehovah's revelation through inspired authors who wrote with intention. The difference between subject matter and meaning safeguards the interpreter from reducing Scripture to trivia, history, or literature. It compels us to ask not only *What is this passage talking about?* but also *What is the inspired author saying about what he is talking about?*

By recognizing subject matter as the content of the text and meaning as the author's communicative act about that content, we honor the nature of Scripture as God-breathed, intelligible, and authoritative.

Defining Understanding in Biblical Interpretation: The Reader's Mental Grasp of Meaning

In the chain of communication between the inspired author, the inscripturated text, and the modern reader, *understanding* plays a crucial role. Understanding is the correct mental grasp of the author's meaning. It does not create meaning, nor does it alter or add to it. Rather, it is the reader's act of apprehending, with the mind, what the author willed to communicate in the text.

Understanding Defined

Understanding is the reader's intellectual alignment with the inspired author's meaning as expressed in the words of Scripture. The author encodes meaning in the text; the reader, by careful exegesis, decodes it. Understanding is achieved when the reader's mental conception corresponds accurately to the meaning the author intended.

This is why Paul exhorted Timothy: "Think over what I say, for the Lord will give you understanding in everything" (2 Tim. 2:7). Paul had already written words with a specific meaning. Timothy's task was to reflect and grasp that meaning correctly. Understanding, then, is the reader's responsibility to comprehend the message conveyed.

Understanding Distinguished from Meaning

Understanding is not meaning itself but the apprehension of it. Meaning exists objectively in the text, independent of the reader's perception. A reader may fail to understand, misunderstand, or distort meaning, but the meaning does not change.

For example, when Paul writes, "For by grace you have been saved through faith" (Eph. 2:8), the meaning is fixed: salvation is a divine gift, not earned by works. A reader who thinks the verse teaches salvation by works has misunderstood. The meaning remains unchanged, but the reader has failed to grasp it correctly.

Thus:

- **Meaning**: the inspired author's willed communication.

- **Understanding**: the reader's accurate mental grasp of that meaning.

Scriptural Evidence for Understanding

Scripture consistently underscores the necessity of understanding.

- In Nehemiah 8:8, the Levites read from the Law of God, "clearly, and they gave the sense, so that the people understood the reading." The meaning of the Law was fixed, but understanding required explanation so that the hearers could mentally grasp it.

- Jesus often rebuked His disciples for lacking understanding. After the feeding of the four thousand, He said, "Do you not yet perceive or understand? Are your hearts hardened?" (Mark 8:17). The meaning of His words and works was clear, but their failure lay in not grasping it mentally.

- In Luke 24:45, after the resurrection, Jesus "opened their minds to understand the Scriptures." The Scriptures already had meaning; understanding required illumination of their minds so they could grasp that meaning accurately.

Barriers to Understanding

Several obstacles hinder correct understanding of Scripture:

1. **Prejudice and Tradition** – When readers impose prior assumptions onto the text, they obscure the author's meaning.

2. **Laziness in Study** – Scripture requires diligence. Paul commands, "Do your best to present yourself to God as one approved... rightly handling the word of truth" (2 Tim. 2:15).

3. **Spiritual Disposition** – While unbelievers *can* mentally grasp meaning, they often dismiss or reject it as folly (1 Cor. 2:14). They may understand the content but not embrace its truth. Understanding requires humility and reverence before the Word.

The Goal of Understanding

The aim of interpretation is not merely to know what the text *says* but to understand what it *means*. Correct understanding precedes faithful obedience. Ezra is praised because he "set his heart to study the Law of Jehovah, and to do it and to teach His statutes" (Ezra 7:10). Understanding is the hinge between study and obedience.

Understanding also guards against error. Misunderstanding Scripture is spiritually dangerous. Peter warns that the untaught distort Paul's letters "to their own destruction" (2 Pet. 3:16). To understand correctly is to safeguard oneself against false teaching and misapplication.

Why Understanding Matters

Without understanding, meaning remains locked in the text and inaccessible to the reader. With understanding, the inspired message is mentally apprehended and ready to be applied in life. The psalmist celebrates this gift: "Give me understanding, that I may keep Your law and observe it with my whole heart" (Ps. 119:34).

Understanding, then, is the vital act by which the interpreter's mind aligns with the inspired author's meaning. It is not optional but necessary for all who would faithfully receive Jehovah's Word.

Defining Interpretation in Biblical Hermeneutics: The Expression of Understanding

Having established *meaning* as the author's willed communication, *implications* as principled extensions of meaning, *significance* as the varied importance of meaning for readers, *subject matter* as the content of the text, and *understanding* as the reader's correct mental grasp of meaning, we now turn to *interpretation*. Interpretation is the act of putting into words—whether spoken or written—one's understanding of the author's meaning.

Interpretation Defined

Interpretation refers to the verbal or written expression of a reader's understanding of an author's meaning. It is not meaning itself, nor is it the act of mental comprehension. Rather, it is the external communication of that comprehension. In other words, understanding is internal; interpretation is external.

For example, when a pastor preaches on Romans 5:1, he is not creating new meaning. The meaning is Paul's inspired declaration that believers, having been justified by faith, now have peace with God through Christ. The preacher's task is to articulate his understanding of that meaning to his hearers. That act of articulation is interpretation.

Distinguishing Interpretation from Other Categories

- **Meaning**: the inspired author's willed communication, fixed in the text.

- **Understanding**: the reader's mental grasp of that meaning.

- **Interpretation**: the verbal or written expression of the reader's understanding.

These distinctions are essential. A person may misunderstand, and then his interpretation will misrepresent the text. Or he may understand correctly, but his interpretation may express it clumsily or inaccurately. Thus, interpretation depends upon accurate understanding and clear communication.

Scriptural Evidence for Interpretation

Interpretation as the expression of understanding is modeled throughout Scripture.

- In Nehemiah 8:8, the Levites "read from the book, from the Law of God, clearly, and they gave the sense, so that the people understood the reading." Here the Levites interpreted by verbally expressing the meaning of the Law so that others could grasp it.

- In Acts 8:30–35, Philip asked the Ethiopian, "Do you understand what you are reading?" When the eunuch confessed his need for guidance, Philip explained Isaiah 53 and preached Jesus. Philip's act of explanation was interpretation—expressing the meaning of the text.

- Jesus Himself often interpreted Scripture for His disciples. In Luke 24:27, "beginning with Moses and all the Prophets, He interpreted to them in all the Scriptures the things concerning Himself." The Scriptures already had meaning; Jesus articulated that meaning to His disciples.

Varieties of Interpretation

Interpretation may occur in various forms:

- **Verbal Interpretation**: Preaching, teaching, or conversation in which one explains the meaning of a passage.

- **Written Interpretation**: Commentaries, study notes, or essays that set forth one's understanding of Scripture.

- **Communal Interpretation**: A church or community declaring together their understanding of meaning, such as in confessions and creeds.

But in all cases, interpretation must faithfully reflect the meaning of the text.

Dangers in Interpretation

Interpretation carries dangers when it drifts from meaning:

- **Speculative Interpretation**: Expressing one's imagination or ideas instead of the author's meaning.

- **Subjective Interpretation**: Basing interpretation on personal impressions rather than exegesis.

- **Ideological Interpretation**: Forcing the text to say what fits human systems (political, philosophical, or theological), rather than yielding to the text itself.

These distortions turn interpretation into invention. Faithful interpretation must always be tethered to the meaning conveyed by the inspired author.

The Goal of Interpretation

The purpose of interpretation is to communicate accurately what the text means so that others may understand and obey it. Paul tells Timothy, "Until I come, devote yourself to the public reading of Scripture, to exhortation, to teaching" (1 Tim. 4:13). The public reading is the text; the exhortation and teaching are interpretation—the expression of its meaning to others.

Faithful interpretation is therefore not creativity but clarity. It is not originality but accuracy. The best interpreter is the one who most faithfully expresses the inspired author's meaning in words that can be grasped by hearers or readers today.

Defining Mental Acts in Biblical Interpretation: Distinguishing Authorial Experience From Authorial Meaning

In the discussion of biblical hermeneutics, it is vital to draw a sharp line between the *mental acts* of an author and the *meaning* of his text. Mental acts refer to the private, inner experiences of an author while writing. These may include thoughts, emotions, struggles, and personal motivations. While such acts were real, they remain inaccessible to us unless the author himself discloses them in writing. The principle that the author willed to communicate, however, is publicly available in the text. Therefore, the interpreter must focus not on speculating about the mental acts of the author, but on the author's communicative intention encoded in shareable, inspired words.

Mental Acts Defined

Mental acts are the subjective experiences of an author during the process of writing. They are part of the psychology of composition— what the writer was feeling, remembering, or pondering at the moment of putting pen to parchment. But these inner acts are not the same as meaning. Meaning resides in the author's willed communication; mental acts are the hidden processes that accompanied the act of writing.

For example, when Paul wrote Philippians 4:4—"Rejoice in the Lord always; again I will say, rejoice"—his meaning is clear: believers are to live in continual joy rooted in the Lord. His mental acts— whether he was smiling, praying, or battling discouragement as he wrote—are irrelevant and inaccessible. The meaning stands in the words; his inner experience is beyond our reach.

The Danger of Confusing Mental Acts With Meaning

Confusing mental acts with meaning leads to what has been called the *intentional fallacy*. This error assumes that interpretation should focus on reconstructing what the author was experiencing internally, rather than on what he communicated through the text. But we cannot relive the author's mental acts; we can only study the communicative symbols he consciously set down.

Paul's letter to the Galatians, for instance, clearly expresses sharp rebuke against false teaching (Gal. 1:6–9). Whether Paul trembled with anger, dictated with tears, or wrote with clenched fists cannot be known. What he willed to communicate is available: a divine warning against deserting the gospel. To speculate about his mental acts adds nothing to our understanding and risks distorting the meaning.

C. S. Lewis and the Impossibility of Recovering Mental Acts

C. S. Lewis's essay "Fern-Seed and Elephants" provides a penetrating critique of attempts to reconstruct an author's mental acts. Lewis observed that reviewers frequently speculated about what prompted him to write, what he was thinking, or what personal circumstances led to his composition. Having lived through those experiences himself, he reported that such speculations were not merely sometimes wrong but always wrong. If contemporaries within the same culture and language fail to reconstruct accurately the mental acts of modern authors, how much more impossible is it to reconstruct the mental acts of biblical writers separated from us by thousands of years, languages, and cultural worlds?

Lewis's point confirms a crucial hermeneutical principle: meaning is public, shareable, and accessible through the text; mental acts are private, hidden, and speculative.

Scriptural Evidence

The Bible itself directs us to the meaning communicated in words, not to speculative reconstructions of mental acts.

- Luke 1:1–4: Luke declares openly his purpose in writing: to provide certainty. We know his meaning because he disclosed it. We do not know his private feelings during the act of writing.

- John 20:31: John explains that his Gospel was written so that readers might believe and have life. The meaning is available; his inner process in recording the signs is not.

- 2 Peter 1:20–21: Men "spoke from God as they were carried along by the Holy Spirit." Their inspired meaning is preserved in the text. Their personal mental state during inspiration is unrevealed and irrelevant.

Why Mental Acts Are Inaccessible and Irrelevant

1. **They Are Private:** Unless disclosed, mental acts remain locked within the author's experience.

2. **They Are Unnecessary:** The author's communicative intention is embedded in the text. To access meaning, we need not relive his private experiences.

3. **They Are Distracting:** Focusing on mental acts shifts attention away from the inspired words that God chose as the vehicle of revelation.

4. **They Are Speculative:** Attempts to reconstruct mental acts usually say more about the interpreter's imagination than the author's reality.

The Interpreter's Task

The faithful interpreter must discipline himself to distinguish between the text's meaning and the author's mental acts. Our calling is to uncover what the author consciously willed to communicate, not to guess at what he was feeling or experiencing while writing. As long as the inspired author has not disclosed his private state in the text itself, it is not our concern.

The meaning of Paul's letters, Moses' laws, David's psalms, or Isaiah's prophecies is accessible and authoritative because Jehovah ensured their communication through inscripturated words. Their mental acts are not, and speculation about them contributes nothing to sound interpretation.

Defining Semantic Range in Biblical Interpretation: The Boundaries of Word Meaning

One of the foundational tasks in biblical interpretation is dealing with words. Since Jehovah chose to communicate His revelation through human language, interpreters must pay careful attention to

47

vocabulary. A crucial concept here is *semantic range*. The semantic range of a word refers to the total set of possible meanings that word may legitimately carry within a given language. It represents the outer boundaries of usage but does not determine which meaning is active in a particular context.

Semantic Range Defined

The semantic range is the limit of possible meanings allowed by the words (verbal symbols) of a text. Every word has a range of senses it may carry depending on context. But in any one instance, only one meaning is intended by the author.

For example, the Greek word *kosmos* can mean:

- the created universe (John 1:10),

- the inhabited earth (John 3:16),

- the world of humanity estranged from God (John 15:18),

- worldly adornment or order (1 Peter 3:3).

All of these fall within the semantic range of *kosmos*. But in John 3:16, only one sense applies: the world of humanity that God loves and redeems through His Son.

Semantic Range and Context

Semantic range reminds us that words are flexible, but context determines the specific sense in any given occurrence.

For instance, the Hebrew word *ruach* may mean "wind," "breath," or "spirit." Its semantic range covers all three. In Genesis 8:1 it means "wind." In Ezekiel 37:9 it refers to "breath." In Numbers 27:18 it designates "spirit." The immediate context, grammar, and literary setting narrow the semantic range down to one precise meaning.

Thus, the semantic range establishes possibilities; the context determines actuality.

Misuses of Semantic Range

Three common interpretive errors arise when semantic range is mishandled:

1. **Illegitimate Totality Transfer** – importing every possible meaning of a word into one occurrence. For example, insisting that *agapē* in every context must carry the full theological weight of divine love, rather than the specific sense intended in that passage.

2. **Etymologizing** – assigning meaning to a word based on its root or component parts rather than actual usage. For example, claiming that *dynamis* must mean "dynamite" because of similarity in sound, ignoring its real range of usage in Greek.

3. **Overextension** – reading meanings outside the semantic range into the word. For instance, attributing modern psychological categories to biblical terms where they never occur.

Faithful exegesis requires respect for semantic range and discipline in letting the context select the appropriate sense.

Scriptural Evidence

Scripture itself demonstrates how semantic range operates under context.

- In John 1:1, *logos* means "Word"—the preexistent Christ as divine communication. But in Acts 19:40, *logos* simply means "reason." Both senses fall within the word's semantic range; the context selects the right one.

- The Hebrew *zera'* may mean "seed" as a unit (Gen. 1:11), "offspring" as collective descendants (Gen. 15:5), or "a specific descendant" (Gen. 21:13). Again, the context decides which meaning within the range is intended.

Edward D. Andrews

Why Semantic Range Matters

Jehovah has chosen to reveal Himself through ordinary human language. That means words function as they do in normal communication—each with a range of possible senses, narrowed to one by context. The interpreter must therefore:

- Establish the legitimate semantic range of a word by examining its usage across Scripture and related literature.

- Avoid the error of smuggling in every possible meaning into each use.

- Rely on grammar, syntax, and literary context to determine the specific meaning willed by the author.

In this way, interpreters respect the way language works and safeguard themselves from distortions that arise from careless word studies.

Defining Specific Meaning in Biblical Interpretation: The Precise Sense Willed by the Author

When studying Scripture, it is not enough to know the *semantic range* of a word—the total set of possible meanings it can bear. The interpreter must also determine the *specific meaning* in each occurrence. Specific meaning refers to the one, precise sense that the inspired author has given to a word, phrase, clause, or sentence within its immediate literary and historical context.

Specific Meaning Defined

The specific meaning is the particular sense willed by the author in a given text. While words may have many possible uses, context narrows the semantic range down to one. This one sense is what the author consciously chose to communicate, and it is the only legitimate meaning in that passage.

50

For example, the Greek word *sarx* ("flesh") has a wide semantic range. It may mean physical flesh (Luke 24:39), humanity in weakness (1 Pet. 1:24), kinship (Rom. 9:3), or the sinful nature (Gal. 5:17). But in Galatians 5:17, Paul's specific meaning is the fallen nature opposed to the Spirit. That particular sense is fixed by the context, not left to the reader's preference.

The Relationship Between Semantic Range and Specific Meaning

Semantic range provides the boundaries; specific meaning identifies the single destination within those boundaries. The process is as follows:

1. **Identify the Semantic Range** – Determine all legitimate senses of the word by studying its usage.

2. **Examine the Context** – Consider the surrounding grammar, syntax, literary form, and historical situation.

3. **Determine the Specific Meaning** – Select the one meaning that fits the context and reflects the author's willed intention.

In this way, interpretation respects both the flexibility of language and the precision of communication.

Scriptural Examples of Specific Meaning

The Bible itself demonstrates how specific meaning emerges from context.

- In John 1:29, when John the Baptist says, "Behold, the Lamb of God, who takes away the sin of the world," the specific meaning of "Lamb of God" is not any lamb, but Christ as the sacrificial substitute. The context of sin-bearing defines the sense.

- In 1 Corinthians 5:7, Paul says, "For Christ, our Passover lamb, has been sacrificed." Here the specific meaning of *Pascha* is not the entire festival but the sacrificial lamb itself, because of its typological fulfillment in Christ.

- In Psalm 1:3, the word "tree" could, in semantic range, refer to any type of tree. But the specific meaning in this poetic context is a flourishing tree planted by streams of water, representing the stability and fruitfulness of the righteous.

In each case, the specific meaning emerges as the one sense the author has chosen from the wider possibilities.

The Danger of Ignoring Specific Meaning

When interpreters fail to identify the specific meaning, they risk two serious errors:

1. **Overgeneralization** – Treating the whole semantic range as active in one passage, which results in illegitimate totality transfer. For example, assuming that *logos* in John 1:1 contains every sense of "word," "reason," and "message," rather than the one specific sense of the eternal Word who was with God and is God.

2. **Subjective Selection** – Choosing a meaning based on preference rather than context. For instance, insisting that *sarx* in Galatians 5 must mean "physical flesh" rather than "sinful nature," simply because it suits a theological bias.

Faithful interpretation avoids both extremes by anchoring specific meaning in contextual analysis.

Why Specific Meaning Matters

The authority of Scripture rests not in vague possibilities but in the precise messages the inspired authors conveyed. Jehovah chose to communicate in human language with clarity and specificity. The task of interpretation is therefore to uncover, not invent, the particular sense the author intended in each passage.

As Proverbs 30:5 declares, "Every word of God proves true." Each word carries a determinate meaning willed by the Author. Identifying that specific meaning is the essential work of the interpreter.

Defining Literary Genre in Biblical Interpretation: Form and Its Governing Rules

Among the most important tools in biblical hermeneutics is the recognition of *literary genre*. Jehovah chose to reveal His Word not in one uniform style but through a variety of literary forms—narrative, law, poetry, prophecy, wisdom, gospel, parable, epistle, and apocalyptic. Each genre has conventions, patterns, and rules that shape how it communicates meaning. To interpret faithfully, the reader must identify the genre being employed and then apply the rules proper to that form.

Literary Genre Defined

Literary genre refers to the literary form an author is using and the rules governing that form. Genre is not merely a label for convenience; it is the framework within which the author's meaning is packaged and delivered. The inspired writers chose specific forms, and each form carries expectations that both limit and guide interpretation.

For example, when reading Proverbs, one must recognize that they are wisdom sayings—general truths for godly living—not absolute promises. Interpreting them as unconditional guarantees distorts the genre and violates authorial intent.

The Role of Genre in Communication

Genre functions as a covenant of understanding between author and reader. Both parties operate with shared expectations:

- A narrative recounts events in sequence, often with theological lessons woven into history.

- A law prescribes obligations and prohibitions.

- A poem compresses truth into parallelism, imagery, and rhythm.

- A prophecy declares divine verdicts and promises concerning the future.

- An epistle develops logical argumentation, exhortation, and instruction.

- A parable conveys spiritual truth by comparison, using story as vehicle rather than literal event.

By selecting a genre, the author signals to the reader how the text should be read. Ignoring genre leads to misinterpretation.

Scriptural Examples of Genre and Its Rules

1. **Narrative** – Genesis 22:1–19 recounts Abraham's offering of Isaac. As narrative, it conveys theological truth through historical events. It is not a parable, so it must be interpreted as a real event with enduring significance.

2. **Law** – Exodus 20 sets forth commands binding on Israel under the covenant. These are not suggestions or symbolic stories but divine statutes to regulate covenant life.

3. **Poetry** – Psalm 19:1 declares, "The heavens declare the glory of God." This is poetic language. The heavens do not literally speak with vocal cords; the psalmist uses imagery and parallelism to express creation's testimony.

4. **Prophecy** – Isaiah 7:14 announces that a virgin will conceive. As prophecy, it looks forward to fulfillment and must be read as divine promise, not as mere poetic imagery.

5. **Epistle** – Romans 8 unfolds through logical argumentation. Each clause builds on the previous. It must be analyzed syntactically and logically, not as if it were a collection of disconnected sayings.

6. **Parable** – The Good Samaritan (Luke 10:25–37) is a parable. Its meaning does not rest in historical detail but in the moral and spiritual lesson Jesus intended to communicate.

Errors From Ignoring Genre

When readers neglect genre, several interpretive errors result:

- **Over-Literalism:** Reading poetry or apocalyptic as if every detail were literal description (e.g., treating "the trees of the field shall clap their hands" in Isa. 55:12 as physical fact rather than poetic imagery).

- **Over-Generalization:** Treating laws or narratives as timeless principles apart from covenantal or redemptive-historical context.

- **Over-Spiritualization:** Treating historical narrative as if it were allegory, ignoring the concrete events Jehovah ordained.

Each of these errors stems from disregarding the author's chosen literary form.

Why Genre Matters in Exegesis

Genre matters because Jehovah inspired His Word in diverse forms that communicate truth in different ways. Faithful interpretation requires honoring the form the author chose, not forcing a foreign one upon the text. The inspired writer expected his audience to read according to the rules of the genre he used. Therefore, interpreters must discipline themselves to read law as law, poetry as poetry, narrative as narrative, and so on.

The recognition of genre guards against distortion, preserves authorial intent, and enables Scripture to be read as its divine Author designed.

Defining Context in Biblical Interpretation: The Surrounding Framework of Meaning

No principle is more vital for sound biblical interpretation than the recognition of *context*. Scripture was not given as a collection of isolated sayings but as coherent communication, with each passage situated within surrounding words, sentences, paragraphs, and books. To grasp meaning accurately, interpreters must always attend to context, for context is the author's willed use of surrounding material to shape and govern the meaning of a passage.

Context Defined

Context refers to the willed meaning that an author gives to the literary materials surrounding a passage in a text. In other words, the words immediately before and after, the paragraph structure, the flow of argument, the book's purpose, and the canonical framework all contribute to the meaning the author intends. Context is not an optional aid; it is the very environment in which meaning resides.

For example, in Philippians 4:13 Paul writes, "I can do all things through Him who strengthens me." Out of context, this could be taken to mean that Christians can achieve any personal goal they desire. But in context—surrounded by verses describing contentment in both abundance and need—the specific meaning is that believers can endure every circumstance faithfully through Christ's strength. The context protects against distortion.

Layers of Context

Biblical context operates at several levels, all governed by the author's willed communication.

1. **Immediate Context** – The surrounding words, phrases, and sentences. These determine the specific sense of vocabulary and grammar. For instance, the word *day* (*yôm*) in Genesis 1 is clarified by its immediate contextual markers: evening and morning.

2. **Literary Context** – The paragraph, section, or discourse. Paul's argument in Romans 3:21–26 must be read within the wider argument of Romans 1–3 concerning universal sin and justification by faith.

3. **Book Context** – The purpose and structure of the entire book. The meaning of Jesus' signs in John must be read in light of John's stated aim: "that you may believe... and that by believing you may have life" (John 20:31).

4. **Canonical Context** – The placement of a passage within the whole of Scripture. Since all Scripture is God-breathed (2 Tim. 3:16), later revelation never contradicts earlier revelation but fulfills and clarifies it. The New Testament use of the Old Testament always affirms, not nullifies, the authorial meaning.

Scriptural Evidence for Context

The Bible itself insists on contextual reading.

- Nehemiah 8:8: "They read from the book, from the Law of God, clearly, and they gave the sense, so that the people understood the reading." Giving "the sense" means situating verses within their context.

- Matthew 22:29: Jesus rebuked the Sadducees, "You are wrong, because you know neither the Scriptures nor the power of God." Their error lay in isolating a verse (Exod. 3:6) without recognizing its contextual testimony to resurrection.

- Acts 17:11: The Bereans were noble because they "examined the Scriptures daily to see if these things were so." They tested Paul's teaching against the context of Scripture, not isolated proof-texts.

Errors From Ignoring Context

Misinterpretation almost always arises from neglecting context.

- **Proof-Texting:** Quoting a verse in isolation to support an idea, without considering its place in the argument.

- **Fragmentation:** Treating Scripture as disconnected sayings rather than coherent revelation.

- **Distortion:** Forcing meanings into verses that the context excludes. For example, using Jeremiah 29:11 ("plans to prosper you") as a universal life promise, ignoring its context as a word to Israel in exile.

Each of these errors undermines authorial intent by severing a passage from its God-given environment.

Why Context Matters

Context is the inspired author's framework for meaning. Jehovah did not inspire words in isolation but embedded them within sentences, discourses, and the canon. To disregard context is to disregard how God chose to communicate. To honor context is to honor authorial intent.

The interpreter, therefore, must always ask: How does the immediate and larger context shape the meaning of this passage? What role does it play in the author's argument, structure, and purpose? Only by answering these questions can one "rightly handle the word of truth" (2 Tim. 2:15).

Conclusion: Terminology for Interpretation

Biblical interpretation demands precision in its categories. Without clear distinctions, interpreters risk blurring the boundaries that safeguard meaning and thereby distort the Word of God. This chapter has established the key terms that govern faithful hermeneutics.

Meaning is the inspired author's willed communication, singular and fixed in the text. *Implications* are the principled extensions of that meaning into contexts not directly named. *Significance* is the varying importance that meaning carries for different readers and communities across time. *Subject matter* is the content under discussion, which must be distinguished from meaning itself. *Understanding* is the reader's correct mental grasp of meaning, while *interpretation* is the verbal or written expression of that understanding. *Mental acts* are the private, inaccessible experiences of the author while writing and are not the concern of exegesis. *Semantic range* is the set of possible meanings a word may bear, while *specific meaning* is the precise sense chosen by the author in context. *Literary genre* refers to the form employed by the author and the rules governing that form, and *context* is the surrounding material the author willed to shape meaning.

Taken together, these terms provide the essential vocabulary for hermeneutics. They guard the interpreter from confusing possibilities with actualities, private impressions with public communication, subject matter with message, and implications with meanings. They remind us that Jehovah has chosen to speak clearly through inspired authors in ordinary human language, and that our duty is to uncover, articulate, and obey what He has revealed.

Faithful interpretation begins with mastering these categories and applying them rigorously. Only then can the interpreter avoid error and stand as a "worker who has no need to be ashamed, rightly handling the word of truth" (2 Tim. 2:15).

Review Questions – Chapter 2: Terminology for Interpretation

1. Why is clear and precise terminology essential for faithful biblical interpretation?

2. What is the difference between *meaning* and *implications* in biblical hermeneutics?

3. How does *significance* differ from *meaning*, and why must this distinction be preserved?

4. What is the difference between *subject matter* and *meaning*?

5. How does the Bible itself demonstrate that meaning is tied to authorial intention rather than subjective impressions?

6. What is the difference between *understanding* and *interpretation*?

7. Why are the *mental acts* of an author not the concern of exegesis?

8. How does recognizing the *semantic range* of a word safeguard against misinterpretation?

9. What role does *genre* play in shaping the meaning of a text?

10. Why is *context* considered the inspired framework for meaning, and how does neglecting context lead to distortion?

CHAPTER 3 The Spirit and Biblical Interpretation

The Role of the Spirit in Inspiration

The starting point for a right doctrine of the Spirit in biblical interpretation is to recognize that the Spirit's role in relation to Scripture is first and foremost the work of inspiration. The Bible is not the product of human genius, religious intuition, or mystical reflection. It is the result of the Spirit of God moving upon chosen men to record the very words of Jehovah. The apostle Paul writes, "All Scripture is inspired by God and is useful for teaching, for reproof, for correction, and for training in righteousness, so that the man of God may be fully qualified, equipped for every good work" (2 Tim. 3:16–17). Likewise, the apostle Peter testifies that "no prophecy of Scripture comes from someone's own interpretation. For no prophecy was ever produced by the will of man, but men spoke from God as they were carried along by the Holy Spirit" (2 Pet. 1:20–21).

These texts define inspiration as the divine act by which the Spirit superintended the writing of Scripture so that the final product is fully the Word of God while at the same time authentically reflecting the vocabulary, style, and personality of the human authors. The Spirit's work did not bypass the mind of the prophets and apostles, nor did it reduce them to passive instruments. Rather, the Spirit bore them along in such a way that what they consciously wrote was precisely what Jehovah intended to communicate.

This inspiration is *verbal* and *plenary*. It is verbal, meaning that inspiration extends to the very words of Scripture, not merely to abstract ideas or concepts. The words themselves, in their grammatical form and lexical selection, are the Spirit's chosen vehicles of meaning. It is plenary, meaning that the whole of Scripture is inspired—every book, every chapter, every line—not only portions that appear especially elevated or theological. Thus, the authority of Scripture is not partial or uneven but absolute and complete.

The role of the Spirit in inspiration guarantees both inerrancy and sufficiency. Because the Spirit is the Spirit of truth (John 16:13), He cannot breathe out error. Therefore, the Scriptures, as God-breathed, are wholly truthful in all they affirm. They are also sufficient, containing everything needed for salvation, faith, and godly living. Paul emphasizes this in 2 Timothy 3:17: Scripture equips the man of God for "every good work." No additional revelation or hidden insight is required, for the Spirit has already provided all that is necessary in the inspired Word.

This understanding of inspiration lays the foundation for the interpreter's task. If the Spirit's role was to inspire the authors to write the inerrant text, then the Spirit's present role in relation to us is not to re-inspire or mystically indwell us with new revelation, but to guide us by means of the inspired revelation He has already given. The Bible itself, as the Spirit's product, is the sole objective authority. The Spirit does not bypass the text; He works through the text.

Therefore, to affirm the Spirit's role in inspiration is to commit oneself to the primacy of Scripture in interpretation. The Bible is not simply a record of past experiences with God; it is the living, authoritative Word of God, breathed out by the Spirit and preserved for the people of God. To treat it as anything less is to deny the very foundation of biblical hermeneutics.

The Role of the Spirit in the Preservation and Restoration of the Bible

When we affirm that "the word of the Lord remains forever" (1 Pet. 1:25; Isa. 40:8), we must do so in harmony with the facts of history and the testimony of Scripture itself. These verses are often misused by charismatics, King James Version Onlyists, and others to teach the notion of *miraculous preservation*—that God kept every letter of Scripture perfectly intact through every copyist's hand from the time of Moses and Paul until today. Such a view is both biblically unfounded and historically disproven. The actual manuscripts that have come down to us—tens of thousands in Hebrew, Aramaic, and Greek—contain hundreds of thousands of variations. This reality demonstrates that while the originals were inspired and inerrant, their transmission involved human scribes who, though often meticulous, were subject to error.

The Spirit's role in preservation must therefore be understood not as direct, ongoing miracle but as providential oversight through ordinary means. Jehovah gave His people the responsibility of copying and transmitting the text. That responsibility was fulfilled with varying degrees of skill, diligence, and accuracy. Over time, textual corruption crept in—through unintentional mistakes such as omissions, misspellings, and transpositions, as well as through intentional changes such as harmonizations and theological clarifications. Yet through these very human processes, God ensured that His Word was never lost and could always be restored through careful examination and comparison of the manuscripts.

Scribal Skills and the Quality of Transmission

The precision of any given manuscript often reflected the scribe's training and background. Four main scribal styles are evident in the ancient manuscripts:

Some copies were made by those with *common handwriting*, often untrained in formal Greek writing. Their work displays inconsistency, uneven lettering, and frequent mistakes. Others reveal the *documentary hand*, produced by scribes accustomed to writing contracts or business records. These texts are functional but uneven, with larger initial letters and crooked lines. More refined are manuscripts in a *reformed documentary hand*, where the scribe recognized he was copying literature of weight and thus showed greater care, uniformity, and legibility. Finally, the highest quality manuscripts are those in *professional bookhand*, where trained scribes carefully formed letters, used spacing and punctuation, and produced aesthetically beautiful and accurate copies. The papyrus Gospel codex known as P4+64+67, with its careful calligraphy and layout, exemplifies such skill.

This diversity of scribal quality explains why textual variants arose. Not all scribes were equally trained, and not all exercised the same diligence. Yet through this variety, a vast manuscript tradition was created that gives us unparalleled resources for restoring the text.

The Greek New Testament: Transmission, Corruption, and Restoration

The New Testament authors, carried along by the Holy Spirit (2 Pet. 1:21), produced inspired, inerrant originals. But once their writings left their hands, copying was not a miraculous process. Scribes, whether professional or ordinary, transmitted these texts with greater or lesser care.

Unintentional errors included simple spelling slips, homophones (confusing words that sound alike), omissions of words or even lines (especially when two lines ended with the same sequence of letters), and transpositions of word order. Intentional changes often took the form of harmonizations—adjusting one Gospel to sound more like another—or theological clarifications, where a scribe might add words to guard against perceived heresy.

By the eighteenth century, as more manuscripts were collected, scholars began the work of *textual criticism*—the science of comparing manuscripts to restore the original text. Johann Jakob Griesbach, Karl Lachmann, Constantin von Tischendorf, Westcott and Hort, Nestle, and later Kurt and Barbara Aland and Bruce Metzger all contributed to the production of eclectic Greek New Testaments. By collating thousands of manuscripts, versions, and patristic quotations, they were able to evaluate readings based on age, geographical distribution, and internal probability.

The result is that the Greek New Testament available today—whether Nestle-Aland, UBS, or Tyndale House editions—represents with 99.9% accuracy the text as it was originally written. The Spirit's role is evident not in a myth of perfect copying but in the fact that through ordinary scribal work, multiplied manuscript witnesses, and the discipline of textual criticism, His Word has been preserved and restored to us with remarkable fidelity.

The Hebrew Old Testament: Preservation and Refinement

The Old Testament followed a similar pattern of preservation and restoration. After the originals were written by Moses, the prophets, and others, scribes known as the *Sopherim* began copying them. Over time, these scribes introduced occasional textual alterations—some out of reverence (such as avoiding direct use of the divine name), others for smoothing difficulties. Jesus Himself criticized some of these traditions.

The *Masoretes*, successors to the Sopherim, developed elaborate systems of vowel pointing, accent marks, and marginal notes (the *Masora*) to preserve correct pronunciation and record textual details. They did not alter the consonantal text but meticulously transmitted it. The Dead Sea Scrolls, discovered in the mid-twentieth century, confirmed the remarkable accuracy of this tradition, with scrolls from the second century B.C.E. showing near identity to medieval Masoretic manuscripts in substance, with only minor orthographic differences.

The history of Hebrew transmission also includes major translations: the Samaritan Pentateuch, the Aramaic Targums, the Greek Septuagint, and the Latin Vulgate. Each reflects both the challenges and benefits of transmission, as translators wrestled with the text and provided valuable witnesses for comparison.

In modern times, critical editions of the Hebrew Bible—beginning with the *Biblia Hebraica* of Rudolf Kittel and refined through later editions—have incorporated manuscript evidence from the Ben Asher tradition and the Dead Sea Scrolls. These scholarly labors have produced a text that represents the inspired originals with extraordinary accuracy.

Preservation Without Miracle, Restoration Through Means

To speak of the Spirit's role in preservation is not to claim that He kept every scribe's hand from error. The manuscript evidence itself disproves such a notion. Rather, the Spirit preserved His Word by ensuring an abundance of witnesses and then guiding the church, through scholarship and faithful study, to restore the text to its original form.

This is a model of preservation and restoration, not of miracle. Jehovah entrusted His people with the responsibility to copy, study, and compare, while overseeing the process so that His Word was never lost and could always be recovered.

Thus, the reality of textual variants does not undermine confidence in Scripture. On the contrary, it demonstrates the Spirit's wisdom: by multiplying manuscripts across regions and centuries, He ensured that no single corruption could ever dominate the tradition. Where one copyist erred, another preserved the correct reading. By comparing them, the original text shines through.

Why This Matters

Understanding the Spirit's role in preservation and restoration strengthens our confidence in Scripture. We are not left with a fragile text corrupted beyond recognition, nor with a naïve myth of perfect copying. Instead, we possess a Bible that, through the Spirit's providential care and the faithful labor of copyists and scholars, has been preserved in all essential details.

As Jesus promised, "Your word is truth" (John 17:17). That truth has been safeguarded not by superstition but by God's wise design: the abundance of manuscripts, the discipline of textual criticism, and the ongoing witness of His people. The Bible in our hands today represents with extraordinary faithfulness the inspired originals. This reality calls us to reverence, diligent study, and unwavering obedience.

The Role of the Spirit in the Interpretation of the Bible

If the Spirit's role in *inspiration* was to breathe out the text and His role in *preservation and restoration* was to safeguard it through ordinary transmission and scholarly restoration, then His role in *interpretation* must be understood with equal precision. Misunderstandings at this point have led to widespread confusion in the church. Many assume that the Spirit gives mystical enlightenment to the believer, directly imparting correct interpretations without the need for disciplined study. But this is neither the teaching of Scripture nor the testimony of history. The Spirit does not bypass the mind of the reader; rather, He works through the Word He has already inspired.

No Direct or Mystical Illumination

1 Corinthians 2:12–16 is often misused to support the idea that unbelievers cannot understand the Bible without a special act of illumination and that believers are guaranteed correct understanding by the Spirit's inward work. Yet the context shows otherwise. Paul explains that the natural man does not *accept* the things of the Spirit because he regards them as foolish. This does not mean that the unbeliever cannot intellectually grasp the meaning of Scripture. Unbelievers can and do understand the content of biblical teaching. What they reject is its truthfulness and authority. They critique it, dismiss it, or mock it.

The Christian, by contrast, has "the mind of Christ" (1 Cor. 2:16). This does not refer to mystical infusion of knowledge but to a biblically shaped mind, renewed by the Word. Believers receive the message as truth, submit to it, and allow it to govern their thinking. Thus, interpretation is not an automatic product of the Spirit's direct action but the result of disciplined engagement with the inspired text.

The Spirit's Guidance Through the Word

Jesus' promises in John 14:16–17 and 16:13 are often cited as if they apply to every believer, guaranteeing direct Spirit-led interpretation. But context shows that these promises were given specifically to the apostles. The Spirit would remind them of Jesus' teaching and guide them into all truth for the purpose of producing the New Testament. This was a unique, unrepeatable work.

Today, Christians are not recipients of new revelation or direct apostolic guidance. Instead, we are guided by the Spirit through the Word He inspired. This guidance is mediated, not immediate. The

Spirit has provided the text, preserved it, and ensured its restoration. Our responsibility is to study it carefully, rightly dividing the Word of truth (2 Tim. 2:15).

The Interpreter's Responsibility

The Spirit does not do the interpreter's work for him. To pray for understanding while neglecting careful study is as futile as praying for employment while refusing to seek work. The Spirit calls us to diligence—learning the languages, studying the historical background, analyzing the grammar, and discerning the literary genre. The Spirit's "illumination" is not the infusion of hidden meanings but the blessing of insight as the believer works carefully through the text.

Thus, believer and unbeliever alike must use the same grammatical-historical method. The difference lies not in cognitive ability but in disposition. The unbeliever may understand the author's meaning yet reject it. The believer, submitting to the authority of Scripture, embraces it as true and seeks to live in obedience. The Spirit's role is not to bypass the text but to press its meaning into the believer's heart and conscience.

The Spirit's Role in the Church

Though the Spirit does not grant mystical insight, He does sustain the church in her interpretive task. He has given teachers, pastors, and evangelists to build up the body of Christ (Eph. 4:11–12). Through the faithful teaching of the Word, the Spirit equips the saints. The Spirit's role here is not to whisper new interpretations but to empower faithful ministers to proclaim the Word already given, and to enable hearers to receive it with reverence.

Why This Matters

This understanding of the Spirit's role in interpretation guards against both arrogance and passivity. It guards against arrogance by reminding us that no one has a private pipeline to divine truth apart from the text. All interpreters, however learned or gifted, must submit to the same inspired words. It guards against passivity by reminding us that serious study is essential. The Spirit does not promise shortcuts; He commands diligence.

Ultimately, the Spirit's role in interpretation is to direct us back to the Word He inspired, so that we may think the thoughts of God after Him. The Bible alone is the voice of the Spirit, and the faithful interpreter is the one who bows before that Word, studying it carefully and embracing it fully.

The Spirit and the Application of Scripture

Having established the Spirit's role in *inspiration* as the divine breathing out of Scripture, His role in *preservation and restoration* as safeguarding the text through ordinary transmission and scholarship, and His role in *interpretation* as guiding us to the text without mystical illumination, we now turn to His role in *application*. Application refers to the bringing of biblical meaning into the lives of readers so that they live in obedience to Jehovah's revealed will.

Application Distinguished From Meaning

The Spirit's inspired Word has one fixed meaning, determined by the author's willed intention. That meaning does not change across time or culture. Application, however, varies as believers in different contexts and circumstances bring that same meaning to bear upon their lives. For instance, Paul's command, "Flee from sexual immorality" (1 Cor. 6:18), always means the same thing—the avoidance of illicit sexual activity. Yet its application differs: to one believer it may mean breaking off an adulterous relationship, to another avoiding pornography, and to another rejecting a sinful cultural practice.

The Spirit does not give new meanings, but He presses the unchanging meaning of Scripture into the diverse circumstances of believers. This is how the living Word speaks afresh in every generation without ever changing its meaning.

Edward D. Andrews

The Spirit's Work in Application

The Spirit works through the Word to confront, convict, and transform the believer. When Paul says, "the word of God is living and active" (Heb. 4:12), he highlights the Spirit's work of bringing Scripture home to the conscience. This does not happen by mystical infusion of guidance apart from the text, but by the Spirit taking the written Word and applying it to the heart of the believer as he or she studies, meditates, and obeys.

Jesus prayed to the Father, "Sanctify them in the truth; Your word is truth" (John 17:17). Sanctification is the Spirit's work (2 Thess. 2:13), but it is accomplished through the means of the Word. Thus, application is not something we wait passively to receive by inner impressions; it comes as the Spirit uses the inspired text to shape our convictions, priorities, attitudes, and actions.

The Responsibility of the Believer

The Spirit's role in application does not excuse laziness. Believers must actively study, meditate, and discipline themselves to obey. James warns that hearing without doing is self-deception (Jas. 1:22–25). The Spirit does not bypass this process; He empowers it. When the believer humbly receives the Word and strives to live it out, the Spirit applies its truths in transforming power.

Application also requires discernment. Just as one must rightly divide the Word in interpretation, one must rightly apply it in life. The Spirit does not whisper custom-fit directives; He equips believers to think biblically so that they discern good and evil (Heb. 5:14). This is how Christians gain the "mind of Christ" (1 Cor. 2:16)—not through mystical downloads of information but through immersion in the Word until its truth governs every thought.

The Spirit's Role in the Church

The Spirit applies Scripture not only to individuals but to the church as a body. Through faithful preaching and teaching, He convicts, encourages, and builds up His people. The Spirit does not

70

add new revelation through the preacher but wields the inspired Word with power. Paul underscores this when he writes, "our gospel came to you not only in word, but also in power and in the Holy Spirit and with full conviction" (1 Thess. 1:5). The Spirit applies the preached Word to hearts, producing repentance, faith, and obedience.

Why This Matters

A proper view of the Spirit in application protects the church from two dangers. First, it guards against subjectivism—the idea that the Spirit speaks through private impressions apart from Scripture. This reduces application to personal feelings and leads to confusion and contradiction. Second, it guards against dead formalism—the idea that application is merely human effort. The Spirit is truly at work through the Word, transforming lives and sanctifying believers.

In short, the Spirit applies Scripture by taking its fixed meaning and pressing it upon the hearts of believers, so that they embrace it as truth and live it out in obedience. The believer's task is to immerse himself in the Word, trusting that the Spirit will use it to renew his mind and conform him to Christ.

Conclusion: The Spirit and Biblical Interpretation

The Spirit's relationship to Scripture must be defined by the roles that God has assigned to Him, not by the assumptions or mystical expectations of men. The Spirit's primary role was in *inspiration*, breathing out the very words of God through chosen authors so that the finished product was both divine and human, perfectly expressing Jehovah's truth without error. Once inspired, the text itself became the Spirit's voice to every generation, fully sufficient for teaching, rebuke, correction, and training in righteousness.

In the matter of *preservation and restoration*, the Spirit did not promise miraculous or automatic copying, nor did He shield every scribe from error. Instead, He worked through the ordinary labors of scribes and the abundance of manuscripts to ensure that His Word was never lost. Through the providential multiplication of witnesses and the discipline of textual criticism, the church has been able to restore the biblical text with remarkable accuracy, demonstrating the Spirit's wisdom in safeguarding Scripture without reliance on myth or superstition.

In *interpretation*, the Spirit does not grant mystical illumination or impart secret insights apart from the text. Both believer and unbeliever are able to understand the meaning of Scripture by using the same grammatical-historical method. The difference lies in reception: the unbeliever rejects God's Word as folly, while the believer, having the mind of Christ, embraces it as truth. The Spirit does not bypass the intellect but works through the inspired words, guiding us as we submit to Scripture's authority.

Finally, in *application*, the Spirit presses the unchanging meaning of Scripture into the diverse circumstances of believers. He sanctifies the people of God by the Word of truth, enabling them to live out its commands and principles in obedience. The Spirit applies the Word through preaching, teaching, meditation, and personal discipline, transforming hearts and renewing minds so that Christ's people become conformed to His image.

Taken together, these roles emphasize one vital truth: the Spirit has already given us everything necessary in the inspired Word of God. He does not add to it, alter it, or bypass it. He calls us to diligence in study, humility in submission, and faithfulness in obedience. The Spirit and the Word are never in conflict, for the Spirit works only through the Word He breathed out. To seek Him apart from Scripture is to seek in vain. To yield to Him in Scripture is to find life, wisdom, and sanctification.

Review Questions – Chapter 3: The Spirit and Biblical Interpretation

1. What is the Spirit's primary role in relation to Scripture, according to 2 Peter 1:20–21 and 2 Timothy 3:16–17?

2. How does the Spirit's act of inspiration differ from mystical or subjective ideas of revelation?

3. Why must interpreters avoid claiming "illumination" apart from the Spirit-inspired Word of God?

4. How does plenary verbal inspiration safeguard the authority of every word of Scripture?

5. Why is it important to distinguish between the Spirit's work in inspiring the authors and His present work in guiding readers through the written Word?

6. How do Nehemiah 8:8 and Acts 17:11 demonstrate the Spirit's role in interpretation through Scripture itself?

7. What dangers arise when interpreters appeal to inner impressions rather than the inspired text?

8. How does recognizing the Spirit's role in inspiration protect against allegory, typology, and subjective speculation?

9. Why is the doctrine of the Spirit's inspiration foundational for a faithful hermeneutic?

10. In what ways does affirming the Spirit's inspiration call the church to submit to Scripture as the final authority?

CHAPTER 4 Words That Shape Hearts and Minds: Decoding Biblical Language and Literary Forms

Speaking to Mind and Heart: The Dual Voices of Biblical Language

The Bible is unlike any other book in history because it is the inspired Word of Jehovah, breathed out through human authors. Yet, in its divine wisdom, it makes use of the full range of human language. One of the most important keys for understanding the Bible is to recognize that it speaks in two distinct voices. One voice addresses the mind, communicating truth with clarity and precision. The other voice stirs the heart, awakening emotion, imagination, and desire for obedience. These two modes of communication—informative and evocative—are woven seamlessly together in Scripture, shaping both thought and affection so that God's people may be transformed in the whole of their being.

Informative Language: Speaking to the Mind

Informative language is the vehicle of factual communication. Its aim is to instruct, to explain, and to transmit accurate content. In everyday life, this is the language of a recipe card that directs one to use "two cups of flour," or a GPS unit that gives step-by-step directions. It is the language of the classroom when a teacher outlines the events of history, or the workplace when a technician details the steps to repair a computer. Informative language serves clarity and precision; its purpose is to make truth understandable and actionable.

In Scripture, informative language appears in passages of law, instruction, and doctrine. When Moses delivers the Ten Commandments (Exod. 20:1–17), the language is factual and directive: "You shall not steal," "You shall not murder," "Remember the Sabbath day." Each command communicates a clear, non-negotiable truth. Likewise, Paul in Romans unfolds doctrine through logical reasoning: "Therefore, since we have been justified by faith, we have peace with God through our Lord Jesus Christ" (Rom. 5:1). The language is not poetic or metaphorical but precise, aiming to inform the mind of the believer of what God has accomplished.

The strength of informative language is its ability to anchor the church in truth. Faith comes by hearing, and hearing by the Word of Christ (Rom. 10:17). Without factual content communicated in clear terms, Christianity would dissolve into mere feeling or mystical impression. Informative language gives the church the doctrinal foundation on which to stand.

Evocative Language: Speaking to the Heart

But Scripture is not only concerned with instructing the mind; it is equally concerned with stirring the heart. Evocative language exists to inspire, persuade, and move. Its purpose is not merely to transmit data but to awaken response—love, fear, joy, hope, repentance, and worship. In ordinary life, this is the language of a wedding vow, a political speech, or a poem. It is the language that makes us weep at a song lyric or feel courage rise during a coach's halftime rally.

The Bible is rich with evocative language. When David cries, "Jehovah is my shepherd, I shall not want" (Ps. 23:1), he is not only stating theological fact but evoking the tender imagery of a shepherd's care. When Isaiah proclaims, "Those who wait for Jehovah shall renew their strength; they shall mount up with wings like eagles" (Isa. 40:31), the language soars, awakening the heart to hope. Jesus Himself often used evocative speech in parables: "A sower went out to sow…" (Matt. 13:3). The purpose was not to provide mere agricultural instruction but to provoke imagination, self-reflection, and spiritual decision.

The strength of evocative language is its ability to penetrate where cold fact cannot. Doctrine alone may inform, but evocative imagery and appeal ignite the affections. A believer is not only to know the truth but to love it, rejoice in it, and live it out with zeal.

The Harmony of the Two Voices

Informative and evocative language are not enemies but partners in Scripture. Often the same passage carries both. When Paul writes of the resurrection in 1 Corinthians 15, he speaks with precision about the historical reality of Christ's rising, grounding faith in fact. Yet he also exclaims with pathos, "O death, where is your victory? O death, where is your sting?" (1 Cor. 15:55). The language is both doctrinal and doxological, factual and poetic. It informs the mind while stirring the heart.

The same harmony is evident in Jesus' Sermon on the Mount. He declares factual truths about righteousness, fasting, prayer, and the Kingdom, but He frames them in vivid, evocative imagery: "You are the salt of the earth... You are the light of the world" (Matt. 5:13–14). Such expressions communicate doctrine while moving disciples to live as salt and light in a dark world.

In this way, the Bible shapes both the intellect and the affections, producing believers who not only know the truth but also love and obey it.

The Danger of Confusion

Misinterpretation often arises when one fails to recognize whether Scripture is speaking primarily in informative or evocative language. To read poetry as if it were literal prose is to distort its meaning, just as to read law as if it were metaphor is to neutralize its authority. For instance, when the psalmist says that the trees of the field "clap their hands" (Isa. 55:12), the evocative nature of the language is clear. To force literalism here is to miss the author's intent. Conversely, when Paul commands, "Do not be conformed to this world, but be transformed by the renewal of your mind" (Rom. 12:2), the language is informative and imperative; to reduce it to mere metaphor is to evade its authority.

Faithful interpretation requires sensitivity to these dual voices, recognizing the author's willed use of language and responding accordingly.

Why This Matters

The Bible's genius lies in its ability to unite precision and passion. It is a book of truth that speaks to the mind and a book of beauty that speaks to the heart. To sever the two is to diminish the fullness of its power. Informative language grounds us in fact; evocative language stirs us to worship and obedience. Together they produce believers whose faith is both rationally sound and spiritually alive.

This dual character reflects the very nature of true religion. Jehovah does not call His people to bare intellectual assent alone, nor to unanchored emotionalism. He calls for worship "in spirit and truth" (John 4:24)—truth to inform the mind and spirit to stir the heart. The Bible, through its two voices, provides the perfect instrument for such worship.

Meaning and Literary Forms

Because Jehovah has chosen to reveal Himself through human language, His Word is clothed in literary form. Meaning never exists in isolation from the genre, structure, and style by which it is expressed. Just as an artist communicates through brushstrokes on a canvas or a composer through the rhythms of a symphony, so the biblical authors communicated their intended meaning through specific literary forms. To grasp their meaning, the interpreter must recognize and respect these forms, allowing them to guide how the text is read and understood.

The Interdependence of Meaning and Form

Meaning is always bound up with form. An author does not first conceive a raw, contentless idea and then clothe it in arbitrary words.

Rather, the words, the syntax, the genre, and the chosen literary style are the very means by which the author conveys his meaning. Therefore, one cannot rightly understand the message without attending to its form.

When David writes, "Jehovah is my shepherd; I shall not want" (Ps. 23:1), he does not merely state a fact about God's providence. He communicates it through the form of pastoral poetry, using imagery and rhythm that both inform the mind and stir the heart. To strip the verse of its poetic form would be to miss the fullness of its meaning. Similarly, when Moses records the Ten Commandments in Exodus 20, the terse, imperative form is inseparable from their meaning as binding covenant stipulations.

The Variety of Biblical Literary Forms

Scripture is a library, not a single-genre book. It contains narrative, law, poetry, prophecy, wisdom, gospel, parable, epistle, and apocalyptic. Each of these literary forms carries conventions that govern how meaning is communicated.

Narrative conveys meaning by recounting events in sequence, showing Jehovah's hand in history. Law communicates through imperatives and prohibitions, defining covenantal obligations. Poetry compresses truth into imagery, parallelism, and rhythm, appealing to both intellect and emotion. Prophecy combines declaration and prediction, often framed in vivid symbolic language. Wisdom literature presents general principles of life in memorable sayings. Parables use story and comparison to provoke moral reflection. Epistles develop meaning through logical argument and exhortation. Apocalyptic reveals future realities through visions, symbols, and cosmic imagery.

To ignore form is to distort meaning. Reading Proverbs as absolute promises rather than wise observations leads to disillusionment. Treating apocalyptic visions as wooden literalism breeds confusion. Interpreting poetry as prose flattens its force. Each form must be read by its rules, for the Spirit inspired the meaning through those forms.

Scriptural Examples of Meaning Expressed in Form

The connection between meaning and form is evident throughout Scripture.

- In Exodus 15, the song of Moses celebrates deliverance from Egypt. The meaning is not merely historical record but worshipful response, communicated through poetic song.

- In Matthew 13, Jesus communicates kingdom truths through parables. The meaning is not in literal agricultural instruction but in the moral and spiritual realities conveyed through story.

- In Paul's epistles, doctrine is expressed through carefully reasoned argument. Romans 3:21–26, for instance, unfolds the meaning of justification through legal and theological categories, not through parable or poetry.

The same truth expressed in a different form would carry different force. Thus, the meaning is inseparable from the form.

The Interpreter's Responsibility

Faithful exegesis requires the interpreter to honor the literary form chosen by the author. The question is never, "What does this mean to me?" but, "What did the author intend to communicate through this form?" Only when meaning is discerned through form can the message be understood and applied rightly.

This demands genre awareness, literary sensitivity, and respect for the rules of communication embedded in each form. The Spirit did not inspire abstract truths but truths clothed in concrete language, literary structure, and style. To misread the form is to misread the meaning.

Why This Matters

By uniting meaning with literary form, the Bible speaks powerfully to mind and heart. Doctrine is given not only in logical propositions but in stories, songs, and symbols. Commands come not only as bare laws but as narratives that display their wisdom and as poetry that sings their beauty. Recognizing the interdependence of meaning and form equips the interpreter to receive the Bible as it is—the living Word of God, speaking through the diverse voices of human authors, yet always conveying the singular truth Jehovah intended.

Review Questions – Chapter 4: Words That Shape Hearts and Minds

1. According to 2 Timothy 2:15, what does it mean to "rightly handle the word of truth," and how does this verse frame the goal of hermeneutics?

2. How is the *goal of hermeneutics* both to understand the meaning God intended and to apply it faithfully in doctrine, worship, and daily living?

3. What role does Nehemiah 8:8 play in demonstrating the process of reading, explaining, and applying Scripture?

4. Why must interpretation involve an author, a text, and a reader, and what happens if one of these elements is removed?

5. How does Luke 1:1–4 illustrate the importance of explicit authorial purpose in biblical communication?

6. Why is the written text itself the God-ordained medium of revelation, rather than mystical impressions or unwritten traditions?

7. How does Acts 17:11 present readers as responsible to test and examine the text carefully?

8. In what ways does recognizing different literary forms (e.g., narrative, poetry, law) protect against misinterpretation?

9. Why is genre a key factor in determining meaning, and how does it shape expectations for interpretation?

10. How does the recognition of rhetoric and form safeguard interpretation from proof-texting and distortion?

Part 2 The Specific Rules for Interpreting Different Genres

Edward D. Andrews

CHAPTER 5 Interpreting Biblical Narrative

Narrative as History: Reading Events as God's Works in Time

Biblical narrative is not myth, allegory, or typological shadowplay. It is history—Jehovah's acts in time, faithfully recorded by inspired authors to reveal His purposes and His truth. To interpret narrative correctly, the interpreter must approach it with unwavering conviction that the events described actually occurred and that the meaning of the narrative lies in what the author intended to communicate about those events.

Narrative as the Vehicle of God's Revelation

Unlike the mythologies of the ancient Near East or the Greco-Roman world, biblical narrative is not the product of human imagination, tribal folklore, or religious storytelling. The inspired writers present real events in history, involving real people, in real places. Abraham left Ur. Israel crossed the Red Sea. David reigned in Jerusalem. Jesus was crucified under Pontius Pilate. These are not metaphors for spiritual truths but concrete acts in space and time. The biblical authors wrote as historians, recording the works of Jehovah in human history to show His covenant purposes unfolding.

Moses declares at the beginning of Genesis, "In the beginning, God created the heavens and the earth" (Gen. 1:1). This is not poetic speculation or mythological imagery; it is the historical assertion that Jehovah is the Creator of all things. Luke likewise grounds his Gospel in history: "Inasmuch as many have undertaken to compile a narrative of the things that have been accomplished among us... it seemed good to me also... to write an orderly account... that you may have certainty concerning the things you have been taught" (Luke 1:1–4). Biblical narrative is rooted in history and aims to provide certainty, not speculation.

The Purpose of Historical Narrative

Biblical narrative does more than report bare facts. It interprets history, showing the hand of God in human affairs. The inspired authors selected events, arranged them, and emphasized details according to the message they willed to communicate. The events are true, but the meaning lies in what the author intended to highlight about God, His people, His promises, and His judgments.

For example, the account of the Exodus is historical record— Israel did leave Egypt under Moses, passing through the Red Sea. But Moses, under inspiration, does not recount every logistical detail of the journey. He narrates the event to display Jehovah's power, His faithfulness to His covenant, and His supremacy over Pharaoh. The meaning of the narrative is tied to the theological point communicated through the historical events.

Guarding Against Allegory and Typology

Many have mishandled biblical narrative by turning it into allegory or uncontrolled typology. In allegory, the narrative is stripped of its historical reality and reinterpreted as a symbolic tale pointing to hidden spiritual truths. In typology, interpreters often go beyond the inspired author's intention, assigning symbolic or foreshadowing meanings that the text itself never claims.

Both approaches violate the principle of grammatical-historical interpretation. They shift authority from the inspired author to the imagination of the interpreter. For instance, treating the crossing of the Jordan River in Joshua 3 as an allegory of the believer entering heaven empties the narrative of its historical and covenantal significance. Likewise, inventing typological parallels between Old Testament characters and New Testament realities, unless directly stated by inspired Scripture, is speculative and distorts the text.

The faithful interpreter rejects these methods and instead honors the narrative as both historical and theological—real events communicated with divine purpose.

Reading Narrative as God's Works in Time

When approaching biblical narrative, the interpreter must recognize that these are not random or neutral stories. They are accounts of Jehovah's works in history, recorded to display His character and will. The chronicling of battles, genealogies, journeys, and kings is not antiquarian curiosity but revelation of God's sovereign rule.

In Genesis, the creation, flood, and patriarchal accounts are presented as real history, demonstrating Jehovah's power, judgment, and covenant faithfulness. In the books of Samuel and Kings, the rise and fall of monarchs reveal Jehovah's standards of righteousness and His judgment upon disobedience. In the Gospels, every miracle, teaching, and act of Christ reveals Him as the incarnate Son who fulfilled the Father's will in time and space.

To read narrative faithfully is therefore to see history as the stage upon which God works out His plan of redemption. The Bible's narratives are not primarily about human achievement but about divine action.

Why This Matters

If narrative is read as allegory or myth, the authority of Scripture is lost, and its meaning becomes fluid. But if it is read as inspired history, it grounds faith in real acts of God and anchors doctrine in concrete reality. Christianity is not built upon ideas or moral tales but upon the fact that God has acted in history, culminating in the death and resurrection of Jesus Christ (1 Cor. 15:3–8).

Biblical narrative, then, must always be interpreted as history— Jehovah's works in time, faithfully recorded to instruct His people. The meaning is found in the author's inspired interpretation of those events, not in speculative allegories or invented typologies.

Theological Purpose in Narrative: More Than Storytelling

Biblical narrative is not bare chronicle, nor is it a collection of entertaining stories designed merely to inspire or amuse. The authors of Scripture, carried along by the Holy Spirit (2 Pet. 1:21), selected, arranged, and recorded historical events in such a way that those events would convey a theological message. Their purpose was not simply to tell what happened but to explain why it mattered in the plan of Jehovah. Every detail of biblical narrative has been included for theological instruction.

Narrative as Theological Communication

Narrative communicates more than sequence; it communicates significance. The inspired author is not a detached historian recounting neutral facts. He writes as a covenant messenger, explaining the meaning of history in light of God's will and purposes. The message of the narrative lies not only in the events themselves but in the author's inspired arrangement and commentary upon them.

Consider the books of Kings. They record centuries of Israel's monarchy, not in exhaustive political detail, but in a theological framework: each king is evaluated by whether he did "what was right in the eyes of Jehovah" or "what was evil." The historical facts of reign length, battles, and alliances are presented, but always with the theological judgment that faithfulness to Jehovah is the true measure of a king's worth.

The Gospels provide another clear example. They record real events from the life of Jesus, but they are not mere biographies. Each Evangelist arranges material to emphasize theological truths. John structures his Gospel around seven signs and seven "I am" statements to demonstrate that Jesus is the Christ, the Son of God, and that by believing, readers may have life in His name (John 20:31). The narrative is history, but its purpose is explicitly theological.

Edward D. Andrews

The Selection and Arrangement of Material

Biblical authors did not attempt to include every possible detail of history. Instead, they selected and arranged what was necessary to convey their theological intent. John acknowledges this explicitly: "Now Jesus did many other signs in the presence of the disciples, which are not written in this book; but these are written so that you may believe…" (John 20:30–31). The selection is theological.

The arrangement also communicates theology. The book of Judges is structured in cycles, showing how Israel repeatedly fell into sin, cried out for deliverance, and was rescued by judges whom God raised up. This cycle reveals the theological truth of Israel's unfaithfulness and Jehovah's mercy. Without recognizing the theological shaping of the narrative, the interpreter misses its meaning.

Examples of Theological Purpose in Narrative

Theological purpose is evident throughout biblical narrative.

- **The Exodus Story**: Israel's deliverance from Egypt is not merely national history but revelation of Jehovah's power over false gods, His faithfulness to covenant promises, and His redemption of His people by blood.

- **David and Goliath (1 Sam. 17)**: This is not simply an inspiring tale of underdog triumph. It is a theological statement about Jehovah's sovereignty, that salvation belongs not to human strength or weaponry but to the God who delivers His people.

- **The Crucifixion Accounts**: The Gospels record the historical execution of Jesus, but they shape the narrative to emphasize theological truth: His death was the fulfillment of Scripture, the sacrifice for sin, and the demonstration of divine love.

These examples demonstrate that meaning is not exhausted by the historical event itself. The meaning is in what the inspired author willed to communicate about God, His purposes, and His covenant relationship with His people through the record of the event.

Guarding Against Mere Storytelling

Modern preaching and teaching often reduce biblical narrative to moral tales or human-centered inspiration. David becomes a model for "facing your giants." Joseph becomes a lesson in career perseverance. These misuses flatten narrative into mere storytelling and miss its theological depth. The text was not given to entertain or provide motivational slogans but to reveal God and His works in history.

The faithful interpreter resists the temptation to treat narratives as fables or inspirational anecdotes. Instead, he seeks to discern the theological truth that the inspired author intended to convey.

Why Theological Purpose Matters

Narrative is never neutral. It always comes to us as God's Word with a theological aim. To read it merely as story is to miss its authority. To read it theologically is to hear the voice of Jehovah, calling His people to faith, repentance, and obedience.

Biblical narrative shows us that history itself is theology in motion. Every event is part of the unfolding plan of redemption, and every inspired record of those events communicates God's purposes for His people. The interpreter must therefore approach narrative not only as history but as theology—truth revealed in and through history.

Identifying Plot, Characters, and Setting Without Allegorizing

Biblical narrative, like all narrative, is built from recognizable literary components: a plot that unfolds, characters who act, and a setting in which the events occur. These elements are not incidental—they are the Spirit-inspired framework through which the author communicates meaning. Yet while narratives make use of these literary features, they are not to be treated as allegories or symbols pointing to hidden spiritual truths. To interpret rightly, the reader must identify these narrative elements carefully, without wandering into speculative allegory.

Plot as the Framework of God's Actions

The plot of a biblical narrative is the sequence of events that moves from a beginning through conflict to resolution. But unlike fictional storytelling, biblical plots are grounded in real history. Their function is not merely to entertain but to reveal Jehovah's purposes at work in time.

Consider the account of Joseph in Genesis 37–50. The plot unfolds with Joseph's dreams, his brothers' betrayal, his slavery and imprisonment, his rise to power in Egypt, and finally his reconciliation with his family. The plot is historical, yet its theological meaning is woven into its development: Jehovah's providence is sovereign, turning human evil into good for the saving of many lives (Gen. 50:20). To allegorize Joseph as "a type of Christ" at every turn misses the author's purpose. The meaning lies in the inspired shaping of the plot to demonstrate divine sovereignty.

The interpreter's task is to follow the movement of the plot, recognizing rising tension, climax, and resolution, and then ask how the inspired author uses that progression to communicate God's truth.

Characters as Agents of Theological Truth

Biblical narratives also communicate through characters. Kings, prophets, apostles, and ordinary men and women act, speak, and respond. Yet these characters are not symbols in an allegorical drama; they are real people whose actions reveal theological realities.

For example, in the book of Judges, characters such as Gideon, Samson, and Jephthah are presented with their flaws and failures. They are not idealized heroes or allegorical figures but historical individuals whose lives expose Israel's spiritual decline and Jehovah's mercy in raising deliverers despite their weakness. Likewise, in the Gospels, Peter's denial of Christ is not an allegory of the church but the real action of a disciple, through which readers learn about human frailty and Christ's forgiveness.

The interpreter must therefore attend to how the inspired author portrays characters—what they say, how they act, and how they are evaluated—not by searching for hidden symbolic correspondences but by discerning the theological truth revealed through their historical reality.

Setting as the Stage of Revelation

Every narrative occurs in a setting—geographical, cultural, and temporal. The inspired authors often highlight setting to underscore theological points. The wilderness, for instance, is more than a physical backdrop; it becomes a place of testing and dependence on Jehovah. Jerusalem is not merely a city; it is the chosen center of worship. Galilee, often despised, becomes the place where the Messiah begins His ministry, highlighting the reversal of human expectations.

Yet even here, the interpreter must resist allegory. The wilderness is not to be spiritualized into "the wilderness of the soul" unless the author himself indicates such a meaning. Jerusalem is not a cipher for the church unless explicitly treated that way in inspired Scripture. The setting is significant, but its significance must be drawn from the author's intent, not the imagination of the interpreter.

Avoiding Allegorical Distortion

Throughout church history, allegory has been a frequent abuse of narrative interpretation. Origen, for instance, allegorized the details of Old Testament narratives to extract hidden meanings that bore little resemblance to the author's purpose. A river becomes "faith," a mountain becomes "prayer," a character becomes "the soul." Such methods abandon the historical reality of the narrative and elevate the interpreter's creativity above the inspired text.

Faithful interpretation avoids this trap by recognizing that plot, characters, and setting are not allegories but the inspired means by which the author communicates theological truth. The narrative communicates in its plain sense, not through hidden codes or symbols waiting to be unlocked.

Why This Matters

If the interpreter allegorizes plot, characters, and setting, he detaches the narrative from its historical grounding and obscures the author's message. But if he attends carefully to these elements as real historical features presented with theological purpose, he honors both the factual truth of the events and the inspired meaning conveyed through them.

Plot, characters, and setting are not literary ornaments but Spirit-inspired vehicles of revelation. To interpret them faithfully is to see God's hand in history, to hear His truth in the lives of real people, and to recognize His purposes in the actual settings where redemption unfolded.

The Role of Repetition, Dialogue, and Structure in Conveying Meaning

One of the most striking features of biblical narrative is the deliberate use of repetition, dialogue, and literary structure. These are not accidents of storytelling, nor are they merely stylistic flourishes. They are Spirit-inspired techniques that the biblical authors employed to emphasize, clarify, and drive home theological truths. The reader who overlooks these features risks missing the weight of the narrative's meaning.

Repetition as a Theological Signal

Repetition in biblical narrative is rarely wasted ink. When details, phrases, or events are repeated, the author is signaling importance. The repetition may occur within a single narrative or across larger sections of Scripture. In either case, it functions to draw the reader's attention to a theological point.

In Genesis 39, the repeated phrase "Jehovah was with Joseph" occurs four times in close succession (vv. 2, 3, 21, 23). This is no accident. The repetition underscores that Joseph's success and preservation were not due to his own ingenuity but to Jehovah's presence. The repeated statement serves as a theological key to the entire narrative.

Similarly, in Judges 17–21, the refrain "In those days there was no king in Israel; everyone did what was right in his own eyes" appears multiple times (Judg. 17:6; 18:1; 19:1; 21:25). This repetition highlights the chaos of Israel's spiritual decline and the need for righteous leadership. By repeating the refrain, the inspired author interprets the narratives of violence and corruption as symptoms of covenantal disorder.

Repetition is therefore a theological spotlight. The interpreter must pay careful attention to it, for it signals what the author most wants the reader to grasp.

Dialogue as a Window into Meaning

Dialogue is another key device in biblical narrative. The words spoken by characters often carry the central message of the passage. In many cases, the turning point of a narrative lies not in action but in speech.

Consider Genesis 22, the account of Abraham's offering of Isaac. The climax of the narrative is found in the dialogue between father and son: "Isaac said to his father Abraham, 'My father!' And he said, 'Here I am, my son.' He said, 'Behold, the fire and the wood, but where is the lamb for a burnt offering?' Abraham said, 'God will provide for Himself the lamb for a burnt offering, my son'" (vv. 7–8). These words interpret the event. The meaning of the narrative lies not merely in Abraham's actions but in his declaration of faith that Jehovah Himself would provide the sacrifice.

The book of Job is almost entirely dialogue. Job's lament, his friends' responses, and ultimately Jehovah's speeches form the heart of the book's theology. To treat Job as mere story without attending to the dialogue would be to miss the inspired message.

Dialogue is not filler; it is often the vehicle of theological revelation. Interpreters must listen carefully to the voices of the characters, discerning how their words convey the meaning of the narrative.

Structure as the Framework of Revelation

Biblical authors also employ structure to shape the meaning of their narratives. Events are arranged in deliberate patterns, often using symmetry, parallels, or contrasts. Recognizing these structures is vital for interpretation.

One common device is the *chiastic structure*, where events or ideas are arranged in a mirrored pattern (A-B-C-B'-A'). For example, the Flood narrative in Genesis 6–9 is structured chiastically, with the statement "God remembered Noah" (Gen. 8:1) at the center. This structure emphasizes that the turning point of the story is not the rising or falling of the waters but Jehovah's covenantal faithfulness.

Parallel accounts also reveal theological design. The repeated cycle in Judges—sin, oppression, cry for help, deliverance—structures the entire book, showing the pattern of Israel's unfaithfulness and God's mercy. In the Gospels, the parallel feeding miracles (feeding of the five thousand in Mark 6 and the four thousand in Mark 8) are structured to highlight the disciples' slowness to grasp Jesus' identity and His sufficiency for Jew and Gentile alike.

Structure is not arbitrary. It is the inspired author's way of directing the reader to the theological center of the narrative.

Guarding Against Overreading

While repetition, dialogue, and structure are crucial for interpretation, the interpreter must guard against overreading them. The goal is not to impose hidden meanings or symbolic layers but to recognize how the author has intentionally shaped the narrative to emphasize his message. Not every repeated phrase is a code, not every dialogue carries hidden allegory, and not every structure is perfectly symmetrical. Faithful interpretation respects the evidence of the text without forcing patterns that the author did not intend.

Why These Features Matter

Repetition, dialogue, and structure remind us that biblical narrative is not a random collection of facts. It is carefully crafted, Spirit-inspired communication. To pay attention to these features is to honor the author's craft and, more importantly, to hear more clearly the truth that God has revealed.

These literary features do not detract from the historical reality of the events. Rather, they show how the inspired authors presented history in such a way that its theological significance would shine through. In the hands of Moses, Samuel, the Chronicler, the Gospel writers, and others, history becomes proclamation: the living God has acted, and here is what it means.

The Danger of Allegorizing and Typologizing Scripture

What is said here about allegorizing and typology is applicable to all genres of Scripture that will follow. Faithful interpretation requires drawing a sharp line between the inspired authors' use of literary devices and the uninspired imagination of later interpreters. The prophets, apostles, and Christ Himself, carried along by the Holy Spirit (2 Pet. 1:21), occasionally employed allegory or typology. When they did so, it was legitimate, authoritative, and divinely sanctioned. However, no interpreter today has the right to replicate that use, because modern readers are not inspired. We must confine ourselves to the Historical-Grammatical method, which seeks to uncover the single, plain meaning of the text as intended by its original author and understood by its first hearers.

Allegory: Literary Device Versus Interpretive Abuse

Allegory, properly understood, is a literary device in which imagery or symbolism conveys truth. Scripture itself sometimes uses allegory in this way. For example, in Psalm 80:8–9 Israel is portrayed as a vine transplanted from Egypt, and in John 10:11 Jesus describes Himself as the Good Shepherd. Both examples communicate spiritual realities through figurative imagery, and both are clear in their meaning. The biblical writers signal the allegory and use it purposefully.

But allegorizing as an interpretive method is something altogether different. It is the attempt to impose hidden, symbolic meanings upon Scripture beyond the literal sense intended by the author. This practice has roots in Greek philosophy, particularly in Philo of Alexandria, who allegorized the details of Genesis to make them fit Platonic categories. The garments of skin in Genesis 3 became, for him, a symbol of the body; the rivers of Eden became abstract virtues. Early Christian interpreters such as Origen and Augustine carried this method into the church, often forcing spiritual meanings onto the text with little concern for context or history.

The Reformers rejected this approach. Luther and Calvin insisted that the text must be allowed to speak for itself, not be bent to the interpreter's imagination. Calvin wrote that the first duty of an interpreter is "to let his author say what he does say, instead of attributing to him what we think he ought to say." Allegorizing shifts authority away from the inspired Word to the mind of the interpreter.

Typology: Inspired Use Versus Human Speculation

Typology differs from allegory in that it deals with historical correspondences between Old Testament persons, events, or institutions and their New Testament fulfillment. Scripture itself sometimes identifies these connections. Paul calls Adam a "type" of Christ in Romans 5:14. Jesus identifies the serpent lifted up in the wilderness as a type of His crucifixion in John 3:14. The writer of Hebrews explains that the sacrificial system and priesthood were shadows pointing to Christ (Heb. 9:11–12; 10:1). These are divinely revealed types, and as such, they are authoritative.

But while the apostles and New Testament writers could employ typology under the Spirit's inspiration, modern interpreters cannot. We are not divinely authorized to create new typological connections. To claim that every Old Testament king foreshadows Christ, or that every battle symbolizes spiritual warfare, or that the ark represents the church, is to indulge in speculation. This practice ignores the grammatical-historical meaning of the Old Testament text and substitutes human imagination.

Typology, like allegory, becomes dangerous when it is employed as a method rather than recognized as a feature of inspired Scripture. The Old Testament should be read in its historical and literary context, not as a coded system of symbols awaiting imaginative discovery.

The New Testament's Use of the Old Testament

It is also important to note how New Testament writers handle Old Testament texts. They do so in two distinct ways.

First, at times they draw directly on the grammatical-historical meaning of an Old Testament passage, treating it as prophecy fulfilled. For example, Matthew cites Micah 5:2 to show that the Messiah would be born in Bethlehem (Matt. 2:5–6). This was the original meaning of Micah's words, and Matthew affirms it.

Second, at other times New Testament writers go beyond the Old Testament author's immediate meaning, assigning an additional sense in light of Christ. For example, Hosea 11:1 originally referred to Israel's exodus from Egypt, but Matthew applies it to Jesus' return from Egypt after Herod's death (Matt. 2:15). Hosea's meaning was historical and covenantal for Israel, while Matthew, under the Spirit's guidance, expands the meaning to show a correspondence with Christ. Both uses are inspired. But this kind of dual-layered interpretation is the privilege of inspired authors only. We do not have the authority to follow their example in creating additional meanings.

The Historical-Grammatical Method as Safeguard

The Historical-Grammatical method alone safeguards the clarity and authority of Scripture. It requires us to ask: What did the author intend? How would his original audience have understood these words? What is the plain meaning in its context? This method leaves no room for allegorizing or speculative typology. It anchors interpretation in facts—grammar, history, culture, and context—rather than imagination.

The Bereans in Acts 17:11 exemplify this approach. They did not seek hidden allegories or speculative types. They examined the Scriptures daily to see whether Paul's teaching corresponded to what was written. This is the model for faithful interpretation.

The Dangers of Allegory and Typology

The use of allegory or typology outside the bounds of inspired Scripture produces serious theological errors. Some deny the historicity of Adam and Eve by allegorizing them into symbols of humanity. Others allegorize the temple into a figure of the human body, detaching it from its covenantal role in Israel's worship. Still others multiply types of Christ throughout the Old Testament until the historical meaning of the text disappears.

Such errors undermine both the authority of Scripture and the clarity of its message. If meaning lies in hidden allegories or types, then every interpreter becomes his own authority, and the text ceases to speak with a single, clear voice.

Conclusion: Honoring the Inspired Word

The biblical writers, under divine inspiration, sometimes employed allegory and typology. Their use is legitimate because it was directed by the Spirit. But modern interpreters are not inspired and have no license to imitate this method. Our responsibility is to read Scripture historically, grammatically, and contextually, uncovering the meaning the Spirit has already placed in the text.

By refusing to allegorize or invent typologies, we honor the sufficiency of the Word and protect ourselves from subjective distortion. The Spirit's Word is clear. Our task is not to create new meanings but to understand, teach, and obey the one meaning He has already given.

Review Questions – Chapter 5: Interpreting Biblical Narrative

1. What distinguishes biblical narrative from other genres, and why is it essential to recognize its historical nature?

2. How does the historical-grammatical method protect narrative interpretation from allegory or typology?

3. Why must the meaning of a narrative be tied to the inspired author's intent and the covenant context?

4. How does the narrator's perspective (e.g., omniscient, selective) shape the way a biblical story communicates truth?

5. What role do characters and dialogue play in conveying the theological message of a narrative?

6. Why is it important to identify the structure of a narrative (beginning, crisis, climax, resolution) in interpretation?

7. How does the immediate literary context influence the meaning of a single episode within a larger narrative?

8. What safeguards prevent interpreters from reading themselves into the story or moralizing every detail?

9. How do narratives reveal Jehovah's redemptive purposes without collapsing into speculation or hidden meanings?

10. In what ways can the lessons of biblical narrative be faithfully applied to the life of the church today?

Exercises in Interpretation – Chapter 5: Interpreting Biblical Narrative

Exercise 1: Joseph and His Brothers (Genesis 45:1–8)

- Read the passage carefully, noting Joseph's words to his brothers.

- Identify the narrator's theological emphasis in verse 5 ("God sent me before you to preserve life").

- How does this statement anchor the meaning of the story in God's sovereign purpose rather than in Joseph's personal triumph?

Exercise 2: David and Goliath (1 Samuel 17:41–51)

- Trace the flow of the story from David's confidence in Jehovah to his victory over Goliath.

- What is the main point of the narrative, and how do details such as David's youth or the size of Goliath serve the central message rather than standing as independent symbols?

- How should this passage be applied today without turning it into allegory or moralistic symbolism?

Exercise 3: The Healing of the Paralytic (Mark 2:1–12)

- Observe how the narrative builds tension through the paralytic's friends, the scribes' objections, and Jesus' climactic declaration of authority to forgive sins.

- What does the narrative structure reveal about the central theological point of the passage?

- How might an overemphasis on side details (e.g., persistence of friends, architecture of the house) distract from the Spirit-inspired meaning?

CHAPTER 6 Interpreting Covenants and Laws

Covenants as the Backbone of Redemptive History

The history of the Bible is the history of God's covenants. These covenants are not minor agreements or isolated promises but the very backbone of redemptive history. Through them Jehovah revealed His character, established His relationship with His people, and unfolded His plan of salvation across time. To interpret Scripture faithfully, one must understand the role of covenants, for they provide the structure and framework by which the entire biblical narrative holds together.

The Nature of a Covenant

A covenant in the biblical sense is a binding agreement initiated by God, sovereignly administered, and often confirmed by oath, sacrifice, or sign. Unlike human contracts, which involve negotiation between equals, divine covenants are gracious acts of condescension whereby Jehovah binds Himself by promise and stipulation to His creatures. The recipients of the covenant do not set its terms; they receive it and are obligated to respond in faith and obedience.

The Hebrew term *berith* and the Greek *diathēkē* both carry the sense of a solemn binding arrangement. The essential feature of the biblical covenant is that it is both relational and legal—relational in that it establishes communion between God and His people, legal in that it involves stipulations, blessings, and curses.

Covenants Across Scripture

From Genesis to Revelation, the covenants serve as the scaffolding on which the story of redemption is built. Each covenant moves the narrative forward, revealing more of God's purposes and clarifying His plan of salvation.

- **The Noahic Covenant (Gen. 9:8–17):** Following the Flood of 2348 B.C.E., Jehovah covenanted never again to destroy all flesh by water. This covenant established the stability of the natural order, ensuring that the world would continue as the arena of redemption.

- **The Abrahamic Covenant (Gen. 12:1–3; 15:1–21; 17:1–14):** In 2091 B.C.E., Jehovah promised Abraham land, descendants, and blessing to all nations through his seed. This covenant is foundational for understanding Israel's role in God's plan and the coming of the Messiah.

- **The Mosaic Covenant (Exod. 19–24):** Instituted at Sinai in 1446 B.C.E., this covenant gave Israel the law, setting forth the terms of their relationship with Jehovah as His chosen nation. It revealed God's holiness, exposed human sin, and pointed forward to the need for a greater covenant.

- **The Davidic Covenant (2 Sam. 7:12–16):** Established in the reign of David around 1000 B.C.E., this covenant promised an eternal dynasty culminating in the reign of the Messiah.

- **The New Covenant (Jer. 31:31–34; Luke 22:20):** Fulfilled in Christ, this covenant brings forgiveness of sins and the law written on the heart. It is the climactic expression of God's covenant purposes, embracing both Jew and Gentile in one redeemed people.

Each covenant is historical, concrete, and progressive, yet together they form a unified plan leading to Christ.

The Theological Significance of the Covenants

The covenants are not side themes but the central thread of Scripture. They reveal the character of God as faithful, merciful, and sovereign. They define the identity of God's people as His covenant community. They disclose His plan to redeem and bless the nations through the seed of Abraham, fulfilled in Christ.

Understanding the covenants protects the interpreter from fragmentation. Without them, the Bible can appear as a collection of disconnected stories and laws. With them, the unity of redemptive history becomes clear: one God, one plan, one unfolding purpose, moving steadily from promise to fulfillment.

Implications for Interpretation

Because covenants are foundational, the interpreter must always read Scripture with covenantal awareness. Law cannot be understood apart from the covenant in which it was given. Prophecy cannot be grasped apart from covenant blessings and curses. Narrative cannot be interpreted apart from the covenant framework in which the events unfold.

For example, Israel's exile cannot be understood without Deuteronomy's covenant warnings. The hope of a coming Messiah cannot be grasped without the Davidic promise of an eternal king. The blessings of forgiveness and new life in Christ cannot be appreciated without Jeremiah's prophecy of a new covenant written on the heart.

Why Covenants Are the Backbone

To call covenants the backbone of redemptive history is to recognize that they give structure, coherence, and direction to the biblical story. Just as a backbone supports and unifies the body, so the covenants support and unify the Bible. They are the Spirit-inspired framework by which the reader sees history not as a random sequence of events but as the ordered unfolding of God's saving plan.

The interpreter who neglects the covenants will miss the central axis of Scripture. The one who studies them carefully will find that they illuminate every part of the Bible, revealing its unity and its focus on Jehovah's covenant faithfulness fulfilled in Jesus Christ.

Edward D. Andrews

The Function of Law in Israel's Covenant Life

The law given at Sinai stands at the center of Israel's covenant life with Jehovah. It was not an arbitrary code of regulations but the divinely revealed stipulations of the Mosaic covenant, governing Israel's relationship with their God and with one another. To understand the law properly, one must see it in its covenantal context. Isolated from that framework, the law can be misread either as a means of salvation or as a mere relic of ancient history. Within its covenantal role, however, the law reveals God's holiness, exposes human sinfulness, and directs His people in covenant faithfulness.

The Law as Covenant Stipulation

When Jehovah brought Israel out of Egypt in 1446 B.C.E., He established them as His covenant people at Mount Sinai. The covenant began with grace—Jehovah had already redeemed them from slavery—and then laid down stipulations for how they were to live as His holy nation (Exod. 19:4–6). The Ten Commandments (Exod. 20:1–17) serve as the core expression of this covenant, with additional laws expanding their application in civil, ceremonial, and moral life.

Thus, the law functioned not as a ladder by which Israel might climb to God, but as the charter of a redeemed people. It clarified how they were to live as those who belonged to Jehovah by covenant. The covenantal sequence is vital: redemption first, law second. Israel was saved out of Egypt before being given the law.

The Law as Revelation of God's Holiness

The law reveals Jehovah's holiness. Its commands reflect His character—His truthfulness, His justice, His purity, His faithfulness. When the law prohibits murder, adultery, theft, and false witness, it reveals that the God who gave it is the God of life, faithfulness, and truth. When it commands love for neighbor and care for the poor, it reflects His mercy and compassion.

In this way, the law was not arbitrary but revelatory. It disclosed to Israel what kind of God Jehovah is and what kind of people they were to be in covenant fellowship with Him.

The Law as Exposure of Human Sin

While the law revealed God's holiness, it also exposed human sinfulness. As Paul later explained, "Through the law comes knowledge of sin" (Rom. 3:20). Israel's repeated failure to keep the covenant demonstrates the inability of fallen humanity to attain righteousness by law-keeping. The sacrificial system itself, embedded within the law, testified that sin was constant and that forgiveness required atonement.

Thus, the law functioned pedagogically, driving Israel to see their need for grace and pointing forward to the ultimate fulfillment of atonement in Christ.

The Law as Covenant Guide for Israel

The law also functioned as a guide, providing wisdom for Israel's life in the land. It addressed matters of worship, justice, economics, health, and community. In doing so, it distinguished Israel from the nations, marking them as a people set apart for Jehovah.

The dietary laws, Sabbath observances, and purity regulations were not arbitrary burdens but covenant signs. They reminded Israel daily that they belonged to Jehovah and were to reflect His holiness in every area of life. Civil laws ordered their society under justice. Ceremonial laws governed their worship. Moral laws defined righteousness in relationships. Together these stipulations ordered Israel's life as God's covenant nation.

The Law in Relation to the Covenants

The law's role must be seen in relation to the broader structure of God's covenants. It did not annul the Abrahamic covenant but built upon it, defining how Abraham's descendants were to live in the land of promise. Nor was it the final covenant; Jeremiah foretold a new covenant in which God's law would be written on the heart (Jer. 31:31–34). In Christ, the law's condemning power is broken, and its covenantal role fulfilled. But this does not nullify its revelatory function; the moral truths it contains continue to reveal God's character and guide His people.

Why the Law Matters for Interpretation

To interpret the law rightly is to understand its covenantal function: it revealed God's holiness, exposed human sin, and directed Israel's life as His redeemed people. To misinterpret the law as a system of works-salvation, or to dismiss it as irrelevant, is to miss its role in the history of redemption.

The interpreter must therefore approach the law with covenantal awareness, discerning its function for Israel in its original context and its theological significance within God's unfolding plan. Only then can the law be understood as part of the unified story of Scripture, pointing forward to the grace fulfilled in Christ.

Moral, Civil, and Ceremonial Distinctions in Context

One of the most vital interpretive tasks in approaching the law is to recognize its threefold character as moral, civil, and ceremonial. These distinctions are not artificial categories imposed later by theologians; they are grounded in the content and function of the law itself. Without understanding these distinctions in their covenantal context, interpreters risk either flattening the law into a single undifferentiated mass or dismissing it altogether as obsolete. Properly understood, these distinctions show how the law governed every dimension of Israel's life under the Mosaic covenant and how it continues to reveal God's holiness today.

The Moral Law: Eternal Principles of Righteousness

At the core of the law stands the moral law, epitomized in the Ten Commandments (Exod. 20:1–17; Deut. 5:6–21). These commands reflect Jehovah's own character and express His unchanging standards of righteousness. Prohibitions against murder, adultery, theft, and false witness are not arbitrary but flow from God's holiness and truth. The call to honor father and mother, to worship Jehovah alone, and to avoid idolatry is grounded in His unique covenant lordship.

The moral law is universally binding, not only upon Israel but upon all humanity, because it expresses eternal principles of right and wrong. Even before Sinai, Cain was guilty of murder, and Sodom of sexual immorality, because the moral law was written on the heart (Rom. 2:14–15). At Sinai it was codified and clarified, serving as the unchanging standard for covenant life.

The Civil Law: Governing Israel as a Nation

Alongside the moral law, Israel received civil laws regulating their life as a covenant nation. These laws governed property rights, inheritance, economic transactions, penalties for crimes, and judicial procedures. For example, Exodus 21–23 contains detailed laws about restitution for theft, liability for injury, and responsibility for property. These civil regulations distinguished Israel as a theocratic society under Jehovah's direct rule.

The civil law was tailored to Israel's unique historical and covenantal context. It was never intended as a universal code for all nations but as the legal structure by which Israel would live in the land as Jehovah's chosen people. With the coming of Christ and the end of the Mosaic covenant, the civil law as a system is no longer binding. Yet its underlying principles of justice, equity, and fairness continue to reveal God's righteousness and provide wisdom for contemporary application.

The Ceremonial Law: Worship and Separation

The ceremonial law regulated Israel's worship and ritual purity. It included the sacrificial system, priesthood, tabernacle regulations, dietary restrictions, and ritual cleansings. These laws served two main purposes. First, they provided atonement and ritual purity, enabling Israel to approach Jehovah's presence. Second, they marked Israel as distinct from the surrounding nations, reminding them that they were set apart as holy.

The book of Leviticus is particularly rich in ceremonial law. Detailed instructions regarding burnt offerings, sin offerings, and guilt offerings pointed to the seriousness of sin and the necessity of blood atonement. Dietary laws distinguished clean from unclean animals, reinforcing Israel's separateness. Regulations for priests and sacrifices ensured that worship was conducted according to Jehovah's holiness.

In Christ, the ceremonial law has reached its fulfillment. Hebrews declares that the sacrifices were shadows pointing to the once-for-all sacrifice of Jesus (Heb. 10:1–14). The dietary and purity laws, likewise, are set aside in the new covenant (Mark 7:19; Acts 10:15). Yet the ceremonial law continues to reveal God's holiness and foreshadows the perfection accomplished by Christ.

The Importance of the Distinctions

Recognizing these three categories prevents misinterpretation of the law. If one treats all laws as equally binding, one may wrongly conclude that Christians must observe dietary regulations or sacrificial rituals. If one dismisses all law as obsolete, one may ignore the abiding authority of the moral law. The distinctions show that while the civil and ceremonial laws were covenant-specific and fulfilled in Christ, the moral law continues to express God's eternal standards of righteousness.

Why This Matters for Interpretation

When reading the law, the interpreter must always ask: Is this law moral, civil, or ceremonial? How did it function for Israel under the Mosaic covenant? How does it reveal God's character, expose human sin, and point forward to Christ? By asking these questions, the interpreter honors both the historical context and the enduring significance of the law.

In the end, the law in all its aspects—moral, civil, and ceremonial—was given to reveal the holiness of Jehovah and to direct

His covenant people. The moral law abides as the standard of righteousness, the civil law teaches principles of justice, and the ceremonial law finds fulfillment in Christ. Together they display the wisdom of God's covenant purposes and point His people to the grace of the gospel.

Law and Its Fulfillment in Christ

The law of Moses was never an end in itself. It was a divinely ordained covenantal arrangement pointing beyond itself to the greater fulfillment found in Jesus Christ. To read the law apart from Christ is to miss its ultimate purpose. To read Christ apart from the law is to misunderstand the depth of His work. The law reveals God's holiness, exposes human sin, and sets forth the covenant framework in which Israel lived, but in Christ we see the law's goal, completion, and perfection.

Christ as the Goal of the Law

Paul declares, "Christ is the end of the law for righteousness to everyone who believes" (Rom. 10:4). The word translated "end" (*telos*) carries the sense of goal, culmination, and completion. The law's purpose was not to provide a system of salvation by works but to lead God's people to Christ. Through its commands, rituals, and sacrifices, the law pointed ahead to the One who would embody righteousness and provide true atonement.

The moral law revealed the perfect holiness of God. Christ fulfilled it by His sinless obedience, living in complete conformity to God's will (Heb. 4:15). The civil law ordered Israel as a nation under God's rule. Christ, as the Davidic King, brings to perfection the theocratic rule of God, establishing His kingdom in righteousness. The ceremonial law pointed through sacrifices, priests, and festivals to the reality of Christ's priesthood and sacrifice. He is the true Passover lamb (1 Cor. 5:7), the true High Priest (Heb. 7:23–28), and the once-for-all sacrifice (Heb. 10:1–14).

Christ and the Moral Law

Christ did not abolish the moral law but fulfilled it. In the Sermon on the Mount, He declared, "Do not think that I have come to abolish the Law or the Prophets; I have not come to abolish them but to fulfill them" (Matt. 5:17). He fulfilled the law in two ways: first, by perfect obedience, keeping every command without fault; second, by bringing the law to its intended depth, exposing its spiritual demands beyond mere external compliance. When He taught that anger is the heart of murder and lust the heart of adultery (Matt. 5:21–30), He revealed the full measure of righteousness.

The moral law remains binding as the standard of righteousness. But in Christ, believers are freed from the law as a condemning covenant. Justification is not by works of the law but by faith in Christ's obedience and sacrifice (Gal. 2:16). Thus, the moral law still reveals God's will, but its condemning power is broken for those who are in Christ.

Christ and the Civil Law

The civil law, given to govern Israel as a covenant nation, reached its fulfillment in Christ. With the coming of the new covenant, the theocratic state of Israel as a political entity under Mosaic law ceased. The principles of justice, fairness, and equity expressed in the civil law still reveal God's character and provide wisdom for governance, but the system itself is no longer binding. Christ reigns as the true King, and His kingdom transcends political boundaries.

Christ and the Ceremonial Law

The ceremonial law finds its clearest fulfillment in Christ. Every sacrifice pointed to His atonement. Every priest prefigured His eternal priesthood. Every festival anticipated His work of redemption. The tabernacle and temple foreshadowed His presence among His people (John 1:14).

Hebrews is emphatic: the blood of bulls and goats could never take away sin (Heb. 10:4). These sacrifices were shadows, not the reality. But Christ, by offering Himself once for all, accomplished eternal redemption (Heb. 9:12). The ceremonial law is therefore no longer binding, for its purpose is completed. To return to it would be to deny the sufficiency of Christ's work.

The Law as Tutor to Christ

Paul describes the law as a "guardian" (Gal. 3:24), whose role was to lead Israel to Christ. Like a tutor who disciplines and instructs a child, the law exposed sin and pointed to the need for a Savior. But now that Christ has come, the tutor's role has ended. Believers are no longer under law but under grace (Rom. 6:14). This does not mean lawlessness but rather life under the Spirit, who writes God's moral law on the heart in the new covenant (Jer. 31:33; Heb. 8:10).

Why This Matters for Interpretation

To interpret the law without reference to Christ is to misread its purpose. The law was not given as a permanent system of salvation but as a temporary covenant arrangement leading to Christ. Every command, ceremony, and regulation must be understood in light of its fulfillment in Him.

This protects interpreters from two errors: legalism, which treats the law as a system of salvation, and antinomianism, which dismisses the law as irrelevant. In Christ, the law is neither our savior nor our enemy. It is the revelation of God's holiness, fulfilled in Christ, who grants righteousness to all who believe.

The Law and the Christian Today

For the believer, the law continues to function as a guide to holy living, though not as a covenant of condemnation. The moral law reveals the righteousness God requires; Christ empowers His people to pursue it in gratitude for grace. The civil and ceremonial laws, though fulfilled, still instruct us by their principles, pointing us to God's justice and holiness.

Thus, the law, fulfilled in Christ, remains profitable for teaching, for reproof, for correction, and for training in righteousness (2 Tim. 3:16). It is no longer a yoke of slavery but a witness to God's holiness and a signpost to the gospel.

Applying Covenant and Law Today Without Distortion

Once the interpreter has grasped the covenantal framework of the law, distinguished between its moral, civil, and ceremonial aspects, and seen its fulfillment in Christ, the crucial question remains: How do we apply covenant and law today? This is where many have erred—either by dragging Christians back under the Mosaic code as though it were still binding in its entirety, or by discarding the law altogether as irrelevant relics of ancient Israel. Faithful interpretation avoids both distortions, applying covenant and law in a way that honors their original context, their fulfillment in Christ, and their abiding revelation of God's holiness.

Avoiding the Error of Legalism

Some interpreters have sought to impose the Mosaic law in its entirety upon Christians. This error appears in movements such as modern-day theonomy, which insists that civil laws given to Israel should be directly enforced in contemporary societies, or in groups that mandate dietary laws and ritual observances. This is a distortion of covenant application. The Mosaic covenant was a temporary arrangement for Israel as a nation until Christ came. With the inauguration of the new covenant, the civil and ceremonial laws have been fulfilled and set aside (Heb. 8:13). To return to them as binding requirements is to ignore Christ's finished work and to re-erect what He has already fulfilled.

Paul warns clearly against such legalism: "Therefore let no one pass judgment on you in questions of food and drink, or with regard to a festival or a new moon or a Sabbath. These are a shadow of the things to come, but the substance belongs to Christ" (Col. 2:16–17).

Applying the law today without distortion means recognizing that Christ has fulfilled the shadows.

Avoiding the Error of Antinomianism

On the opposite side, some dismiss the law entirely, claiming that under grace Christians have no relationship to the law at all. This view, called antinomianism, wrongly pits grace against law. It fails to see that the moral law reflects God's eternal holiness and continues to serve as the standard of righteousness for His people.

Paul is clear: "Do we then overthrow the law by this faith? By no means! On the contrary, we uphold the law" (Rom. 3:31). While believers are freed from the law as a covenant of condemnation, they are not freed from its moral demands. Grace does not abolish righteousness; it empowers obedience.

The Moral Law as Abiding Standard

The moral law, epitomized in the Ten Commandments, continues to function as the guide for Christian living. It reveals what love for God and neighbor requires (Matt. 22:37–40). It sets forth the boundaries of holiness in speech, conduct, and worship. While justification is not by works of the law, sanctification involves conformity to God's moral will as revealed in His commandments.

Thus, applying covenant and law today means recognizing the moral law as still authoritative, not for salvation but for obedience grounded in grace.

The Civil and Ceremonial Laws as Instruction

Though not binding, the civil and ceremonial laws remain profitable for instruction. They reveal God's concern for justice, fairness, and community order. They display His holiness in worship and the seriousness of sin requiring atonement. They provide principles of wisdom that can inform Christian ethics and discipleship today.

111

For example, laws about honest weights and measures (Lev. 19:35–36) reveal God's concern for economic justice. While the specific regulation belonged to Israel's civil code, the principle remains applicable. Ceremonial laws about purity point to the necessity of holiness in approaching God, even though the rituals themselves are fulfilled in Christ.

The New Covenant as the Lens of Application

All application must take place through the lens of the new covenant. Jeremiah foretold a covenant in which God's law would be written on the heart (Jer. 31:33). In Christ, this promise is fulfilled, and the Spirit uses the inspired Word to shape believers' minds and wills. Christians are not under the Mosaic covenant but under the law of Christ (Gal. 6:2)—a law that encompasses the moral demands of God, now lived out in the power of the gospel.

This means that the law's abiding role must always be seen in light of Christ's fulfillment. The moral law continues as the expression of God's holiness. The civil and ceremonial laws instruct and point to Christ's work. But none of them are to be applied as though Christians live under the Mosaic covenant itself.

Why This Matters

Applying covenant and law today without distortion safeguards the church from both extremes—legalistic bondage and lawless freedom. It preserves the unity of the Bible, showing continuity between the Old and New Testaments, while also recognizing the decisive fulfillment of the law in Christ.

The interpreter who understands the covenants and their laws rightly will lead God's people into mature obedience: not seeking salvation by law-keeping, not discarding the law as useless, but walking in the holiness that God revealed from Sinai to Calvary and beyond, fulfilled perfectly in Christ and written now on the hearts of His redeemed.

Conclusion: Interpreting Covenants and Laws

The Bible cannot be understood apart from the covenants. They are not minor side agreements, nor are they theological curiosities for specialists. They are the backbone of redemptive history, the framework by which Jehovah has revealed Himself, structured His people's lives, and unfolded His plan of salvation. Each covenant—from Noah to Abraham, from Moses to David, and culminating in the new covenant in Christ—serves as a vital link in the chain of God's dealings with mankind.

The law, given within the Mosaic covenant, must likewise be interpreted in its covenantal role. It was never a ladder by which Israel could climb to salvation. It was the stipulation of a redeemed people's relationship with their God. It revealed His holiness, exposed their sin, and directed their life together. Divided into moral, civil, and ceremonial dimensions, the law governed every aspect of Israel's existence, setting them apart as Jehovah's holy nation.

Yet the law was never the end. It pointed beyond itself to Christ, who is its fulfillment. In Him, the moral law is perfectly obeyed, the civil law reaches its purpose, and the ceremonial law finds its completion. He is the true King, the eternal High Priest, and the perfect sacrifice. To interpret the law apart from Him is to misread its design.

For the Christian today, the law remains relevant, but only when read through the lens of the new covenant. The moral law continues as God's eternal standard of holiness, guiding believers in sanctification. The civil and ceremonial laws, though no longer binding, instruct us in principles of justice, purity, and worship, always pointing to Christ's sufficiency.

To apply covenant and law without distortion requires balance: resisting the pull of legalism that seeks to reimpose the Mosaic code, and rejecting the lure of antinomianism that discards God's standards entirely. In Christ, the law is neither abolished nor binding as a covenant of condemnation. It is fulfilled, transformed, and applied in the power of the gospel.

The interpreter who grasps this covenantal and Christ-centered perspective will read the Bible with unity and clarity. He will see that history, law, prophecy, and gospel are not disconnected fragments but parts of one divine plan: Jehovah's faithful covenant purpose, revealed in His Word and fulfilled in His Son.

Review Questions – Chapter 6: Interpreting Covenants and Laws

1. Why are covenants described as the "backbone of redemptive history"?

2. How does a biblical covenant differ from a human contract?

3. What role does the Noahic covenant play in stabilizing the arena of redemption?

4. How did the Abrahamic covenant shape Israel's role and anticipate the Messiah?

5. In what ways did the Mosaic covenant reveal God's holiness and expose human sin?

6. What was promised in the Davidic covenant, and how does it point to Christ?

7. How does the New Covenant fulfill the promises of earlier covenants?

8. Why must the law always be interpreted within its covenantal framework?

9. How are the distinctions between moral, civil, and ceremonial laws important for interpretation?

10. How does the fulfillment of the law in Christ prevent both legalism and antinomianism?

Exercises in Interpretation – Chapter 6: Interpreting Covenants and Laws

Exercise 1: The Abrahamic Covenant (Genesis 15:1–21)

- Read the passage, noting the unilateral nature of God's covenant promise.

- How does the covenant ceremony demonstrate that fulfillment rests on Jehovah's faithfulness rather than Abraham's performance?

- How does this covenant anticipate the coming of Christ?

Exercise 2: The Giving of the Law (Exodus 19:1–8; 20:1–21)

- Observe how the covenant framework ("You shall be my treasured possession") precedes the Ten Commandments.

- What does this order teach about grace preceding law?

- How should this covenantal context prevent misinterpretation of the law as a works-based system of salvation?

Exercise 3: The New Covenant (Jeremiah 31:31–34; Luke 22:20)

- Compare Jeremiah's prophecy with Jesus' words at the Last Supper.

- How does the promise of the law written on the heart contrast with the external administration of the Mosaic covenant?

- What does this teach about continuity and discontinuity between covenants?

CHAPTER 7 Interpreting Poetry

Poetry as a Vehicle of Truth: Parallelism and Imagery

Poetry in Scripture is not ornamental fluff nor artistic decoration meant to entertain the reader. It is a Spirit-inspired mode of revelation chosen by God to convey His truth with precision, depth, and power. Nearly one-third of the Bible is poetry, which means that interpreting poetry faithfully is indispensable to a full understanding of God's Word. Poetry, with its parallelism and imagery, is not less true than prose; it is simply truth conveyed in a different form—designed to speak to the heart and the mind, sharpening clarity, stirring memory, and pressing truth upon the soul.

The Purpose of Poetry in Scripture

Jehovah chose poetry to capture dimensions of truth that ordinary prose cannot fully express. Where prose gives direct statement, poetry brings intensity, rhythm, and imagery that linger in the heart. The Psalms teach the believer how to worship, lament, and rejoice. Proverbs distill wisdom into brief, memorable lines. The prophets employ poetry to confront sin, warn of judgment, and promise hope.

Poetry communicates truth not by logical progression alone but by evoking reflection, emotion, and meditation. Its structure invites readers not only to understand but to feel the weight of truth and to carry it in memory.

Parallelism as the Core of Biblical Poetry

The hallmark of Hebrew poetry is parallelism—the arrangement of lines so that the second echoes, contrasts, or develops the first.

Unlike Western poetry, which often relies on rhyme or meter, biblical poetry achieves its power through this balanced correspondence of thought.

Synonymous Parallelism

Here the second line restates the first in slightly different words, reinforcing the meaning. For example:

"The heavens declare the glory of God,
and the sky above proclaims His handiwork" (Ps. 19:1).

The two lines say essentially the same thing, intensifying the point by repetition.

Antithetic Parallelism

Here the second line contrasts the first, sharpening meaning through opposition.

"For Jehovah knows the way of the righteous,
but the way of the wicked will perish" (Ps. 1:6).

The contrast between righteous and wicked highlights the certainty of God's judgment.

Synthetic (or Formal) Parallelism

Here the second line adds to or completes the thought of the first.

"Commit your work to Jehovah,
and your plans will be established" (Prov. 16:3).

The second line develops the first, showing the consequence of the action.

Climactic Parallelism

Here the second line repeats part of the first but carries it forward to a climax.

"Ascribe to Jehovah, O families of the peoples,
ascribe to Jehovah glory and strength!" (Ps. 96:7).

The repetition builds intensity, moving the worshipper upward in praise.

Parallelism, in all its forms, functions to make truth memorable, emphatic, and clear. It is not mere repetition for its own sake but the inspired design of the author to impress theological truths on the mind and heart.

Imagery as a Window into Truth

Alongside parallelism, imagery is the lifeblood of biblical poetry. Metaphor, simile, and symbol convey truth through vivid pictures.

David does not merely say that God protects; he declares, "Jehovah is my rock and my fortress and my deliverer" (Ps. 18:2). The imagery communicates strength, stability, and safety in a way far more potent than abstract description. Isaiah does not simply say that God's Word endures; he declares, "The grass withers, the flower fades, but the word of our God will stand forever" (Isa. 40:8). The fading of grass and flowers makes the truth tangible and unforgettable.

Imagery does not obscure truth; it clarifies it. By appealing to the senses and imagination, it makes the invisible visible and the abstract concrete.

Theological Weight of Poetic Devices

Parallelism and imagery are not aesthetic embellishments but theological tools. Through them, God confronts His people with the seriousness of sin, the beauty of holiness, the certainty of judgment, and the comfort of His promises. The prophets employed poetry to drive truth home in unforgettable ways. The Psalms use it to lead worshippers in prayer and song. Proverbs use it to condense wisdom into portable form.

Every poetic device serves the Spirit's purpose of making God's truth grip the whole person—mind, heart, and will.

Why This Matters for Interpretation

To interpret biblical poetry faithfully, the reader must respect its form. Treating poetry as though it were prose misses its power. Ignoring parallelism blinds us to how meaning is reinforced. Flattening imagery into bare literalism robs it of its evocative force. The faithful interpreter seeks the author's meaning as conveyed through these poetic devices, understanding that the Spirit inspired not only the content but the form.

Poetry in Scripture is therefore not a secondary mode of revelation but a primary vehicle of truth. Its parallelism and imagery are not obstacles to meaning but the very means by which God has chosen to speak with beauty, clarity, and power.

Recognizing Evocative Versus Informative Elements

Biblical poetry operates with a dual purpose: to inform the mind and to stir the heart. These two functions—informative and evocative—are woven together throughout the Psalms, Proverbs, Prophets, and other poetic texts. Failing to distinguish between them leads to interpretive mistakes, either by reducing poetry to dry instruction or by dissolving it into pure emotion without doctrinal substance. Faithful interpretation requires careful recognition of which elements of poetry are meant primarily to convey factual truth and which are meant to evoke reflection, feeling, and response.

Informative Elements in Poetry

Informative elements communicate direct truth claims. They tell us who God is, what He has done, and what He requires. In Psalm 19:7–8, for example, the psalmist writes:

"The law of Jehovah is perfect, reviving the soul;
the testimony of Jehovah is sure, making wise the simple;
the precepts of Jehovah are right, rejoicing the heart;
the commandment of Jehovah is pure, enlightening the eyes."

Here the poetic form conveys informative content: God's law is perfect, sure, right, and pure. These statements, though framed poetically, are declarative truths about the Word of God. The poetry does not diminish their factual nature but enhances their memorability and impact.

The Proverbs also abound with informative elements. "A false balance is an abomination to Jehovah, but a just weight is His delight" (Prov. 11:1). This is a direct moral statement framed in parallelism. It informs the reader about God's view of dishonesty and fairness.

In such cases, the poetic form is a vehicle for instructive truth. The content must be understood as declarative, binding, and doctrinal.

Evocative Elements in Poetry

Evocative elements, by contrast, aim to stir the heart and imagination, moving the reader beyond cognitive understanding to awe, repentance, joy, or lament. These are not abstract ideas but vivid images, metaphors, or hyperboles designed to engage the emotions and the will.

Psalm 42:1–2 provides a clear example:

"As a deer pants for flowing streams,
so pants my soul for You, O God.
My soul thirsts for God, for the living God."

This is not a zoological observation about deer. It is an evocative metaphor expressing the psalmist's deep longing for God. The informative element ("I long for God") is wrapped in evocative imagery that makes the truth more compelling and experiential.

The prophets often employ evocative language to confront sin or inspire hope. Isaiah 1:18 declares: "Though your sins are like scarlet, they shall be as white as snow." The contrast of scarlet and snow is not scientific description but vivid imagery intended to impress upon the hearer the magnitude of forgiveness.

Blending of Informative and Evocative

Often, poetry blends informative and evocative elements, with each serving the other. Psalm 23 illustrates this perfectly:

"Jehovah is my shepherd; I shall not want."

Informative: Jehovah provides and cares for His people. Evocative: The metaphor of a shepherd evokes security, intimacy, and dependence.

Both elements work together to convey the truth in a way that informs the mind and moves the heart.

Errors to Avoid

A common interpretive mistake is to flatten evocative language into literalistic information. For example, to ask, "How many waters does a deer need to drink per day?" misses the metaphorical point of Psalm 42. Another mistake is to treat informative elements as merely evocative, reducing doctrinal assertions to poetic feeling. When Psalm 19 declares that the law of Jehovah is perfect, it is not simply an emotional outburst but a doctrinal statement about God's Word.

The faithful interpreter discerns whether the line functions primarily to inform, to evoke, or to blend both, and then handles it accordingly.

Why This Matters

Recognizing evocative versus informative elements ensures that the interpreter respects both the mind and the heart in Scripture. God communicates not only to inform His people but to transform them. He speaks in propositions and in poetry, in facts and in feelings, in truths and in images. Both are inspired. Both are necessary.

Poetry, therefore, must not be reduced to cold instruction, nor must it be romanticized into mere emotion. Its dual function reflects the wisdom of God, who addresses the whole person. To interpret it faithfully is to allow its informative content to shape belief and its evocative imagery to stir devotion.

Reading Metaphor, Simile, and Symbol with Care

One of the defining marks of biblical poetry is its frequent use of metaphor, simile, and symbol. These figures of speech are not optional flourishes but essential devices chosen by the Spirit-inspired authors to convey truth with clarity, power, and memorability. Proper interpretation of biblical poetry requires handling these devices carefully, recognizing both their purpose and their limits. If the interpreter flattens them into literal descriptions, he misses their evocative power. If he spiritualizes them into allegories, he distorts their meaning. Faithful exegesis respects metaphor, simile, and symbol as the Spirit's chosen way of communicating truth without twisting them into imaginative speculation.

Metaphor in Biblical Poetry

A metaphor speaks of one thing in terms of another, transferring qualities for the sake of vivid expression. In Psalm 18:2 David declares:

"Jehovah is my rock and my fortress and my deliverer."

Jehovah is not literally a rock or a fortress. The metaphor communicates His stability, strength, and protection. The meaning lies in the shared qualities, not in a one-to-one correspondence of every detail.

Metaphors in biblical poetry often convey relational truths about God and His people. He is a shepherd, and His people are sheep (Ps. 23:1). He is a sun and shield (Ps. 84:11). He is a consuming fire (Deut. 4:24). Each metaphor opens a window into His character, not by discarding His transcendence but by illuminating aspects of His nature in terms humans can grasp.

The interpreter must resist the temptation to overextend metaphors into allegory. God as shepherd does not mean He is limited by the weaknesses of literal shepherds. The metaphor conveys His care and guidance, not every imaginable detail of shepherding.

Simile in Biblical Poetry

A simile compares one thing to another using words such as *like* or *as*. Psalm 103:12 provides a striking example:

"As far as the east is from the west,
so far does He remove our transgressions from us."

The simile does not assign mathematical measurement but evokes the immeasurable extent of God's forgiveness. Similarly, Isaiah 55:10 compares the rain and snow watering the earth to God's Word accomplishing His purpose. The simile clarifies abstract truth by linking it to familiar experience.

Similes, like metaphors, must be read in their intended sense. They communicate theological truth by drawing a comparison, not by inviting the reader to press every detail of the imagery.

Symbol in Biblical Poetry

Symbols go a step further, using objects, actions, or images as recurring representations of larger truths. The vine often symbolizes Israel (Ps. 80:8–16; Isa. 5:1–7). Light symbolizes God's revelation and salvation (Ps. 27:1; Isa. 60:1–3). Water symbolizes cleansing, refreshment, and life (Isa. 55:1; Ezek. 36:25; John 7:37–39).

Symbols in biblical poetry are not arbitrary. They arise from the world of Israel's experience and are reinforced by repeated use throughout Scripture. To understand them, the interpreter must consider the cultural, historical, and canonical context. For instance, the image of light carried rich connotations in Israel's world, where light was rare and precious, making it a powerful symbol of God's presence and guidance.

As with metaphors and similes, symbols must not be pressed into uncontrolled allegory. They convey a particular theological meaning, not limitless possibilities.

Balancing Figurative and Literal

The presence of metaphor, simile, or symbol in poetry does not mean the text is less true than prose. These devices are not evasions of truth but vehicles of truth. The psalmist is not less accurate when he says, "Jehovah is my shepherd," than when Moses states, "Jehovah brought us out of Egypt." Both are true. One communicates by historical fact, the other by figurative imagery. Both are inspired and authoritative.

The interpreter must discern whether a statement is figurative or literal and then interpret accordingly. Misreading figurative speech as literal can lead to absurdities. Misreading literal statements as figurative can rob the text of its doctrinal force. Careful attention to genre, context, and usage guards against both errors.

Why Careful Reading Matters

Metaphors, similes, and symbols are the Spirit's chosen means of revealing God's truth in poetry. They are designed to move the mind and heart together, giving vivid expression to truths that might otherwise remain abstract. When interpreted with care—neither flattened into literalism nor twisted into allegory—they serve as windows into the richness of God's revelation.

To read them well is to allow poetry to accomplish its purpose: to make God's truth clear, memorable, and compelling for His people.

The Theological Force of Poetic Structure

Biblical poetry does not simply communicate truth in isolated lines. Its arrangement, its deliberate structure, and its progression all carry theological force. The Spirit-inspired authors did not scatter verses randomly; they shaped them into patterns that emphasize, highlight, and press forward the truths God intended. The structure of poetry is therefore not ornamental but revelatory. Paying attention to the shape of a psalm, proverb, or prophetic oracle is as vital as attending to its words.

The Unity of Poetic Composition

Biblical poems, whether psalms of lament, hymns of praise, or prophetic oracles, are unified wholes. Each has an internal logic and progression, even though expressed in poetry rather than prose. For example, Psalm 13 begins in lament—"How long, O Jehovah? Will You forget me forever?"—but progresses toward confidence and ends in praise—"I will sing to Jehovah, because He has dealt bountifully with me." The structure reveals a theological movement from despair to faith, teaching readers how to bring their struggles to God honestly yet trust Him fully.

Interpreters who treat biblical poetry as disconnected fragments miss this theological flow. The structure itself embodies the message.

Patterns of Emphasis

The structure of poetry often emphasizes key truths through placement, repetition, or arrangement. Hebrew poetry frequently places the most important line at the beginning or the end of a unit, creating a frame that highlights the central idea. In some cases, the central verse of a poem stands as the pivot or climax.

For instance, the chiastic structure of Lamentations highlights chapter 3, where Jeremiah confesses both affliction and hope: "The steadfast love of Jehovah never ceases; His mercies never come to an end" (Lam. 3:22). The structure drives the reader to this theological center, showing that divine mercy is the turning point amid judgment.

Progression of Thought

Biblical poetry often develops by progression rather than by strict logical argument. A psalm may begin with a statement of trust, expand it through imagery, and climax in a vow of praise. A prophetic poem may begin with accusations, move to judgment, and end with promises of restoration. The structure carries the theology forward.

Take Isaiah 40 as an example. The chapter begins with words of comfort ("Comfort, comfort my people"), develops by contrasting the frailty of humanity with the permanence of God's Word, climaxes with the greatness of the Creator, and concludes with promises of renewed strength for those who wait on Jehovah. The structure reinforces the theology: comfort is grounded in God's unchanging Word and sovereign power.

Parallelism as Structural Force

Parallelism, the heartbeat of Hebrew poetry, also carries theological force at the structural level. Entire psalms are arranged by parallel sections. Psalm 29, for example, repeats the command "Ascribe to Jehovah" and the phrase "the voice of Jehovah" to build an escalating storm scene, climaxing in Jehovah's enthronement over the flood and His blessing of His people with peace. The repetition and arrangement of these parallels are not accidental; they declare Jehovah's power and sovereignty.

Refrains and Repetition

Refrains, or repeated lines, often serve as structural anchors, reinforcing theological truths. In Psalm 136, the refrain "for His steadfast love endures forever" appears in every verse. The structure engrains this theological truth in the mind of the reader: all of God's works, from creation to redemption, flow from His steadfast covenant love.

Theological Implications of Structure

The structure of biblical poetry is itself theology in form. It demonstrates that God's truth is not merely delivered in propositions but shaped in patterns that embody His message. The lament psalms show that grief and faith coexist, moving the worshiper from complaint to trust. Wisdom poetry shows the contrast of the righteous and the wicked through balanced structure. Prophetic oracles show judgment and salvation in carefully ordered stanzas, reinforcing the justice and mercy of God.

Structure is not neutral. It is part of the inspired design through which the Spirit communicates theology. Ignoring it diminishes the message. Paying attention to it allows the reader to grasp not only what God says but how He presses that truth upon His people.

Safeguarding Against Over-Spiritualization

Biblical poetry, with its rich imagery and evocative language, is especially vulnerable to misuse through over-spiritualization. Because it speaks in pictures, metaphors, and symbols, some interpreters have wrongly assumed that every detail hides a deeper meaning, as though Scripture were a code to be cracked rather than the plain Word of God. This tendency has led to imaginative allegories, fanciful interpretations, and doctrinal distortions that obscure rather than clarify the inspired message. To handle biblical poetry faithfully, one must learn to safeguard against over-spiritualization and allow the text to speak in the sense intended by its author.

The Nature of the Danger

Over-spiritualization occurs when interpreters detach imagery or poetic form from its intended meaning and invent hidden truths beyond what the author communicated. This is not reverence for Scripture but abuse of it. It elevates human imagination above the inspired Word and shifts authority from the text to the interpreter.

For example, some have treated the Song of Solomon as an extended allegory of Christ and the church, ignoring its plain sense as a celebration of marital love. Others have turned poetic references to Israel's enemies into symbols of "personal struggles" without regard for their historical reality. Such approaches may sound spiritual but are, in fact, distortions of the inspired message.

Distinguishing Figurative from Allegorical

Poetry often employs figurative language, but figurative is not the same as allegorical. A metaphor such as "Jehovah is my rock" (Ps. 18:2) communicates strength, protection, and stability. It is figurative, but its meaning is clear and grounded in the historical relationship between God and His people. Allegorizing that same line into elaborate symbolic schemes—for example, seeing the rock as representing hidden mystical truths about creation or the church—goes far beyond the inspired intent.

The faithful interpreter must discern the difference. Figurative language conveys real, straightforward meaning through imagery. Allegorizing imposes hidden meanings that the author never intended.

Respecting Authorial Intent

The safeguard against over-spiritualization is a rigorous commitment to authorial intent. The question is never, *What hidden meaning can I find in this image?* but always, *What did the inspired author intend this image to communicate to his original audience?* The meaning lies in the author's words, not in the interpreter's imagination.

When Isaiah declares, "The mountains shall depart and the hills be removed, but My steadfast love shall not depart from you" (Isa. 54:10), the imagery is grand, but the intent is clear: God's covenant love is more enduring than the natural world. The meaning is not hidden or mystical; it is communicated directly through poetic imagery.

The Role of Context

Another safeguard is close attention to literary and historical context. Imagery cannot be pulled out of its setting and spiritualized at will. In Psalm 23, the image of the shepherd has specific meaning in the context of ancient Israel, where shepherds protected and guided their flocks. In the psalm, it communicates God's care and guidance for His people. To turn it into a generalized allegory of psychological comfort or to spiritualize every detail of shepherding misses the context and dilutes the theological force.

The Dangers of Subjective Interpretation

Over-spiritualization is inherently subjective. Because it is not bound by grammar, history, or context, it produces as many meanings as there are interpreters. This leads to confusion and undermines the clarity of Scripture. If every image can mean whatever the interpreter decides, then the authority of the text is lost, and the church is left adrift in speculation.

Affirming the Sufficiency of the Plain Sense

The safeguard is to affirm the sufficiency of the plain sense of poetry. The imagery of Scripture is already rich, powerful, and transformative. It does not require hidden allegories to make it meaningful. The Spirit-inspired words carry their own force when understood in their context. To over-spiritualize is to imply that God's Word as given is inadequate, when in reality it is sufficient for teaching, for reproof, for correction, and for training in righteousness (2 Tim. 3:16).

Why This Matters

Poetry is meant to grip both the mind and the heart, but only as the inspired author intended. Over-spiritualization substitutes imagination for revelation and undermines the authority of Scripture. By resisting this distortion and embracing the grammatical-historical method, interpreters can preserve both the clarity and the power of biblical poetry, hearing in it not the inventions of men but the voice of God Himself.

Conclusion: Interpreting Poetry

Poetry is not an ornament in Scripture but a chosen vehicle of divine revelation. Jehovah, in His wisdom, inspired nearly a third of the Bible in poetic form because poetry presses truth into both the mind and the heart. It instructs with clarity, stirs with imagery, and lodges truth deep within memory and devotion. Its parallelism sharpens meaning, its imagery makes the invisible tangible, its structure embodies theological force, and its cadence engraves the Word of God upon the soul.

To interpret biblical poetry rightly, one must honor its unique features. Parallelism—whether synonymous, antithetic, synthetic, or climactic—serves as the backbone of Hebrew verse, guiding the reader to see truth in balance, contrast, and development. Imagery through metaphor, simile, and symbol is not decoration but revelation, chosen to communicate God's holiness, mercy, judgment, and salvation in ways no abstract statement could capture. Structure, whether through refrains, chiastic patterns, or progression of thought, is never random but deliberately crafted to highlight the theological center of the text.

The interpreter must also recognize the interplay between informative and evocative elements. Biblical poetry does not simply state facts; it shapes affections. It informs the believer of who God is and what He has done, while evoking worship, fear, lament, and joy. To reduce poetry to dry propositions strips it of power; to reduce it to emotion empties it of doctrine. Both mind and heart must be addressed, as the inspired text intends.

Safeguarding against misuse is equally vital. Poetry must not be flattened into literalism, nor must it be distorted into hidden allegories or speculative typologies. Figurative language is to be understood as figurative, communicating real truth in accessible imagery. Over-spiritualization shifts authority from the text to the interpreter, while the grammatical-historical method preserves the plain sense that God Himself placed in the inspired words. The sufficiency of the plain sense is the safeguard against distortion.

Ultimately, biblical poetry reveals a God who communicates not only to the intellect but to the whole person. It is not less true than prose, nor less authoritative. It is simply another form chosen by the Spirit to convey the same inerrant Word. To interpret it faithfully is to hear God's voice as He intended—majestic in its imagery, powerful in its structure, and transformative in its truth.

Review Questions – Chapter 7: Interpreting Poetry

1. How does Hebrew poetry differ from Western poetry, and what role does parallelism play in its meaning?

2. Why is it important to recognize that poetry is not less inspired than prose, but equally God-breathed?

3. What is the function of imagery in biblical poetry, and how does it communicate truth powerfully?

4. How does historical and cultural context help us avoid misreading poetic expressions?

5. Why must poetic figures (e.g., metaphors, similes) be interpreted in light of the author's intended meaning rather than through speculation?

6. How do Psalms display the interplay between personal emotion and theological truth?

7. What dangers arise when interpreters flatten poetic language into literal statements?

8. How do parallel lines in Hebrew poetry clarify, intensify, or contrast meaning?

9. Why is it necessary to read biblical poetry as covenantal instruction rather than as mere human reflection?

10. In what ways does biblical poetry train believers to respond to Jehovah in worship, lament, and trust?

Exercises in Interpretation – Chapter 7: Interpreting Poetry

Exercise 1: Psalm 23:1–6

- Identify the imagery used for Jehovah as Shepherd.

- How does the use of parallel lines expand the meaning of His provision and protection?

- How should this psalm be applied without over-allegorizing every image (e.g., green pastures, still waters)?

Exercise 2: Psalm 19:1–6

- Observe how the heavens are personified in declaring God's glory.

- How does parallelism in verses 1–4 reinforce the central message?

- How does the poetic form intensify the reality of general revelation?

Exercise 3: Lamentations 3:19–26

- Note the shift from despair to hope within the poetic structure.

- How does imagery such as "steadfast love" and "mercies new every morning" serve the theological point?

- What safeguards prevent us from reading this passage as exaggerated optimism rather than Spirit-inspired confidence in God's faithfulness?

CHAPTER 8 Interpreting Psalms

The Psalter as Israel's Inspired Songbook

The book of Psalms, or the Psalter, stands as the inspired hymnbook of Israel. It is not a humanly compiled anthology of spiritual reflections but a Spirit-breathed collection of songs, prayers, and liturgical poems designed for worship, meditation, and instruction. The Psalter uniquely combines profound theology with heartfelt devotion, giving voice to the full range of human experience in relation to Jehovah. To understand the Psalms rightly is to recognize both their literary form as poetry and their function as the worship songs of God's covenant people.

The Nature of the Psalter

Unlike any other portion of Scripture, the Psalter is intentionally crafted as a collection of songs. Many of them were written with musical notations, references to instruments, or instructions for public use. Terms such as *Selah*, references to choirs, and superscriptions mentioning the chief musician (e.g., Ps. 4; Ps. 6) reveal their use in temple worship. Yet these are not merely songs of human genius—they are inspired songs, breathed out by God through human authors, including David, Asaph, the sons of Korah, Solomon, Moses, and others.

Thus, the Psalter functions both as divine revelation and as the prayer book of God's people. It teaches doctrine, reveals God's character, and guides His people in how to approach Him. The Psalms speak not only to Israel in their historical setting but also to the church in every generation, for their theology is timeless and their voice universal.

The Psalms as Worship

The primary function of the Psalter was worship. Israel was a redeemed people called to praise Jehovah for His mighty acts of salvation, and the Psalms gave words and melodies to their devotion. In the temple, they were sung by Levitical choirs, accompanied by instruments, and used in public festivals. In the home, they were recited in family and personal devotion.

The Psalms reveal that worship is not limited to joy and triumph. They give expression to lament, complaint, confession, and even despair. Nearly one-third of the Psalms are laments, showing that bringing grief before God is as much a part of worship as offering praise. By including both cries of anguish and songs of thanksgiving, the Psalter teaches that worship encompasses the whole of life under God's covenant care.

The Psalms as Theology

The Psalms are not merely emotional expressions; they are theological instruction. They teach about Jehovah's attributes—His sovereignty, holiness, justice, mercy, and steadfast love. They rehearse His works in creation, exodus, covenant, and kingship. They set forth the reality of human sin, the hope of forgiveness, and the promise of redemption.

Psalm 33 declares Jehovah as Creator and Sovereign: "By the word of Jehovah the heavens were made, and by the breath of His mouth all their host" (v. 6). Psalm 51 teaches the reality of sin and the necessity of repentance. Psalm 103 celebrates God's mercy: "As far as the east is from the west, so far does He remove our transgressions from us" (v. 12). These are not private reflections but inspired doctrines sung by the congregation.

The Psalter is therefore as much a theological book as it is a hymnbook. It instructs God's people even as it leads them in worship.

The Psalms as Prayer

The Psalms also function as inspired prayers. They show God's people how to bring every emotion, circumstance, and need before Him. From cries for deliverance in Psalm 3, to confessions of sin in Psalm 51, to thanksgivings for victory in Psalm 118, the Psalms encompass the entire spectrum of human experience.

As prayers, they demonstrate that God invites His people to be honest before Him. The laments express anguish without fear of irreverence. The imprecatory psalms call upon God to bring justice against the wicked. These prayers show that covenant relationship with God is not one of cold ritual but of heartfelt communion.

The Structure of the Psalter

The Psalms are not randomly arranged but carefully shaped into five books (Pss. 1–41; 42–72; 73–89; 90–106; 107–150), each ending with a doxology. This structure mirrors the five books of the Torah, suggesting that the Psalter was intended to serve as a counterpart to the Law. If the Torah is God's instruction, the Psalter is God's provision for the worshipful response of His people. Together they form the foundation of Israel's covenant life.

The final psalms (146–150) form a crescendo of praise, each beginning and ending with "Hallelujah," signaling that the ultimate goal of the Psalter—and indeed of all redemptive history—is the glory of Jehovah in the praise of His people.

The Psalter for Christians Today

Though rooted in Israel's covenant worship, the Psalms remain vital for Christians. They reveal the same God, display the same holiness, and proclaim the same steadfast love fulfilled in Christ. The New Testament itself quotes the Psalms more than any other Old Testament book, showing their enduring authority. They instruct the church in worship, prayer, and theology, reminding believers that all of life is to be brought before God in prayer and praise.

Christ Himself sang the Psalms, prayed them, and fulfilled them. On the cross He cried out the words of Psalm 22:1, "My God, my God, why have You forsaken Me?" To sing the Psalms today is to join the voice of Christ, the church, and the saints of every age in declaring the glory of Jehovah.

Classifying Psalms: Lament, Praise, Royal, Wisdom, and More

The Psalter is not a random collection of disconnected hymns and prayers. It is a carefully organized body of inspired poetry with identifiable patterns, themes, and purposes. Classifying the Psalms helps the interpreter to recognize their function, discern their theological message, and apply them rightly. While many psalms contain overlapping features, scholars and faithful interpreters alike have long recognized several major categories that serve as interpretive guides.

Lament Psalms

Lament is the single largest category in the Psalter. These psalms give voice to grief, suffering, and the experience of divine silence. They usually follow a pattern: a cry to God, a description of distress, a plea for deliverance, a confession of trust, and often a vow of praise.

Psalm 13 illustrates this form: it begins with complaint ("How long, O Jehovah? Will You forget me forever?"), continues with supplication ("Consider and answer me, O Jehovah my God"), and concludes with confidence and praise ("But I have trusted in Your steadfast love; my heart shall rejoice in Your salvation").

The theological importance of lament psalms lies in their honesty. They teach believers that bringing sorrow, doubt, and frustration before God is not unbelief but covenant faith. These psalms guard against superficial worship and remind us that God invites His people to cry out to Him in every circumstance.

Praise Psalms

Praise psalms, often called hymns, are songs of adoration that celebrate God's greatness, majesty, and works. They typically begin with a call to praise, followed by reasons for praise, and end with renewed exhortation to praise.

Psalm 100 provides a classic example: "Make a joyful noise to Jehovah, all the earth! Serve Jehovah with gladness! Come into His presence with singing!" The psalm then gives reasons for praise: Jehovah is God, He made us, we are His people, His steadfast love endures forever.

The theology of praise psalms centers on God's attributes and mighty acts. They exalt Him as Creator, Redeemer, and King, reminding worshippers that the purpose of life and history is the glory of Jehovah.

Royal Psalms

Royal psalms focus on the Davidic king, his reign, and his relationship to God's covenant purposes. Some celebrate the king's enthronement (Ps. 2), others pray for his success in battle (Ps. 20), and still others look forward to the eternal reign of the promised Messiah (Ps. 110).

The royal psalms are vital for understanding the Davidic covenant and the messianic hope. They show that Israel's kingship was not merely political but theological, bound up with God's promise of an everlasting throne. While rooted in the historical monarchy, these psalms ultimately point to the reign of Christ, the greater Son of David, who fulfills their hope.

Wisdom Psalms

Wisdom psalms reflect themes common to Proverbs and other wisdom literature. They contrast the righteous and the wicked, call believers to fear Jehovah, and extol the blessings of obedience.

Psalm 1 sets the tone for the entire Psalter: "Blessed is the man who walks not in the counsel of the wicked ... but his delight is in the law of Jehovah, and on His law he meditates day and night." The psalm contrasts the way of the righteous, likened to a fruitful tree, with the way of the wicked, likened to chaff driven by the wind.

Wisdom psalms emphasize practical godliness, showing that true wisdom begins with reverence for Jehovah and obedience to His Word.

Thanksgiving Psalms

Distinct from general praise, thanksgiving psalms celebrate God's specific acts of deliverance. They recount distress, acknowledge God's intervention, and offer thanks for His salvation.

Psalm 30, for example, is a thanksgiving for recovery from illness: "O Jehovah my God, I cried to You for help, and You have healed me." These psalms highlight God's faithfulness in answering prayer and invite the congregation to join in thanksgiving.

Imprecatory Psalms

Imprecatory psalms call upon God to bring judgment upon the wicked. They include strong language, asking God to defeat enemies and vindicate His people (Ps. 69; Ps. 109).

These psalms must be interpreted carefully, recognizing that they are not expressions of personal revenge but appeals for God's justice. They remind the faithful that vengeance belongs to Jehovah (Deut. 32:35) and that His covenant people may entrust ultimate justice to Him.

Songs of Zion and Liturgical Psalms

Some psalms focus on Jerusalem, the temple, and worship (Ps. 48; Ps. 84). Others were written for specific liturgical use, such as pilgrim psalms sung on the way to festivals (Pss. 120–134, the Songs of

Ascents). These psalms emphasize God's presence among His people and the joy of gathering to worship Him.

Why Classification Matters

Classifying the Psalms helps interpreters to respect their diversity and their function. A lament should not be read as though it were a praise psalm; a wisdom psalm should not be interpreted like a royal psalm. Each type has its own theological role within the Psalter.

At the same time, all psalms, whatever their type, share the same ultimate purpose: to direct God's people to Him in worship, faith, and obedience. The diversity of forms mirrors the diversity of life itself, showing that every circumstance can be brought before God in song.

The Use of Parallelism and Figurative Language in Psalms

The Psalms stand as the richest and most concentrated collection of Hebrew poetry in the Bible. To interpret them properly, the reader must understand the literary devices that give them their unique power. Chief among these are parallelism and figurative language. These devices are not decorative ornaments but essential means of communicating truth. Through parallelism, ideas are reinforced, contrasted, or expanded. Through figurative language—metaphor, simile, imagery, and symbol—the invisible realities of God's character and works are made visible and memorable.

Parallelism as the Backbone of the Psalms

Parallelism is the defining feature of Hebrew poetry, and nowhere is it more fully displayed than in the Psalms.

Synonymous Parallelism

The second line restates the first in different words, reinforcing the truth.

"The heavens declare the glory of God,
and the sky above proclaims His handiwork" (Ps. 19:1).

The repetition deepens the reader's grasp of the same reality—creation's witness to God's glory.

Antithetic Parallelism

The second line contrasts with the first, sharpening the meaning through opposition.

"For Jehovah knows the way of the righteous,
but the way of the wicked will perish" (Ps. 1:6).

This form sets two paths before the reader, highlighting the seriousness of covenant obedience versus disobedience.

Synthetic (or Constructive) Parallelism

The second line adds to or completes the thought of the first.

"Blessed is the man who walks not in the counsel of the wicked,
nor stands in the way of sinners,
nor sits in the seat of scoffers" (Ps. 1:1).

Each line builds upon the previous one, progressing the idea from walking to standing to sitting, emphasizing a deepening involvement in sin.

Climactic Parallelism

The second line repeats part of the first but carries it to a climax.

"Ascribe to Jehovah, O families of the peoples,
ascribe to Jehovah glory and strength!" (Ps. 96:7).

The repetition is not redundant but intensifies the call to worship.

Emblematic Parallelism

One line presents a figure of speech, and the second explains or applies it.

"As a father shows compassion to his children,
so Jehovah shows compassion to those who fear Him" (Ps. 103:13).

Here the comparison clarifies the truth by drawing on human experience.

Parallelism in the Psalms functions to emphasize meaning, create rhythm, and ensure memorability. It is the Spirit's chosen form for inscribing truth in the minds and hearts of God's people.

Figurative Language in the Psalms

Alongside parallelism, the Psalms make extensive use of figurative language. These images convey theological truths in vivid and experiential ways.

Metaphor

"Jehovah is my rock and my fortress and my deliverer" (Ps. 18:2). This imagery portrays God's protection and stability in ways that abstract words could never capture.

Simile

"As a deer pants for flowing streams, so pants my soul for You, O God" (Ps. 42:1).
The simile expresses spiritual longing with intensity and familiarity.

Personification

"Let the rivers clap their hands; let the hills sing for joy together" (Ps. 98:8).

Here creation is pictured as worshiping, underscoring the universal scope of God's reign.

Symbol

"Jehovah is my light and my salvation" (Ps. 27:1).
Light is a recurring biblical symbol of life, guidance, and truth.

Figurative language in the Psalms is not a diversion from truth but a Spirit-inspired method of making truth vivid and memorable.

The Function of These Devices

Parallelism and figurative language serve a theological purpose. They do not obscure meaning but make it clearer, sharper, and more powerful. They enable the Psalms to communicate not only to the intellect but also to the imagination and emotions. By means of these devices, truth is not merely understood but felt, remembered, and lived.

Guarding Against Misuse

The interpreter must handle parallelism and figurative language with care. The temptation to over-spiritualize or allegorize must be resisted. The meaning is not hidden but revealed in the imagery itself, as the inspired author intended. To force additional symbolic layers is to go beyond Scripture. To flatten imagery into wooden literalism is to rob it of its power. The key is to discern what truth the author intended to communicate through the chosen poetic device.

Why This Matters

The Psalms endure in the hearts of God's people because their poetic devices communicate eternal truth in unforgettable form. They teach us how to worship, pray, lament, and hope. They do so not only by what they say but by how they say it—through parallelism and figurative language chosen by the Spirit to grip mind and heart together.

Historical Setting and Theological Message

The Psalms were not written in a vacuum. Each psalm has a historical setting—whether explicitly identified in its superscription or implied in its content—and each psalm conveys a theological message that transcends that setting. Faithful interpretation requires attention to both. Ignoring the historical setting risks detaching the psalm from its covenantal context. Ignoring the theological message risks leaving the psalm bound in the past, rather than hearing it as the living Word of God for today.

Historical Setting of the Psalms

The Psalter spans centuries of Israel's history. The earliest psalm is attributed to Moses (Ps. 90), dating to the wilderness period around 1400 B.C.E. Many psalms were written by David during his reign (1010–970 B.C.E.), reflecting personal struggles, national victories, and covenant promises. Others come from the era of Solomon, Asaph, and the sons of Korah, connected to temple worship in Jerusalem. Still others were composed during the exile in Babylon (e.g., Ps. 137) or after the return (e.g., Ps. 126).

The superscriptions attached to many psalms are part of the inspired text and provide valuable clues to their setting. For example:

- **Psalm 3**: "A Psalm of David, when he fled from Absalom his son."

- **Psalm 51**: "A Psalm of David, when Nathan the prophet went to him, after he had gone in to Bathsheba."

- **Psalm 90**: "A Prayer of Moses, the man of God."

These notes help the reader to hear the psalm in its historical context, linking the poetry to specific events in Israel's covenant life.

Even when no superscription is present, internal clues can often locate a psalm within Israel's story. References to the temple suggest the monarchy period. Longing for Jerusalem suggests exile. Celebration of God's kingship points to festival use in the gathered assembly.

The Psalms as Theological Reflection

Yet the psalms are not mere historical documents. They are Spirit-inspired reflections on God's character and works, framed in Israel's covenant relationship. Each psalm expresses a theological truth that transcends the moment of its writing.

- Psalm 23 reflects David's personal trust but communicates timeless theology: Jehovah is the Shepherd of His people.

- Psalm 46 arises from national crisis but proclaims an enduring truth: "God is our refuge and strength, a very present help in trouble."

- Psalm 51 confesses David's sin, yet it teaches every generation the theology of repentance, forgiveness, and renewal.

The historical occasion gives the psalm its form, but the theology gives it universal significance.

Covenant Context of the Psalms

The Psalms must be read within the covenantal framework of Israel's relationship with Jehovah. They presuppose the law given at Sinai, the promises made to Abraham, and the covenant with David. Their cries for deliverance, confessions of sin, and hopes for future blessing are all rooted in the covenant.

For example, when Psalm 89 laments the apparent failure of the Davidic covenant, it does so from the perspective of exile. The theology of the psalm is bound to the promise of an eternal throne and the hope that Jehovah's steadfast love will not fail.

Theological Themes of the Psalms

The Psalms consistently proclaim the central truths of biblical theology:

- **God as Sovereign King:** "Jehovah reigns, He is robed in majesty" (Ps. 93:1).

- **God's Steadfast Love:** "His steadfast love endures forever" (Ps. 136, repeated in every verse).

- **God as Creator:** "By the word of Jehovah the heavens were made" (Ps. 33:6).

- **God as Refuge:** "Jehovah is my rock and my fortress" (Ps. 18:2).

- **Human Sin and Divine Forgiveness:** "Blessed is the one whose transgression is forgiven" (Ps. 32:1).

These themes are not bound to Israel's past but speak to every generation, because they reveal the unchanging character of Jehovah.

Why Historical Setting and Theological Message Matter Together

The danger of ignoring historical setting is to misinterpret the psalm by lifting it out of context. The danger of ignoring theological message is to treat the psalm as only ancient history, irrelevant to today. The faithful interpreter holds both together: the psalm arose from a real historical moment in covenant life, and it communicates a timeless theological truth for God's people in every age.

Thus, the Psalms teach us not only how Israel worshiped, lamented, and prayed, but also how we, as God's people today, are to do the same. They are historical songs with enduring theological voice, the inspired hymnbook of the covenant community across all generations.

The Role of the Psalms in Christian Life and Worship

The Psalter was not given to remain locked in Israel's past. It was inspired to shape the worship, faith, and life of God's people in every generation. The Psalms are as vital for the church today as they were for the nation of Israel, because they speak to the full range of human experience in relationship to Jehovah. They inform the mind with theology, stir the heart with devotion, and direct the will in obedience. To neglect the Psalms is to deprive ourselves of the Spirit-given guide to worship and prayer.

The Psalms as a Pattern for Prayer

The Psalms provide the vocabulary of prayer for God's people. They show us how to approach Jehovah in praise, thanksgiving, lament, confession, and petition. They teach that prayer is not limited to moments of joy but extends to times of grief, doubt, and even despair.

Psalm 13 begins with complaint—"How long, O Jehovah?"—but ends with trust—"I will sing to Jehovah, because He has dealt bountifully with me." Psalm 51 models repentance, Psalm 23 expresses confidence, and Psalm 150 bursts into praise. Together they provide believers with a comprehensive guide to bring every circumstance of life before God.

By praying the Psalms, Christians learn to speak to God in the language He Himself has inspired.

The Psalms as a School of Worship

The Psalms teach not only how to pray but how to worship. They are filled with calls to praise: "Sing to Jehovah a new song; sing to Jehovah, all the earth!" (Ps. 96:1). They remind us that worship is centered on God's attributes—His holiness, mercy, and steadfast love—and on His works—creation, redemption, and covenant faithfulness.

In corporate worship, the Psalms provide a model for singing and rejoicing together as God's people. In private devotion, they guide the heart in meditation and praise. Their repeated emphasis on God's steadfast love and eternal kingship ensures that worship remains God-centered rather than man-centered.

The Psalms as a Guide for Faith

The Psalms are not merely prayers and songs; they are theology set to music. They shape the believer's faith by teaching the truth about God and His ways. They remind us that God is sovereign in suffering, faithful in covenant, merciful in forgiveness, and certain in judgment.

They train the heart to trust Him when circumstances seem dark and to rejoice in Him when blessings abound.

Psalm 46, for example, instills confidence: "God is our refuge and strength, a very present help in trouble." Psalm 73 teaches that God's presence is better than earthly prosperity. These theological truths, sung and prayed, take deep root in the soul.

The Psalms in the Life of Christ and the Church

The New Testament shows that the Psalms remain central in the life of Christ and the church. Jesus prayed the Psalms, quoted them, and fulfilled them. On the cross He cried out the words of Psalm 22:1, "My God, my God, why have You forsaken Me?" The apostles quoted the Psalms more than any other Old Testament book to explain Christ's work and the life of the church.

The early church continued to sing the Psalms, and faithful Christians throughout history have found them indispensable for worship and devotion. They remain God's inspired hymnbook for His people, not replaced but enriched by the fuller light of Christ's fulfillment.

The Psalms in the Christian's Daily Walk

For the believer today, the Psalms are a resource for every season of life. In sorrow, they give words of lament. In joy, they supply songs of thanksgiving. In guilt, they teach confession. In fear, they provide assurance. They anchor the soul in the unchanging character of God and remind the believer that every experience of life is to be lived before His face.

The Psalms are not optional extras; they are central to the Christian life. They are as much Scripture as the epistles and the narratives, and they are to be studied, memorized, prayed, and sung.

Why the Psalms Must Shape Our Worship

The Psalter reminds the church that worship must be God-centered, Word-driven, and Spirit-inspired. It keeps us from trivializing worship into entertainment or reducing it to mere emotional release.

True worship is grounded in the truth about who God is and what He has done, expressed with reverence, joy, and devotion.

The Psalms give us this balance: theology and doxology, mind and heart, truth and passion. They are the inspired pattern by which God's people may worship Him in spirit and in truth across all generations.

Conclusion: Interpreting Psalms

The Psalter is far more than an anthology of ancient songs; it is the Spirit-inspired hymnbook of God's people. It unites worship and theology, prayer and doctrine, lament and praise. By classifying the psalms into laments, hymns of praise, royal psalms, wisdom psalms, songs of thanksgiving, and others, the interpreter sees their diversity of form and function, yet also their common purpose: to lead the covenant community in a life of faith before Jehovah.

The Psalms are poetry at their richest, employing parallelism, imagery, and symbol to impress God's truth upon mind and heart alike. They are also deeply historical, often arising from specific moments in Israel's life, yet they never remain bound to the past. Each psalm proclaims theological truth about God's character and works that endures for every generation.

Above all, the Psalms teach the church how to pray, how to worship, and how to live before the face of God. They show that worship includes joy and sorrow, thanksgiving and confession, confidence and lament. They keep believers from shallow expressions of faith and anchor them in the unchanging reality of God's sovereignty, holiness, steadfast love, and mercy.

For the Christian, the Psalms remain indispensable. They are Scripture to be read, sung, memorized, and prayed. They are a school of worship, shaping how we approach God in every circumstance. And they are theology set to music, reminding the church that the end of all things is the glory of Jehovah in the praise of His people.

Review Questions – Chapter 8: Interpreting Psalms

1. Why is it essential to read the Psalms as part of Israel's covenant life rather than as isolated poems?

2. How does Hebrew poetry (parallelism, imagery, rhythm) shape the meaning of the Psalms?

3. In what ways do the Psalms function both as prayers of individuals and as the worship of the covenant community?

4. Why must interpreters avoid using the Psalms as mystical formulas or detached devotional fragments?

5. How does Psalm 1 set the theological tone for the entire Psalter?

6. What is the significance of the historical settings (superscriptions) attached to many Psalms?

7. How do the Psalms demonstrate the interplay of human experience and divine truth?

8. Why is it crucial to see the Psalms in their Messianic and Christ-centered fulfillment without forcing Christ into every verse?

9. How do laments, thanksgiving, and praise function theologically within the Psalter?

10. In what ways do the Psalms shape the worship, prayer, and hope of the church today?

Exercises in Interpretation – Chapter 8: Interpreting Psalms

Exercise 1: Psalm 1:1-6

- Identify the contrast between the righteous and the wicked.

- How does parallelism strengthen the Psalm's teaching on two ways of life?

- What covenantal truth does this opening Psalm establish for reading the rest of the Psalter?

Exercise 2: Psalm 51:1–12

- Read David's confession after his sin with Bathsheba.
- How does the Psalm balance deep personal grief with covenantal hope in God's mercy?
- What dangers arise if interpreters universalize David's personal details rather than focusing on the central point of sin, repentance, and forgiveness?

Exercise 3: Psalm 110:1–7

- How does this royal Psalm point forward to Christ as priest-king?
- What role does divine speech ("Jehovah says to my Lord...") play in the authority of the Psalm?
- How is this Psalm used in the New Testament, and what does that teach us about the Spirit-inspired application of the Psalms?

CHAPTER 9 Interpreting Proverbs

The Nature of Wisdom Sayings as General Principles

The book of Proverbs occupies a unique place within Scripture. Unlike narrative, which recounts God's mighty acts in history, or psalms, which express worship and prayer, Proverbs presents short, pithy sayings that distill the essence of wise living before Jehovah. These sayings are not random folk maxims but Spirit-inspired wisdom, designed to instruct God's people in practical righteousness. Yet to interpret Proverbs correctly, one must grasp their nature: they are general principles, not ironclad promises.

The Character of Proverbs

Proverbs are concise statements of truth expressed in memorable form. They are crafted to be easily remembered, repeated, and applied. Their brevity requires compression of thought, so that a profound truth is expressed in only a few words. For example:

"A soft answer turns away wrath,
but a harsh word stirs up anger" (Prov. 15:1).

This short statement captures a profound principle of interpersonal conduct. Its form makes it portable, ready to guide speech in daily life.

Proverbs are therefore not exhaustive laws but distilled wisdom. They do not cover every exception, nuance, or circumstance. Their power lies in their clarity and brevity, which make them effective guides for everyday living.

Proverbs as General Principles

A common interpretive mistake is to treat every proverb as a universal, exceptionless rule or as an unconditional promise. Instead, proverbs are general observations of how life normally works under God's moral order.

For example: "Train up a child in the way he should go; even when he is old he will not depart from it" (Prov. 22:6). This is not a promise that every well-trained child will remain faithful. It is a principle that faithful instruction normally bears lasting fruit, even if exceptions exist. To treat it as a guarantee would be to misread its nature and create false expectations.

Similarly, "The hand of the diligent will rule, while the slothful will be put to forced labor" (Prov. 12:24) does not mean that every hardworking person will always rise to power. It expresses the general truth that diligence leads to advancement while laziness leads to hardship.

Proverbs in the Context of Wisdom

Proverbs belong to the broader biblical category of wisdom literature, which also includes Job and Ecclesiastes. Wisdom is not mere cleverness but skillful living in covenant relationship with Jehovah. Proverbs reflects the principle that God has ordered the world morally and practically, so that righteous living generally leads to blessing while folly leads to ruin.

The proverbs, therefore, are not detached observations but covenantal instruction. They teach Israel, and by extension the church, how to live wisely under God's lordship.

Why Recognizing Proverbs as Principles Matters

Failure to recognize the nature of proverbs as general principles leads to two distortions. On one side, interpreters turn them into unconditional promises, only to be disillusioned when reality does not match expectation. On the other, some dismiss them as simplistic or naïve because exceptions exist. Both errors miss the point.

Proverbs teach the normal patterns of life in God's world. They do not deny that exceptions occur, nor do they pretend that life is mechanical. Rather, they call believers to pursue wisdom, knowing that God blesses righteousness and judges folly, even if the timing and details vary.

The Interpreter's Task

The faithful interpreter approaches Proverbs not as a code of guarantees but as a treasury of Spirit-inspired wisdom. He seeks to understand the principle expressed, its application to daily life, and its place within the larger framework of biblical theology. By recognizing proverbs as general principles, the interpreter preserves their authority, avoids misapplication, and allows them to function as they were intended: guides for godly living under Jehovah's covenant rule.

Parallelism and Antithesis in Proverbs

The book of Proverbs is not only a treasury of wisdom but also a masterpiece of literary craft. Its sayings are designed for memorability, clarity, and impact. Much of this power comes from the use of parallelism and antithesis, features that characterize Hebrew poetry in general but find particularly sharp expression in Proverbs. To interpret the book rightly, one must understand how these devices function to convey truth with precision and force.

Parallelism in Proverbs

Parallelism is the basic structural feature of Hebrew poetry, and Proverbs is saturated with it. By setting one line alongside another, the inspired writer reinforces, develops, or contrasts ideas, making wisdom memorable and emphatic.

Synonymous Parallelism

Here the second line repeats the thought of the first in slightly different words, reinforcing the principle.

"The fear of Jehovah is the beginning of knowledge;
fools despise wisdom and instruction" (Prov. 1:7).

While the second line introduces a contrast, it still serves to underscore the truth of the first: reverence for Jehovah is foundational, and rejection of wisdom is folly.

Synthetic (or Constructive) Parallelism

Here the second line adds to or expands upon the first.

"Trust in Jehovah with all your heart,
and do not lean on your own understanding" (Prov. 3:5).

The two lines together present a fuller picture: trust in God requires not only positive reliance but also the rejection of self-reliance.

Emblematic Parallelism

Here one line presents a figure of speech, while the other explains its meaning.

"Like a gold ring in a pig's snout
is a beautiful woman without discretion" (Prov. 11:22).

The vivid image in the first line is clarified in the second, driving home the point about the emptiness of beauty without virtue.

Antithesis in Proverbs

If parallelism reinforces or expands an idea, antithesis sharpens meaning through contrast. Antithetic proverbs are among the most memorable, because they set wisdom and folly side by side in stark relief.

"The way of the wicked is an abomination to Jehovah, but He loves him who pursues righteousness" (Prov. 15:9).

Here the contrast between wickedness and righteousness highlights God's moral order. The reader is forced to choose between two clearly opposed paths.

Antithesis often appears in the form of short, sharp contrasts:

"A wise son makes a glad father,
but a foolish son is a sorrow to his mother" (Prov. 10:1).

"The mouth of the righteous is a fountain of life,
but the mouth of the wicked conceals violence" (Prov. 10:11).

By pairing opposites, Proverbs emphasizes the practical and moral consequences of each choice, underscoring the urgency of wisdom.

Why Parallelism and Antithesis Matter

These literary features are not mere stylistic flourishes; they are theological tools. Parallelism ensures clarity by restating or elaborating truth. Antithesis highlights the sharp divide between wisdom and folly, righteousness and wickedness, life and death. Together they embody the moral polarity of biblical wisdom.

The interpreter must respect these structures, recognizing how they shape meaning. To overlook them is to flatten the text into disconnected sayings. To attend to them is to hear the full force of the Spirit-inspired wisdom, sharpened by repetition and contrast.

Theological Force of Contrast

The prevalence of antithesis in Proverbs reflects a profound theological truth: there are only two paths. Just as Psalm 1 divides humanity into the righteous and the wicked, Proverbs consistently sets before the reader the choice between fearing Jehovah or despising His wisdom. The form of the proverb enforces the reality of covenant life: neutrality is impossible, and the consequences are eternal.

Avoiding Misuse: Promise Versus Probability

Among the most common interpretive mistakes with Proverbs is the assumption that each proverb functions as an absolute promise from God, guaranteeing a fixed outcome. This misunderstanding often leads to disappointment, disillusionment, or distorted theology when life does not match such expectations. The truth is that proverbs are Spirit-inspired wisdom sayings that set forth general principles—probabilities rooted in God's moral order—not unconditional promises. Recognizing this distinction is vital for faithful interpretation.

The Nature of Proverbs

A proverb is a compact expression of a principle, not a universal law without exception. It points to the way life normally works under Jehovah's governance of the world. Proverbs are therefore neither speculative musings nor ironclad guarantees; they are observations shaped by divine wisdom, intended to guide the covenant community into righteous living.

The proverb's brevity requires generalization. It highlights what is generally true, leaving aside exceptions that may arise in a fallen world. This is why the wise interpreter treats proverbs as Spirit-given guidance for godly living, while also remembering that God's providence sometimes permits outcomes that appear to contradict the general pattern.

Illustrations of Principle, Not Promise

Consider Proverbs 22:6: "Train up a child in the way he should go; even when he is old he will not depart from it." This is not a guarantee that every child raised in the fear of Jehovah will persevere in faith without exception. Instead, it is a principle that faithful instruction normally shapes the life of a child in enduring ways. The proverb's purpose is to stress parental responsibility and the effectiveness of godly training, not to promise unfailingly positive results in every case.

Similarly, Proverbs 10:27 declares, "The fear of Jehovah prolongs life, but the years of the wicked will be short." This does not mean that every godly person will live a long earthly life, or that every wicked person will die young. It communicates the principle that reverence for

God tends toward life and blessing, while rebellion brings destruction. Exceptions may occur, but the principle remains valid as a reflection of God's moral order.

Proverbs in the Context of the Whole Bible

The misinterpretation of Proverbs as promises is corrected when viewed in the broader context of Scripture. Other wisdom books, such as Job and Ecclesiastes, remind us that exceptions exist. Job was a righteous man who suffered greatly. Ecclesiastes observes that "in the place of justice, even there was wickedness" (Eccl. 3:16). These books do not contradict Proverbs but complement it, balancing principle with the reality of a fallen world.

The Psalms also show that the wicked sometimes prosper temporarily, while the righteous suffer. Yet the end of both is consistent with the principles of Proverbs: the wicked will ultimately perish, and the righteous will ultimately be vindicated (Ps. 1:6).

The Danger of Misuse

When proverbs are misapplied as promises, the results can be pastorally harmful. Parents may wrongly conclude that a wayward child proves their failure or God's unfaithfulness. Believers may assume that diligent labor always guarantees prosperity, only to become embittered when hardship comes. Such misapplications impose expectations on the text that God never placed there.

The misuse of Proverbs also distorts theology by implying that God is bound to act in mechanical ways. This undermines the biblical teaching that God works according to His sovereign wisdom and that His providence may permit suffering for purposes beyond human understanding.

The Interpreter's Task

The wise interpreter must discern the difference between principle and promise. Proverbs describe the normal patterns of God's moral order, urging the believer to live wisely in covenant obedience.

They are true, authoritative, and profitable, but their truth lies in their function as general principles, not as unconditional guarantees.

By treating Proverbs rightly, the interpreter avoids the snares of false expectation and preserves the rich value of these sayings as practical guides to godliness. They teach not how to manipulate God for desired outcomes but how to live faithfully under His rule, trusting Him with results.

The Fear of Jehovah as the Interpretive Key

If there is a single thread that ties the book of Proverbs together, it is the theme of the fear of Jehovah. This is not a marginal idea but the theological foundation of biblical wisdom. Proverbs declares at the outset: "The fear of Jehovah is the beginning of knowledge; fools despise wisdom and instruction" (Prov. 1:7). This theme is repeated and reinforced throughout the book (Prov. 9:10; 10:27; 14:26–27; 15:33; 19:23; 22:4). Without the fear of Jehovah, there is no true wisdom. To interpret Proverbs apart from this key is to miss its very heart.

The Meaning of the Fear of Jehovah

The fear of Jehovah is not servile terror, nor is it casual respect. It is reverential awe toward God, rooted in recognition of His holiness, majesty, and authority. It includes trust in His promises, submission to His will, and dread of dishonoring Him. It is covenantal in nature, acknowledging Jehovah as both Redeemer and King.

This fear is the posture of faith. It does not drive believers away from God but draws them near in humility and obedience. It is the soil in which wisdom grows, because wisdom is nothing less than skillful living in light of God's character and covenant.

The Fear of Jehovah as Beginning

Proverbs calls the fear of Jehovah the "beginning" of wisdom (Prov. 9:10). This does not mean it is merely the first step, to be left behind once wisdom matures. Rather, it is the foundation and controlling principle of all wisdom. Just as a building cannot stand without a solid foundation, so wisdom cannot exist apart from reverent submission to God.

The fear of Jehovah guards wisdom from degenerating into mere pragmatism. It ensures that wisdom is not simply about living effectively but about living rightly in relationship to God. Without this fear, what passes for wisdom is merely cleverness or cunning, often employed for selfish ends.

The Fear of Jehovah in Daily Life

The book of Proverbs shows how the fear of Jehovah shapes every area of life:

- **In Speech:** "By steadfast love and faithfulness iniquity is atoned for, and by the fear of Jehovah one turns away from evil" (Prov. 16:6).

- **In Conduct:** "The fear of Jehovah is hatred of evil" (Prov. 8:13).

- **In Security:** "The fear of Jehovah leads to life, and whoever has it rests satisfied" (Prov. 19:23).

- **In Prosperity:** "The reward for humility and fear of Jehovah is riches and honor and life" (Prov. 22:4).

These proverbs do not teach a mechanistic formula but show that reverence for God shapes character, directs behavior, and secures blessing under His providence.

The Fear of Jehovah Versus Folly

The contrast between wisdom and folly in Proverbs is ultimately the contrast between fearing Jehovah and rejecting Him. The wise embrace God's authority, while fools despise it. Proverbs 1:29–31 warns of those who "hated knowledge and did not choose the fear of Jehovah." Their rejection of God's rule results in ruin.

The stark polarity of Proverbs underscores that wisdom is not neutral. Every decision, word, and action flows from either reverence for God or rebellion against Him. The fear of Jehovah is thus the dividing line of human existence.

The Fear of Jehovah and Christ

In the fuller light of the New Testament, the fear of Jehovah finds its ultimate expression in Christ. He is wisdom incarnate (1 Cor. 1:24, 30), and those who follow Him walk in the fear of the Lord (Acts 9:31). The reverence, trust, and submission called for in Proverbs are now directed toward the risen Christ, who embodies and fulfills the wisdom of God.

Thus, to interpret Proverbs through the fear of Jehovah is to see that wisdom begins and ends with Christ, the One greater than Solomon (Matt. 12:42). The interpreter must never separate Proverbs' moral instruction from its theological root in reverence for God, now revealed fully in His Son.

Why This Is the Interpretive Key

Without the fear of Jehovah, Proverbs becomes a manual of moralism or a collection of secular advice. With the fear of Jehovah, it is understood as Spirit-inspired wisdom that leads to godliness, holiness, and blessing. The key to interpretation, then, is not clever analysis or cultural insight but a posture of reverent submission to God's Word.

The fear of Jehovah ensures that Proverbs is read not merely as ancient sayings but as divine instruction for covenant living. It binds the book together, safeguards it from misuse, and directs the reader to true wisdom found only in humble reverence before God.

Applying Proverbs in Daily Living

The book of Proverbs is not designed for detached study alone. Its Spirit-inspired wisdom was written to be lived. To interpret Proverbs faithfully is to allow its principles to shape character, guide decisions, and transform conduct. The sayings are concise, memorable, and portable because they are meant to accompany God's people in the practical realities of daily life.

Proverbs and the Formation of Character

At its heart, Proverbs aims to cultivate godly character. It contrasts the wise and the foolish, the righteous and the wicked, the diligent and the lazy. These categories are not merely intellectual but moral and spiritual. To live wisely is to walk in reverence before Jehovah, reflecting His holiness in the ordinary routines of life.

For example, Proverbs consistently praises diligence: "The hand of the diligent will rule, while the slothful will be put to forced labor" (Prov. 12:24).

It warns against dishonesty: "A false balance is an abomination to Jehovah, but a just weight is His delight" (Prov. 11:1).

It extols kindness: "Whoever oppresses a poor man insults his Maker, but he who is generous to the needy honors Him" (Prov. 14:31).

Each proverb presses truth into the heart, calling for transformation in character as well as action.

Proverbs and Decision-Making

The wisdom of Proverbs equips believers to make decisions in daily life. Because the book addresses matters of speech, work, relationships, money, justice, and integrity, it provides guidance in countless situations. Its principles are not bound to ancient culture but are universally applicable because they are grounded in God's moral order.

When facing conflict, Proverbs 15:1 counsels: "A soft answer turns away wrath, but a harsh word stirs up anger." When weighing financial dealings, Proverbs 13:11 reminds: "Wealth gained hastily will dwindle, but whoever gathers little by little will increase it." When tempted to gossip, Proverbs 26:20 instructs: "For lack of wood the fire goes out, and where there is no whisperer, quarreling ceases."

These sayings do not guarantee outcomes in every circumstance, but they provide divine wisdom to guide godly choices.

Proverbs and Relationships

A major focus of Proverbs is relationships. It teaches children to honor parents (Prov. 1:8–9), friends to be loyal (Prov. 17:17), spouses to be faithful (Prov. 5:18–19), and rulers to act justly (Prov. 29:4). The book addresses every sphere of human interaction, pressing God's wisdom into family life, friendships, marriage, community, and leadership.

Applying these truths means measuring one's relationships not by cultural norms but by the standard of covenant faithfulness and reverence for Jehovah.

Proverbs and the Fear of Jehovah

The application of Proverbs is always rooted in the fear of Jehovah. Without reverence for God, the sayings could be twisted into tools for self-advancement or mere pragmatism. With the fear of Jehovah, they are recognized as divine instruction for holy living. Every decision, every action, every word is shaped by the awareness that life is lived before the face of God.

Living Proverbs in Christ

The New Testament reveals that the wisdom of Proverbs finds its fulfillment in Christ, who is "the wisdom of God" (1 Cor. 1:24, 30). To live out Proverbs today is to walk in Him, embodying the wisdom that He perfectly displayed. Jesus lived with perfect diligence, integrity, compassion, and reverence for God. The believer who abides in Him, by faith and obedience, applies Proverbs not as abstract sayings but as a Christ-centered pattern of life.

Why Application Matters

If Proverbs is studied only as ancient literature, its power is lost. If it is memorized but not obeyed, its purpose is thwarted. But when Proverbs is received as Spirit-inspired wisdom and applied in daily life, it produces character that reflects God's holiness, decisions that display His wisdom, and relationships that honor His covenant.

Proverbs was written to be lived. Its wisdom is for the marketplace, the family, the workplace, and the heart. To apply it faithfully is to walk in the fear of Jehovah, skillfully navigating life's complexities with integrity, humility, and devotion to Him.

Conclusion: Interpreting Proverbs

The book of Proverbs is Jehovah's inspired guide to skillful living. Its sayings are concise, memorable, and practical, designed to form godly character and direct the daily choices of His people. Yet to interpret Proverbs rightly, one must remember its essential nature: it is a collection of general principles, not absolute promises.

Proverbs does not operate on the principle of rigid cause and effect, as though life were a formula where obedience always guarantees immediate blessing and disobedience always guarantees immediate ruin. Instead, it declares how life normally works under God's moral order. Generally speaking, diligence leads to prosperity, honesty leads to honor, reverence for God leads to life, and folly leads to destruction. Living by the principles of Proverbs—and of the Bible as a whole—greatly increases the likelihood of a life free from the worst adversities brought by human imperfection, sinful choices, and the wickedness of the world. But it is not an absolute guarantee. In Satan's world, bad things do happen to faithful people, as Job and countless other saints have shown.

Understanding this distinction protects against misapplication. When a proverb such as "Train up a child in the way he should go;

even when he is old he will not depart from it" (Prov. 22:6) is treated as an unconditional promise, parents may suffer needless guilt or doubt God's faithfulness if a child strays. When "The fear of Jehovah prolongs life" (Prov. 10:27) is read as a guarantee, believers may stumble when a righteous man dies young. But when these sayings are understood as principles, their power is preserved: they encourage godliness, warn against folly, and point to the moral structure of God's world, while leaving the outcomes in His sovereign hands.

At the heart of Proverbs is the fear of Jehovah, the interpretive key that unlocks every saying. Reverence for God ensures that Proverbs is not reduced to moral pragmatism but embraced as divine wisdom. When applied in daily living, the book trains believers to walk in diligence, integrity, humility, compassion, and righteousness. It shapes families, friendships, marriages, work, and speech. It directs the believer to wisdom incarnate, Jesus Christ, in whom these sayings find their ultimate fulfillment.

Proverbs is not a set of guarantees but a map of wisdom. Those who walk its paths will, generally speaking, enjoy lives marked by stability, righteousness, and blessing, even though adversities may still come in a fallen world. Its purpose is not to offer formulas of certainty but to equip God's people to live faithfully before Him, trusting His providence, fearing His name, and walking in His wisdom until the day when all adversity is removed in His kingdom.

Review Questions – Chapter 9: Interpreting Proverbs

1. How do biblical proverbs differ from absolute promises or universal guarantees?

2. Why is it essential to read Proverbs as general truths rooted in God's created order?

3. What is the danger of misapplying Proverbs as if they were unconditional promises?

4. How does the "fear of Jehovah" function as the interpretive key for the entire book of Proverbs?

5. Why must Proverbs be understood within the covenant framework of Israel's life before God?

6. How do the short, memorable form and parallel structure of proverbs contribute to their impact?

7. In what ways can Proverbs be wrongly reduced to secular moralism if separated from their covenantal and theological foundation?

8. How does the Christ-centered perspective safeguard against treating Proverbs as merely human wisdom?

9. Why must interpreters be cautious in transferring cultural specifics of Proverbs directly into modern settings without context?

10. How does the collection of Proverbs shape practical godliness in speech, work, family, and community life?

Exercises in Interpretation – Chapter 9: Interpreting Proverbs

Exercise 1: Proverbs 3:5-6

- Identify the command ("Trust in Jehovah with all your heart") and the promise ("He will make straight your paths").

- How does this proverb teach reliance on divine wisdom over human understanding?

- Why should this not be treated as a mechanical formula for success but as a call to covenantal faithfulness?

Exercise 2: Proverbs 22:6

- Read the proverb, "Train up a child in the way he should go; even when he is old he will not depart from it."

- What does this teach as a principle rather than as a guarantee?

- How does interpreting it correctly protect parents from misplaced guilt or false expectations?

Exercise 3: Proverbs 10:27

- "The fear of Jehovah prolongs life, but the years of the wicked will be short."
- How should this proverb be understood in the context of general patterns rather than absolute outcomes?
- What covenantal truth underlies this statement, and how does it guard against misinterpretation when a righteous person dies young?

CHAPTER 10 Interpreting Prophecy

Prophecy as Covenant Proclamation and Prediction

The prophetic books of the Bible stand as some of the most challenging yet rewarding portions of Scripture to interpret. Their richness lies in their dual function: the prophets proclaimed God's covenantal truth to their immediate audience, and at the same time, under divine inspiration, they often predicted future events tied to God's unfolding plan of redemption. To grasp their message faithfully, interpreters must first recognize prophecy as covenant proclamation and then as prediction, always holding both together within the framework of the historical-grammatical method.

Prophecy as Covenant Proclamation

At its foundation, biblical prophecy is covenantal. The prophets were not religious innovators or detached seers offering vague spiritual insights. They were covenant prosecutors, men raised up by Jehovah to call Israel and Judah back to the stipulations of the covenant made at Sinai and renewed through Moses and Joshua.

This covenantal foundation explains why so much of prophetic literature consists of warnings, indictments, and calls to repentance. The prophets were bringing charges against a rebellious people who had violated God's law. For example, Isaiah's opening chapter sounds more like a courtroom indictment than a fortune-teller's prediction:

"Hear, O heavens, and give ear, O earth; for Jehovah has spoken: 'Children have I reared and brought up, but they have rebelled against Me'" (Isa. 1:2).

Similarly, Hosea presents Jehovah's case against Israel's unfaithfulness in covenant terms, portraying their idolatry as spiritual adultery. Micah declares God's controversy with His people (Mic. 6:1–8), reminding them that covenant blessing is contingent on covenant faithfulness.

In this sense, prophecy is primarily proclamation—declaring God's truth into the present, confronting sin, and urging repentance in light of the covenant relationship.

Prophecy as Prediction

Yet prophecy is not only proclamation; it is also prediction. Under divine inspiration, the prophets foretold events that lay beyond their own day. Some of these predictions concerned near-term events, such as the fall of Samaria (722 B.C.E.) or the destruction of Jerusalem (586 B.C.E.). Others extended far beyond the immediate horizon, pointing to the coming of the Messiah, the outpouring of the Spirit, and the consummation of God's kingdom.

For example, Isaiah predicted the virgin conception and birth of Immanuel (Isa. 7:14), the suffering of the Servant (Isa. 53), and the glory of the Messianic kingdom (Isa. 11). Micah foretold the Messiah's birth in Bethlehem (Mic. 5:2). Daniel spoke of successive kingdoms and the ultimate triumph of God's everlasting reign (Dan. 2:44; 7:13–14).

The predictive element of prophecy demonstrates the supernatural character of Scripture. These were not educated guesses or general observations about the cycles of history. They were specific declarations, often centuries in advance, which came to pass exactly as Jehovah had spoken.

Holding the Two Together

The mistake of many interpreters is to emphasize one aspect of prophecy at the expense of the other. Some reduce prophecy to mere covenant proclamation, denying its predictive element, as if the prophets only spoke to their contemporaries. Others treat prophecy as little more than a codebook of predictions, detached from its covenantal context and exploited for speculative timelines.

The faithful interpreter holds both together. Prophecy is covenant proclamation in the present, rooted in the law of Moses, and it is prediction of the future, rooted in the sovereignty of God. Its authority lies in both aspects, since both were inspired by the Spirit.

The Practical Implications

Recognizing prophecy as covenant proclamation and prediction guards the interpreter from distortion. It prevents us from misusing the prophets as if they were fortune-tellers for modern events, while also preventing us from stripping their words of their predictive power. It shows us that prophecy is deeply relevant to every generation, calling for covenant faithfulness today while strengthening hope for God's promised future.

The message of the prophets is therefore not limited to ancient Israel, nor is it exhausted by future fulfillment. It is the living Word of God, proclaiming His holiness, warning of judgment, promising salvation, and directing all history toward its consummation in Christ.

The Role of Symbolism and Poetic Imagery in Prophetic Texts

One of the most striking features of prophetic literature is its heavy use of symbolism and poetic imagery. The prophets did not limit themselves to straightforward prose; under the Spirit's inspiration, they employed vivid pictures, dramatic symbols, and poetic devices to impress God's truth upon His people. These elements are not random embellishments but integral to the message. To interpret prophecy faithfully, one must carefully distinguish between the image and the truth it conveys, appreciating the power of figurative language without losing sight of the literal meaning intended by the inspired author.

The Function of Symbolism in Prophecy

Symbolism in prophecy serves to make the message unforgettable. Symbols arrest attention, stir imagination, and drive home truth with force. When Isaiah compared Judah to a vineyard (Isa. 5:1–7), his audience could not miss the indictment: they were the vineyard Jehovah had planted, yet they produced only wild grapes of injustice and unrighteousness.

Prophetic symbolism often functioned as a parable in action. Jeremiah smashed a clay jar before the leaders of Jerusalem (Jer. 19), symbolizing the coming destruction of the city. Ezekiel lay on his side for hundreds of days, bearing the iniquity of Israel and Judah (Ezek. 4). Hosea's marriage to Gomer symbolized Israel's unfaithfulness and Jehovah's redeeming love (Hos. 1–3). These enacted symbols were not theatrical performances for their own sake but visual sermons conveying covenant truth with unmistakable clarity.

The Nature of Prophetic Imagery

Prophetic books also employ rich poetic imagery, much like the Psalms, but often with heightened intensity. Nations are described as raging seas (Isa. 17:12–13), rulers as trees felled by God's axe (Ezek. 31:3–18), judgment as fire consuming stubble (Mal. 4:1). Such imagery is not to be flattened into literal description; it conveys theological realities in ways that plain speech could never capture.

For example, when Daniel described four beasts rising from the sea (Dan. 7), he was not reporting zoological anomalies but symbolizing successive empires rising in rebellion against God. The image communicates truth by evoking the chaos, terror, and inhumanity of these kingdoms. The reader must discern the meaning intended by the imagery rather than pressing the details into speculative allegory.

Symbolism and Historical Context

Symbolism in prophecy is deeply rooted in Israel's historical and cultural context. Images drawn from agriculture, warfare, temple worship, and creation were immediately recognizable to the original audience. Interpreters today must therefore study these contexts carefully to grasp the force of the imagery. For example, Joel's locust plague (Joel 1–2) reflects the devastation familiar to an agrarian society, while also pointing to a greater day of judgment.

Understanding the context prevents misinterpretation. Without it, interpreters may over-spiritualize the imagery, detaching it from its covenant setting. Proper interpretation requires grounding symbolic language in the realities known to the original audience.

Symbolism and Prophetic Certainty

It is important to emphasize that symbolism does not diminish the certainty of prophecy. A symbolic vision still communicates literal truth, even if it does so figuratively. The beasts of Daniel 7 represent real kingdoms. The statue of Daniel 2 symbolizes actual historical empires. The symbolic language is the Spirit's means of revealing reality, not concealing it.

The danger lies in confusing symbol with allegory. The inspired author had a specific truth in mind when using a symbol, and it is the interpreter's task to uncover that intended meaning through the historical-grammatical method. To press every feature of the imagery into hidden significance is to fall into speculation and to distort the message.

Why Prophecy Employs Symbolism

The prophets used symbolism because the realities they proclaimed were too vast, too awe-inspiring, or too dreadful for plain description. Judgment, redemption, and the consummation of history demand imagery that engages both imagination and conscience. By employing symbols and poetic pictures, the prophets spoke to the whole person—mind, heart, and will.

Moreover, symbolism allows prophecy to speak across generations. A vision of beasts, fire, or mountains communicates timeless truths about God's sovereignty, human rebellion, and final redemption. The imagery transcends its immediate setting while remaining anchored in historical reality.

The Interpreter's Responsibility

The interpreter must therefore approach prophetic symbolism with reverence and care. He must discern what is figurative and what is literal, what is intended as symbol and what is straightforward statement. He must resist both wooden literalism and uncontrolled allegorizing. His task is to ask: *What did this image mean in its historical context? What truth did the inspired author intend it to convey?*

By handling prophetic imagery in this way, the interpreter preserves its power without distorting its meaning. He allows the Spirit-inspired pictures to do their work: to warn of judgment, to assure of salvation, and to direct hope toward the consummation of God's covenant promises.

Distinguishing Near and Distant Fulfillment Without Speculation

One of the greatest interpretive challenges in prophecy is discerning the relationship between near and distant fulfillment. The prophets frequently spoke of events that were both imminent in their own day and ultimate in God's unfolding plan. The Spirit sometimes compressed these horizons into a single prophetic message, so that the near and the distant appear side by side. To handle these texts faithfully requires careful use of the historical-grammatical method, vigilance against speculation, and a commitment to let Scripture itself set the boundaries of interpretation.

The Reality of Dual Horizons

The prophets often addressed their contemporaries directly, warning of judgments or promising deliverance in terms of their historical situation. At the same time, those same oracles often carried significance far beyond the immediate horizon. This dual horizon of prophecy is sometimes compared to a mountain range: peaks appear close together when viewed from a distance, even though valleys may lie between them.

For example, Isaiah 7:14 promised a child called Immanuel as a sign to King Ahaz, tied to events in the eighth century B.C.E. Yet Matthew 1:23 identifies that prophecy with the virgin conception of Christ centuries later. The prophecy had an immediate relevance to Ahaz and his day, but also an ultimate fulfillment in the coming of the Messiah.

Similarly, Joel's prophecy of the Spirit poured out (Joel 2:28–32) carried an initial application to Israel's restoration but found climactic fulfillment at Pentecost (Acts 2:16–21).

Guarding Against Speculation

Because prophecy often carries both near and distant horizons, interpreters must guard against the temptation to indulge in speculation. The prophets did not intend their words to be used as coded forecasts for every modern event. Their primary audience was their own generation, and their message was framed within Israel's covenant context.

Speculative interpretation arises when interpreters detach prophecy from its historical grounding and force it into alignment with contemporary headlines. This not only distorts the inspired message but undermines the authority of Scripture by turning it into a malleable tool of personal opinion.

The faithful interpreter must resist the urge to ask, *How does this prophecy fit into my timeline?* and instead ask, *What did this prophecy mean for its first audience? How does Scripture itself explain its fulfillment?*

The Historical-Grammatical Safeguard

The historical-grammatical method provides the safeguard against speculation. Every prophecy must first be interpreted in light of its original context—its historical setting, audience, language, and covenant framework. Only then should its broader fulfillment be considered, and only where Scripture itself provides warrant for such an extension.

For example, Daniel's prophecy of four kingdoms (Dan. 2; 7) can be identified with historical empires because the text itself provides clues. By contrast, to assign every symbol in prophecy to modern nations or events apart from textual warrant is speculation, not exegesis.

Progressive Revelation

Another safeguard is to recognize the role of progressive revelation. Later Scripture often clarifies how earlier prophecy is fulfilled. The New Testament interprets many Old Testament prophecies, showing their ultimate realization in Christ. The interpreter should follow this inspired pattern, allowing the New Testament to provide the lens through which the prophetic word is seen in its fullness.

Where the New Testament applies a prophecy directly to Christ or the church, the meaning is secure. Where it is silent, interpreters must exercise restraint, acknowledging the limits of what has been revealed.

Theological Purpose of Near and Distant Fulfillment

The blending of near and distant fulfillment serves a theological purpose. It demonstrates that God is sovereign over history, bringing His word to pass both in immediate judgments and in ultimate redemption. The near fulfillments validate the prophet's authority and confirm the certainty of God's word. The distant fulfillments reveal the larger scope of God's plan, culminating in Christ and His kingdom.

This dual horizon keeps the reader rooted in history while also lifting his eyes to eternity. It grounds prophecy in real events yet directs hope toward the final consummation of God's covenant promises.

Why Caution Is Essential

To speculate about the timing or manner of fulfillment beyond what Scripture reveals is to presume upon God's revelation. Jesus Himself warned against date-setting and unwarranted curiosity about "times or seasons that the Father has fixed by His own authority" (Acts 1:7). The interpreter's task is not to decode hidden timelines but to proclaim the truth of prophecy as God has revealed it, urging repentance and hope in light of His promises.

Christ and the Prophetic Hope

The prophetic writings, while deeply rooted in their historical contexts, ultimately converge on the person and work of Christ. He is not hidden under every detail of prophecy, nor should interpreters force Him into passages where He is not present. Yet taken as a whole, the prophetic corpus points forward to the ultimate redemption that Jehovah would accomplish through His Messiah. Christ is the fulfillment of the covenant promises, the embodiment of prophetic hope, and the assurance that God's word never fails.

The Prophets and the Messianic Promise

From the earliest stages of prophecy, the hope of a coming deliverer is present. Genesis 3:15 promises that the seed of the woman would crush the serpent's head. This promise is clarified in the Abrahamic covenant: "In your offspring shall all the nations of the earth be blessed" (Gen. 22:18). The Davidic covenant narrows the focus further, promising an everlasting throne (2 Sam. 7:12–16).

The prophets continually returned to these promises, interpreting Israel's history and future in light of God's covenant commitment. Isaiah spoke of a child born to rule (Isa. 9:6–7), a Servant who would suffer for the sins of many (Isa. 53), and a coming age of righteousness and peace (Isa. 11). Micah identified Bethlehem as the birthplace of the Messiah (Mic. 5:2). Zechariah foretold a king coming in humility, "righteous and having salvation, humble and mounted on a donkey" (Zech. 9:9).

These were not imaginative guesses or literary ideals but Spirit-inspired promises, preparing the covenant people for the coming of Christ.

Christ as the Fulfillment of Prophecy

The New Testament repeatedly affirms that Christ fulfills the prophetic hope. Matthew presents His birth, ministry, and death as the realization of specific Old Testament prophecies (Matt. 1:23; 2:6; 21:5). Luke records Jesus' own declaration that "everything written about Me in the Law of Moses and the Prophets and the Psalms must be fulfilled" (Luke 24:44).

The apostles consistently proclaimed Christ as the one whom the prophets foretold. Peter declared that "all the prophets who have spoken, from Samuel and those who came after him, also proclaimed these days" (Acts 3:24). Paul testified that his gospel was nothing other than what "the prophets and Moses said would come to pass: that the Christ must suffer and that, by being the first to rise from the dead, He would proclaim light both to our people and to the Gentiles" (Acts 26:22–23).

Christ is not a forced addition to the prophetic word but its God-ordained fulfillment.

The Prophetic Hope in Christ's First Coming

Prophecy found dramatic realization in the first coming of Christ. He was born of a virgin (Isa. 7:14; Matt. 1:23), in Bethlehem (Mic. 5:2; Matt. 2:6), entered Jerusalem on a donkey (Zech. 9:9; Matt. 21:5), was betrayed for thirty pieces of silver (Zech. 11:12; Matt. 26:15), and suffered as the righteous Servant who bore the sins of many (Isa. 53; 1 Pet. 2:24).

These fulfillments validate the authority of the prophetic word and confirm that God's promises are certain. They demonstrate that the prophets were not speaking of vague ideals but of specific historical realities realized in Jesus Christ.

The Prophetic Hope in Christ's Return

Yet prophecy does not end with Christ's first coming. The prophets also looked ahead to the day when Jehovah's kingdom would be fully established. The New Testament connects this hope with Christ's return.

Passages such as Isaiah 2:2–4, envisioning nations streaming to Zion and peace covering the earth, await their final fulfillment. Daniel's vision of a kingdom that will crush all others and endure forever (Dan. 2:44) finds its consummation in Christ's millennial reign (Rev. 20:1–6). Zechariah 14 anticipates a day when Jehovah will reign as King over all the earth, fulfilled in Christ's second coming.

The prophetic hope is therefore both "already" and "not yet." Christ has fulfilled much, but the fullness of prophecy still awaits His return.

Christ as the Center, Not the Obsession

The faithful interpreter must recognize Christ as the center of prophetic hope without turning every prophetic image into a direct Christological symbol. The prophets proclaimed real judgments on real nations and spoke to real covenant violations. Their words cannot be reduced to allegories about Christ. Yet, at the same time, to ignore the prophetic anticipation of the Messiah is to miss the very trajectory of redemptive history.

The historical-grammatical method safeguards this balance. It allows the interpreter to see Christ where the prophets intended and where the New Testament confirms, without forcing Him into every detail. This preserves both the integrity of the text and the glory of Christ as the fulfillment of the prophetic hope.

Why Christ Is the Prophetic Hope

Christ is the one who embodies the justice, mercy, and kingship the prophets longed for. He is the Servant who bore our sins, the King who reigns in righteousness, and the Judge who will set all things right.

All prophecy—whether covenant proclamation, near fulfillment, or ultimate prediction—finds its coherence and consummation in Him.

Thus, prophecy teaches the church to look back in gratitude for Christ's first coming and forward in hope for His return. It assures believers that history is not chaotic but governed by God's sovereign plan, which reaches its climax in the reign of Christ.

The Interpreter's Responsibility in Prophetic Study

Prophecy is one of the most stirring and complex portions of Scripture. It addresses the present with covenant proclamation, unveils the future with divine prediction, and uses rich symbolism to impress God's truth upon His people. Because of its unique features, prophecy demands great care from the interpreter. Mishandling it can lead to confusion, speculation, or even false teaching. To interpret prophecy responsibly, one must approach it with reverence, discipline, and fidelity to the historical-grammatical method.

Anchoring Prophecy in the Historical-Grammatical Method

The first responsibility of the interpreter is to read prophecy in its historical and grammatical context. The prophets spoke to real people in real times, addressing the covenant community in specific circumstances. Their words cannot be understood apart from that setting. The language, culture, and historical situation must be examined before broader application is made.

For example, Isaiah's words to Ahaz in Isaiah 7:14 had immediate meaning in the political crisis of the eighth century B.C.E. before finding ultimate fulfillment in Christ. The interpreter must not skip past the historical horizon in eagerness to reach the distant. Only by honoring the near meaning can the distant fulfillment be rightly understood.

Avoiding Speculation and Date-Setting

Another responsibility is to resist speculation. The temptation to turn prophecy into a codebook for current events has plagued interpreters throughout history. Whether assigning modern nations to the symbols of Daniel or forcing contemporary headlines into Revelation, such methods depart from sound exegesis. Jesus Himself warned against attempts to fix dates and times: "It is not for you to know times or seasons that the Father has fixed by His own authority" (Acts 1:7).

The interpreter's duty is not to indulge curiosity but to proclaim the truths God has revealed—His holiness, His judgment, His mercy, His promises, and His sovereignty over history. Speculation undermines confidence in Scripture when predictions fail; disciplined exegesis strengthens confidence by showing how God's Word has always proven true.

Respecting the Role of Symbolism

Because prophecy often employs symbolic language, the interpreter must carefully distinguish between what is literal and what is figurative. To read everything literally is to miss the richness of prophetic imagery. To allegorize everything is to drain prophecy of its concrete meaning. The balance is to let the context determine how the language functions, recognizing that figurative symbols convey real truths.

For instance, the beasts of Daniel 7 are not literal animals but symbolize actual empires. The point is not zoology but theology: human kingdoms are beastly in rebellion against God, yet they are subject to His sovereign rule.

Letting Scripture Interpret Scripture

The faithful interpreter allows later Scripture to explain earlier prophecy. The New Testament often identifies the fulfillment of Old Testament prophecies, and these inspired explanations must govern interpretation. Matthew applies Isaiah 7:14 to the virgin conception of

Christ (Matt. 1:23). Peter applies Joel 2:28–32 to the outpouring of the Spirit at Pentecost (Acts 2:16–21). Such Spirit-given interpretations provide sure guidance where otherwise uncertainty might remain.

Where the New Testament is silent, restraint is required. Not every detail is explained, and not every image should be forced into a system. The interpreter's responsibility is to teach what God has revealed, not to speculate about what He has concealed.

Keeping Christ Central Without Losing Balance

Since prophecy culminates in Christ, the interpreter must always bear in mind that the prophetic hope points to Him. Yet this Christ-centeredness must not become forced or obsessive. Not every image or phrase is directly about Christ, though all prophecy finds its coherence in Him. The interpreter's responsibility is to see Christ where the prophets intended and where the New Testament affirms, guarding against imaginative excesses that distort the plain sense of the text.

Applying Prophecy Faithfully

The interpreter must not leave prophecy in the realm of academic analysis. Its purpose is to call God's people to repentance, faith, and hope. Covenant warnings are meant to stir the conscience. Predictions of judgment are meant to awaken fear of God. Promises of restoration are meant to anchor faith in His covenant love. Visions of future glory are meant to sustain perseverance in the present.

To interpret prophecy responsibly is to press its truths upon the heart, urging believers to walk in covenant faithfulness while awaiting the fulfillment of God's promises in Christ.

The Weight of Responsibility

Because prophecy has been so frequently misused, the responsibility of the interpreter is weighty. He must resist curiosity, avoid speculation, honor context, respect symbolism, follow Scripture's own interpretations, keep Christ central, and apply the message to the lives of God's people. By doing so, he safeguards the integrity of God's Word and strengthens the faith of the church.

Prophecy is not given to satisfy idle curiosity but to reveal Jehovah's holiness, sovereignty, and redemptive purpose. The interpreter's calling is to handle it with fear, humility, and faithfulness, proclaiming its message with clarity and confidence until all is fulfilled in Christ.

Conclusion: Interpreting Prophecy

Prophecy is one of the most demanding genres of Scripture, yet one of the richest in its testimony to Jehovah's holiness, covenant faithfulness, and sovereign rule over history. To interpret it rightly is to hold together all the features we have studied: its nature as covenant proclamation and prediction, its use of symbolic and poetic imagery, its dual horizons of near and distant fulfillment, its culmination in Christ, and the sober responsibilities it places upon the interpreter.

At its core, prophecy is not a cryptic codebook for the curious but a covenant summons from God Himself. The prophets confronted Israel and Judah with their sin, called them back to faithfulness, and warned them of judgment if they persisted in rebellion. Yet they also proclaimed hope, pointing forward to a day when Jehovah's promises would be fulfilled in His Messiah. Their words were both immediate and ultimate, addressing their contemporaries while anticipating God's redemptive plan across the ages.

Symbolism and imagery gave prophetic truth unforgettable force, but these devices never obscured reality. They conveyed literal truths in vivid form, pressing the message into the hearts of God's people. Near fulfillments validated the prophet's authority, while distant fulfillments anchored hope in God's sovereign plan. The blending of these horizons demonstrates both the relevance of prophecy to its first hearers and its abiding significance for all generations.

Christ stands as the fulfillment and center of the prophetic hope—not forced into every phrase, but clearly the One toward whom the prophets pointed. He is the Servant who bore sin, the King who reigns in righteousness, and the Judge who will return to set all things right. The prophetic word finds coherence and consummation in Him, assuring the church that God's promises are certain and His purposes unstoppable.

Because prophecy has often been misused—through speculation, allegorizing, or obsessive attempts to find hidden meanings—the responsibility of the interpreter is weighty. He must anchor his work in the historical-grammatical method, respect symbolism without distortion, let Scripture interpret Scripture, and apply prophecy with reverence and clarity. To do otherwise is to twist God's Word to human imagination; to do so faithfully is to proclaim His Word as He intended.

Ultimately, prophecy reveals the God who rules history, judges sin, redeems His people, and brings all things to their appointed end in Christ. To interpret prophecy rightly is to hear that voice and to proclaim it with faith and fear, knowing that "no prophecy of Scripture comes from someone's own interpretation" (2 Pet. 1:20). Prophecy belongs to God; the interpreter's calling is to handle it with integrity, proclaim it with boldness, and live in hope of its sure fulfillment.

Review Questions – Chapter 10: Interpreting Prophecy

1. Why must prophecy be understood first as covenant proclamation before it is considered prediction?

2. How did the prophets function as covenant prosecutors rather than independent seers?

3. What role did near-term fulfillments (e.g., fall of Samaria, destruction of Jerusalem) play in validating prophetic authority?

4. How does the predictive element of prophecy demonstrate the supernatural character of Scripture?

5. Why is it dangerous to reduce prophecy to proclamation only or prediction only?

6. How does symbolic action (e.g., Jeremiah's broken jar, Ezekiel lying on his side) serve the prophetic message?

7. Why must symbolism and imagery in prophecy always be interpreted within their historical and cultural context?

8. How do dual horizons of fulfillment (near and distant) function in prophecy, and how do they safeguard interpretation?

9. Why is Christ the fulfillment and center of prophetic hope without forcing Him into every verse?

10. What responsibilities does prophecy place upon the interpreter in handling God's Word faithfully?

Exercises in Interpretation – Chapter 10: Interpreting Prophecy

Exercise 1: Isaiah 5:1-7 – The Vineyard Song

- Identify the covenantal imagery used in this passage.

- How does the vineyard metaphor communicate Jehovah's indictment against His people?

- Why is this not to be allegorized beyond the author's intended meaning?

Exercise 2: Micah 5:2 – The Birthplace of the Messiah

- Read the prophecy and its fulfillment in Matthew 2:1–6.

- How does this illustrate the predictive nature of prophecy?

- What safeguards prevent us from treating every Old Testament detail as predictive in the same way?

Edward D. Andrews

Exercise 3: Daniel 7:1–14 – The Vision of the Beasts and the Son of Man

- Observe the symbolism of the four beasts.

- How should these images be interpreted in their historical context rather than as arbitrary speculation?

- How does the vision climax in the sovereignty of God and the exaltation of the Son of Man?

CHAPTER 11 Interpreting Idioms

Idioms as Expressions Rooted in Culture and Language

Among the most frequent and misunderstood features of biblical language are idioms. An idiom is a fixed expression whose meaning cannot be derived by analyzing the literal sense of its individual words. Instead, idioms draw meaning from cultural usage, linguistic convention, and shared assumptions of the original audience. To interpret the Bible accurately, the reader must recognize idioms for what they are—expressions rooted in Hebrew and Greek culture and language, not wooden statements to be pressed into literalism.

The Nature of Idioms

Idioms are not unique to the Bible; they exist in every language. In English, to say "it's raining cats and dogs" is not to suggest animals are falling from the sky but to communicate heavy rainfall. To "kick the bucket" is not about striking a container with one's foot but about dying. These phrases cannot be understood by dissecting their words but only by recognizing their cultural usage.

The same principle applies to biblical idioms. They are linguistic shortcuts, condensed expressions of meaning understood by their original hearers but often obscure to modern readers. Because idioms lose clarity when translated literally, interpreters must take care to discern their intended sense in context.

Idioms in Hebrew

The Hebrew Bible abounds in idioms. For example:

- **"His nose burned"** (אַף חָרָה, *'aph charah*) means "he became angry" (Gen. 30:2). The image of a hot or flaring nose reflects cultural associations of anger with heavy breathing.

- **"Lift up the face"** means "to show favor" (Num. 6:26). The idiom reflects the gesture of raising one's face toward another in acceptance.

- **"To walk in the ways of"** means "to follow the example or conduct of" (1 Kgs. 22:52). The idiom uses walking as a metaphor for moral and spiritual conduct.

These phrases would confuse or mislead if pressed into literal translation. Their meaning lies in the idiomatic usage familiar to the ancient audience.

Idioms in Greek

The New Testament also contains idioms inherited from both Greek language and Jewish thought. For example:

- **"To have in the belly"** (*en tē koilia*) means "to feel deeply" (John 7:38). The belly was considered the seat of emotions.

- **"To gird up the loins of your mind"** (1 Pet. 1:13) means "to prepare your mind for action," drawn from the practice of tucking robes into a belt before strenuous work.

- **"To heap burning coals on his head"** (Rom. 12:20) does not mean literal fire but refers to bringing shame and repentance upon an enemy through kindness.

Again, the key is recognizing that the meaning is determined by idiomatic usage, not by the literal image itself.

The Interpreter's Responsibility

The responsibility of the interpreter is to identify idioms and interpret them according to their cultural and linguistic context. To read them literally is to misrepresent the text. To treat them as vague metaphors without grounding in context is also an error. The faithful interpreter must ask: *What did this idiom communicate to the original audience?*

Modern translations often render idioms in equivalent contemporary expressions ("be patient with me" instead of "lengthen your nose"), but interpreters must still be alert to underlying idiomatic forms in the original languages.

Why Idioms Matter in Biblical Interpretation

Idioms remind us that Scripture was written in real human languages, with all their cultural richness. They show that meaning is not locked in individual words but in how those words are used. Recognizing idioms prevents misinterpretation, protects against false doctrines built on literalism, and opens the door to a deeper appreciation of the beauty and power of biblical language.

In sum, idioms are expressions rooted in culture and language, given by the Spirit through human authors. To interpret them rightly is to honor both their human context and their divine authority.

Identifying Idiomatic Speech in Hebrew and Greek

Because idioms are fixed expressions whose meanings cannot be determined by literal word-for-word analysis, identifying them is one of the essential skills in biblical interpretation. The challenge is that idioms, by their very nature, make perfect sense to the original audience but can be obscure or misleading to readers centuries later, especially across languages and cultures. Recognizing idiomatic speech in Hebrew and Greek is therefore a crucial step in sound exegesis.

Principles for Identifying Idioms

Several principles can guide the interpreter in discerning idiomatic expressions:

1. **Literal Impossibility**: If the literal sense of the phrase would result in nonsense, exaggeration, or impossibility, it may be

idiomatic. For example, in Genesis 43:34 the Hebrew says Benjamin's portion was "five hands" larger than the others. This does not mean literal hands but portions of food.

2. **Cultural Expressions**: Many idioms reflect cultural practices unfamiliar to modern readers. When a phrase relates directly to ancient customs, gestures, or worldviews, it often carries idiomatic meaning.

3. **Repetition Across Texts**: When an unusual phrase recurs in multiple contexts with consistent meaning, it is likely idiomatic rather than literal.

4. **Translation Difficulty**: Phrases that are difficult to render literally into another language, or that vary significantly across translations, often signal idiomatic usage.

5. **Lexical and Grammatical Study**: Consulting lexicons and grammars often reveals when a phrase is recognized by scholars as an idiom, preventing misinterpretation.

Identifying Idioms in Hebrew

The Hebrew Scriptures contain a wealth of idiomatic expressions. A few examples illustrate the principle:

- **"To uncover the feet"** (Ruth 3:7): In Hebrew culture, this action was idiomatic for lying at someone's feet in a posture of dependence, not an immoral act.

- **"To sleep with one's fathers"** (1 Kgs. 2:10): An idiom for death, rooted in the practice of family burial.

- **"To lengthen the nose"** (Exod. 34:6): Literally odd, but idiomatic for being slow to anger.

- **"To eat the bread of idleness"** (Prov. 31:27): Not literal bread but an idiom for laziness or unproductive living.

Each of these would be misunderstood if read in a strictly literal sense without attention to Hebrew idiomatic usage.

Identifying Idioms in Greek

The Greek of the New Testament also carries idiomatic speech, some native to Greek itself, others shaped by the influence of Hebrew thought expressed in Greek words (known as *Semitisms*). Examples include:

- **"To have the bowels yearn"** (*splagchnizomai*, Mark 1:41): An idiom for deep compassion, since the bowels were considered the seat of emotion.

- **"To kick against the goads"** (Acts 26:14): An agricultural idiom meaning to resist authority, drawn from oxen rebelling against the farmer's prod.

- **"To gird up the loins of your mind"** (1 Pet. 1:13): An idiom for mental readiness, reflecting the custom of tucking in robes before strenuous activity.

- **"To heap burning coals on his head"** (Rom. 12:20): An idiom for producing shame and repentance in an enemy by treating him kindly.

Without recognition of these idioms, interpreters might mistake bodily organs for emotions, agricultural practices for spiritual realities, or imagery of fire for cruelty.

Tools for Identifying Idioms

Identifying idiomatic speech requires careful study and the use of reliable tools. Lexicons (such as HALOT for Hebrew and BDAG for Greek), specialized studies in idioms, and exegetical commentaries often flag idiomatic expressions. Comparing translations can also highlight idioms, since translators often render them into equivalent phrases in the target language rather than sticking with a literal word-for-word form.

Why Identification Matters

If idioms are not recognized, the interpreter risks misunderstanding the text, creating false doctrines, or misrepresenting God's Word. For example, to interpret "sleep with one's fathers" literally would confuse death with sleep, while "to heap burning coals" could be distorted into teaching cruelty rather than kindness. Properly identified, idioms reveal the richness of biblical language and prevent error in both study and application.

The faithful interpreter must therefore train himself to spot idiomatic expressions and handle them carefully, always seeking the meaning intended by the inspired author within the cultural and linguistic context of the original audience.

Avoiding Literalism in Idiomatic Phrases

One of the most common interpretive pitfalls in handling idioms is pressing them into a literal sense. Because idioms do not convey their meaning through the surface value of their words, reading them literally leads to distortion, confusion, or even false teaching. The faithful interpreter must guard against this error by recognizing idioms for what they are—fixed cultural expressions whose meaning lies in usage, not in a woodenly literal rendering.

Why Idioms Cannot Be Taken Literally

Idioms function on the level of cultural convention, not individual word meaning. To interpret them literally is to impose meanings the inspired author never intended. Just as modern English speakers know that "kick the bucket" refers to death, not striking a pail with one's foot, so the original audience of Scripture instinctively understood their own idioms. When readers today press these phrases into literal sense, they obscure the meaning and replace God's Word with human imagination.

Examples of Misinterpreted Idioms

- **"To sleep with one's fathers" (1 Kgs. 2:10):** A Hebrew idiom for death. If read literally, it would suggest continued life or family intimacy rather than burial. Misreading this idiom has sometimes fueled false doctrines about "soul sleep."

- **"The apple of His eye" (Deut. 32:10):** Literally "the little man of His eye," referring to the reflection seen in the pupil. The idiom means someone is precious and carefully protected. Literalism obscures the beauty of the expression.

- **"To heap burning coals on his head" (Rom. 12:20):** A Greek idiom for bringing shame and repentance through kindness. Pressed literally, it could suggest cruelty, the very opposite of Paul's intent.

- **"Gird up the loins of your mind" (1 Pet. 1:13):** An idiom for readiness and discipline. Literalizing it would lead to bizarre mental images rather than clear exhortation.

The Dangers of Literalism

When idioms are forced into literal sense, several dangers arise:

1. **Doctrinal Error:** Misunderstanding idioms can produce unbiblical teachings (e.g., reading "sleep" in death texts as denial of resurrection or consciousness).

2. **Loss of Meaning:** Literalism often flattens or obscures the intended force of the idiom. The richness of imagery and the power of expression are lost when reduced to nonsense.

3. **Distortion of God's Word:** By imposing meanings never intended by the inspired author, literalism undermines the authority of Scripture. It replaces the true message with human invention.

Guarding Against Literalism

To avoid literalism, interpreters must:

- **Study Historical Usage**: Research how phrases functioned in Hebrew or Greek culture, using lexicons, grammars, and commentaries.

- **Attend to Context**: Let the surrounding passage clarify whether a phrase is idiomatic. If the literal sense does not fit the context, an idiom is likely in view.

- **Compare Translations**: Divergent renderings often signal idiomatic speech. Many modern translations convert idioms into contemporary equivalents.

- **Exercise Humility**: Resist the temptation to create new interpretations based on a wooden reading. Trust that the Spirit inspired human authors to use the idioms of their day, and meaning lies in how those idioms functioned for their audience.

Misunderstandings Produced by Literalism

Scripture itself provides many examples where literalism would lead to serious error. When the Old Testament reports that a king "slept with his fathers," the phrase is a Hebrew idiom for death and burial in the family tomb. If taken literally, it has been misused to support the false doctrine of "soul sleep." Likewise, when Moses describes Israel as "the apple of Jehovah's eye," the Hebrew literally says "the little man of His eye," a reference to the reflection seen in one's pupil. The meaning is that Israel was precious and carefully guarded, not that God possesses anatomical features like human eyes.

The New Testament also demonstrates idiomatic usage. Paul exhorts believers to feed their enemies, explaining that this will "heap burning coals on his head." This does not describe physical cruelty but is an idiom for shaming an adversary into repentance through acts of kindness. Peter urges believers to "gird up the loins of your mind," borrowing a cultural image of tucking in robes before strenuous work. Pressed literally, such expressions become confusing or absurd, and their true meaning is lost.

The Consequences of Wooden Readings

Treating idioms as if they were straightforward statements produces multiple dangers. It can foster doctrinal error when figurative phrases are forced into theological systems that the text does not support. It flattens the richness of Scripture's language, draining idioms of the vividness and force that the Spirit intended. Most seriously, it misrepresents God's Word by obscuring what the inspired author actually meant to communicate, substituting human invention for divine revelation.

Preserving Meaning Through Careful Interpretation

The task of the interpreter is to preserve the meaning of idioms by handling them with historical and linguistic sensitivity. This requires attention to the cultural background that produced these expressions, a careful reading of the immediate context, and comparison with other passages where the idiom occurs. Reliable lexicons, grammars, and exegetical commentaries often signal idiomatic usage, helping the interpreter avoid literalism. Even modern translations, which sometimes smooth idioms into contemporary equivalents, can highlight where idiomatic expressions are in play. Above all, the interpreter must remember that God communicated His Word through real human languages, complete with their cultural conventions.

Faithful Handling of Biblical Idioms

To avoid literalism in idiomatic phrases is not to weaken Scripture but to uphold its meaning. Idioms are part of the Spirit-inspired text, chosen to impress truth upon the original audience in vivid and memorable ways. The faithful interpreter must therefore recognize them, resist the pull of literalism, and communicate their meaning clearly. When rightly understood, idioms reveal the depth and richness of biblical language; when misread, they obscure God's Word and mislead God's people. Responsible interpretation safeguards both the beauty of the expression and the truth it was designed to convey.

Why This Matters

Avoiding literalism in idioms is not about softening Scripture but about preserving its meaning. Jehovah communicated His Word through real human languages, complete with cultural expressions. To honor His Word is to interpret it as intended, which means handling idioms with sensitivity and accuracy. When properly understood, idioms enrich the text, providing vivid, memorable expressions of truth. When mishandled through literalism, they obscure that truth and mislead the reader.

Examples of Common Biblical Idioms and Their Meaning

Idioms in Scripture reflect the life, culture, and worldview of the people through whom God chose to reveal His Word. They provide vivid, memorable expressions that often cannot be translated literally without obscuring the meaning. To interpret them properly, the interpreter must recognize that these expressions were part of the living languages of Hebrew and Greek, carrying a sense that was immediately clear to the original hearers but often obscure to us today. By recovering their idiomatic force, we better understand both the text itself and the theological truths it conveys.

Hebrew Idioms

The Old Testament contains a wide range of idiomatic expressions that grew naturally out of Hebrew life and culture. When Scripture says someone's "nose burned" (Gen. 30:2), it refers to anger, not a physical condition. To "lift up the face" (Num. 6:26) means to show favor, reflecting a gesture of acceptance and welcome. To "walk in the ways of" another (1 Kgs. 22:52) means to imitate their conduct, whether righteous or wicked. Death itself is described by the idiom "to sleep with one's fathers" (1 Kgs. 2:10), not to suggest unconsciousness, but to convey the reality of burial in the family tomb.

These idioms reveal how ancient Israel spoke about emotions, relationships, and experiences of life and death. To interpret them literally would distort their meaning; to interpret them idiomatically preserves their power and conveys the author's intent.

Greek Idioms

The New Testament, written in Koine Greek but deeply influenced by Hebrew thought, also employs idiomatic expressions. When Paul writes of "heaping burning coals on his head" (Rom. 12:20), he uses a cultural expression for bringing shame and repentance to an adversary through kindness. When Peter urges believers to "gird up the loins of your mind" (1 Pet. 1:13), he borrows an everyday idiom for readiness drawn from the act of tucking in one's robe before strenuous activity. When the Gospels describe Jesus being "moved in His bowels" (*splagchnizomai*, Mark 1:41), this idiom expresses compassion, since the bowels were regarded as the seat of emotion.

Each of these idioms would confuse the modern reader if pressed literally. Instead, they must be understood as fixed cultural expressions that convey theological truths with striking imagery.

The Richness of Idioms in Biblical Language

Far from being obstacles to interpretation, idioms enrich the texture of Scripture. They reveal how God's Word was spoken into the real cultures and daily lives of His people. They also remind us that the Bible is not a sterile collection of abstract propositions but a book that speaks through the languages, customs, and expressions of living communities. Idioms are part of the Spirit's inspired design, not mere accidents of culture, and they carry His intended meaning.

Why This Matters

Recognizing idioms and interpreting them according to their cultural meaning prevents distortion and preserves the truth of God's Word. If idioms are misread literally, the interpreter risks false doctrine and misses the force of the text. When they are handled with care, idioms bring clarity, color, and richness to Scripture, allowing modern readers to grasp the text as the original audience did. This honors the authority of Scripture, upholds the historical-grammatical method, and reminds us that God's Word, though written in ancient cultural settings, speaks with power and precision to His people today.

Guarding Against Misinterpretation of Figurative Language

Idioms belong to the broader category of figurative language, and therefore the interpreter must exercise care in distinguishing between literal statements and figurative expressions. Figurative language is not ornamental fluff but a Spirit-inspired means of communication, chosen to press truth upon the heart and memory. When figurative expressions are misunderstood—whether by being flattened into literalism or by being spiritualized into imaginative speculation—the meaning intended by the biblical author is lost. The interpreter's task is to preserve the balance, respecting figures as figures, and allowing them to communicate the realities for which they were chosen.

The Dangers of Misinterpretation

Two opposite errors commonly arise when dealing with figurative expressions in Scripture. On one hand, some readers collapse every figure into literal terms, producing nonsense and distorting doctrine. If one treats Jesus' statement that believers are "the salt of the earth" (Matt. 5:13) literally, the metaphor of moral preservation and covenant faithfulness is lost. If one insists that "mountains skip like rams" (Ps. 114:4) describes geology rather than poetry, the image of creation rejoicing at God's deliverance is flattened into absurdity.

On the other hand, others run to the opposite extreme, treating figurative expressions as an invitation for spiritualizing or allegorizing. Instead of asking what the author meant by the figure, they assign symbolic meanings that have no basis in the text or its context. A psalmist's image of God as a shepherd (Ps. 23:1) may be pressed into a fanciful system where every element—the rod, the staff, the green pastures—becomes a hidden picture of later events or doctrines, none of which were in view for the inspired writer. Both extremes—

literalism and allegorizing—violate the author's communicative intention and undermine the historical-grammatical method.

The Interpreter's Safeguards

To guard against these errors, the interpreter must first respect genre. Figurative language is common in poetry, prophecy, and wisdom, where imagery and parallelism carry meaning. Recognizing the literary form alerts the reader that figures of speech are likely in play. Second, context always determines meaning. A figure never floats free of its surroundings but contributes to the overall message of the passage. Third, the interpreter must ask how the figure functioned in the original culture and language. What a metaphor or idiom conveyed to an ancient Hebrew or Greek audience is the true key to its meaning.

In addition, Scripture itself often explains its own figures. Jesus calls Himself the "bread of life" (John 6:35) and immediately clarifies the figure, identifying Himself as the one who sustains eternal life. Paul speaks of the "armor of God" (Eph. 6:11–17) and then interprets each piece as a spiritual reality. Letting Scripture interpret its own figures is a safeguard against imagination running loose.

Why This Matters

Figurative language, including idioms, is part of the inspired form of God's Word. To mishandle it is to mishandle the message. Flattening figures into literal nonsense dishonors the beauty and vividness chosen by the Spirit. Allegorizing them into imaginative speculation imposes human ideas onto the text rather than drawing out what the author meant to convey. The faithful interpreter must therefore guard against both extremes, handling figurative language with historical sensitivity, literary awareness, and theological discipline. By doing so, he preserves the integrity of God's Word, upholds its clarity, and allows its truth to shape the heart and mind as the Spirit intended.

Edward D. Andrews

Conclusion: Interpreting Idioms

Idioms stand as one of the clearest reminders that God revealed His Word in real human languages, shaped by culture, usage, and shared understanding. They are not puzzles for imaginative speculation nor lifeless phrases to be dissected literally. They are fixed expressions, chosen by the Spirit, that carried immediate meaning for their original audiences and continue to communicate timeless truth when handled faithfully.

To interpret idioms rightly, the reader must approach them with the discipline of the historical-grammatical method. This requires recognizing idiomatic expressions, discerning their meaning within Hebrew and Greek usage, and avoiding the twin dangers of wooden literalism and uncontrolled allegorizing. Each idiom must be understood as the inspired author and the first hearers would have understood it, within the covenantal and cultural context in which it was spoken.

By identifying idioms carefully, avoiding literalistic missteps, and guarding against imaginative speculation, the interpreter preserves the clarity of God's Word and protects the church from error. Idioms, like all forms of figurative language, are not obstacles but gifts—vivid, memorable, Spirit-inspired ways of impressing truth on the heart and mind. When honored for what they are, idioms enrich Scripture with color and force, reminding us that Jehovah's Word is living, personal, and perfectly suited to communicate His will across all ages.

If idioms are misunderstood, they obscure rather than clarify God's Word, leading to confusion or false doctrine. But when interpreted rightly, they display the beauty of the Bible's languages and deepen the reader's grasp of truth. The interpreter's responsibility is therefore to approach idioms with humility and care, always asking what the author willed to communicate. In doing so, he honors the inspired text, upholds the authority of Scripture, and allows its vivid expressions to shape hearts and minds as God intended.

Review Questions – Chapter 11: Interpreting Idioms

1. What is an idiom, and how does it differ from a literal phrase?

2. Why is it essential to interpret idioms within their cultural and linguistic context?

3. How do Hebrew idioms (e.g., "his nose burned," "lift up the face") communicate meaning beyond their literal wording?

4. How do Greek idioms in the New Testament (e.g., "heap burning coals on his head") function within their cultural setting?

5. What are the dangers of pressing idioms into wooden literalism?

6. Why is allegorizing idioms equally dangerous for sound interpretation?

7. How does the historical-grammatical method safeguard the meaning of idiomatic expressions?

8. How does recognizing idioms enrich our understanding of the Bible's inspired languages?

9. Why is it important to ask what the author willed to communicate when encountering idioms?

10. In what ways does faithful interpretation of idioms protect the clarity and authority of Scripture?

Exercises in Interpretation – Chapter 11: Interpreting Idioms

Exercise 1: Genesis 30:2 – "His Anger Was Kindled"

- How does the Hebrew idiom "his nose burned" communicate anger?

- Why would a strictly literal reading distort the meaning?

- What does this idiom reveal about the vividness of Hebrew expression?

Exercise 2: Numbers 6:24–26 – "Jehovah Make His Face Shine Upon You"

- How does this idiomatic blessing express favor and acceptance?
- Why is it important not to over-spiritualize the imagery?
- What covenantal truth is communicated through this idiom?

Exercise 3: Romans 12:20 – "Heap Burning Coals on His Head"

- What cultural background helps explain this idiom?
- How should this phrase be understood in light of Paul's call to love one's enemy?
- What dangers arise from interpreting it literally or speculatively?

CHAPTER 12 Interpreting Parables

The Nature of Parables as Comparisons, Not Allegories

Parables stand as one of Jesus' most distinctive teaching methods. They are striking in their simplicity and profound in their impact. Yet, precisely because of their narrative form and symbolic elements, parables have often been subjected to allegorizing, where interpreters search for hidden meanings in every detail rather than discerning the single intended point. Such an approach risks obscuring the very message Jesus sought to deliver. Therefore, to properly interpret the parables of Scripture, we must anchor ourselves in the historical-grammatical method, treating them as comparisons rooted in everyday life rather than allegories filled with secret codes.

The inspired Gospel writers consistently portray parables as teaching devices intended to engage the audience at the level of heart and conscience. They draw on familiar imagery—seeds, soils, lamps, banquets, vineyards—not to obscure meaning but to illuminate spiritual truth through common experience. Jesus Himself introduced parables as a way to confront both receptive listeners and hardened hearts, exposing disbelief and calling for repentance. The plain sense of the parable is what carries divine authority, not hidden interpretations invented by later readers.

Exposition

The Greek term *parabolē* literally means "to place alongside." In the first-century Jewish context, it described an illustrative comparison in which a story or picture from common life was set next to a spiritual or moral reality. Parables were not meant to be puzzles for intellectual speculation but vivid, memorable comparisons that drove home a single central point.

Consider the Parable of the Sower in Matthew 13. Jesus describes a sower scattering seed on various types of soil. The picture is drawn from agricultural life in Galilee, instantly recognizable to His audience. The meaning rests on the comparison between the soils and the human responses to the Word of God. When Jesus interprets the parable for His disciples, He does not assign symbolic meaning to every detail—such as the bag the sower carried, the season of sowing, or the clothing of the farmer. Instead, He highlights the central comparison: the seed is the Word of God, and the soils represent the varied conditions of human hearts. The parable makes its point not by elaborate allegorizing but by a straightforward contrast between fruitful and fruitless hearing.

Another example is the Parable of the Good Samaritan in Luke 10. The parable answers the lawyer's question, "Who is my neighbor?" Jesus tells of a man beaten by robbers and ignored by religious figures, only to be compassionately helped by a Samaritan. Here, too, the parable hinges on a comparison: true neighborly love is not defined by ethnicity, status, or religious standing but by mercy and action. The point is clear and direct. To allegorize the beaten man as humanity, the Samaritan as Christ, the inn as the church, and the two denarii as the sacraments—as was done by many in church history—is to miss the plain lesson. Jesus' intent was to confront the lawyer's heart, not to provide a coded theological chart.

Historical context reinforces this understanding. Jewish teachers in the Second Temple period frequently used parables and mashalim (sayings or illustrations) in their instruction. These were practical comparisons meant to clarify moral and theological truths, not vehicles for hidden mystical codes. Jesus' use of parables aligns with this cultural background, while also uniquely sharpening them to expose unbelief and summon repentance.

Application and Clarification

Recognizing parables as comparisons rather than allegories safeguards faithful interpretation in several ways. First, it restrains us from speculative readings that fracture the text into disconnected symbols. Instead of searching for hidden codes, we focus on the central point that Jesus intended. Second, it keeps us anchored in the historical realities familiar to the original audience, which preserves authorial intent. The agricultural, social, and economic settings of the parables were not random but carefully chosen illustrations from daily life in first-century Palestine. Third, this approach ensures that application flows naturally from the text rather than being imposed by the interpreter.

For example, when modern readers approach the Parable of the Lost Sheep in Luke 15, they should not assign arbitrary meaning to the ninety-nine sheep, the wilderness, or the shoulders of the shepherd. The central comparison is unmistakable: Jehovah's joy in recovering the lost far exceeds human expectations of mercy. The parable communicates the extravagant grace of God toward sinners, and that message must be embraced and proclaimed without distortion.

Why This Matters

Understanding the nature of parables as comparisons rather than allegories protects both the authority of Scripture and the clarity of the gospel. Allegorizing parables elevates the imagination of the interpreter above the inspired meaning of the text, leading to confusion and error. But recognizing parables as comparisons grounds interpretation in the author's intended message, which alone carries divine authority.

For the church today, this matters immensely. Parables are among the most beloved portions of Scripture, frequently cited in preaching, teaching, and personal devotion. When rightly understood, they confront the conscience, expose unbelief, and call hearers to faith and obedience. When mishandled through allegorizing, they become obscured, their convicting power blunted, and their message distorted. The parables of Jesus are not riddles filled with secret keys but clear comparisons that reveal the heart of God's kingdom. To hear them rightly is to be confronted with truth that demands response.

Edward D. Andrews

Recognizing the Central Point of a Parable

If parables are to be understood as comparisons rather than allegories, the next essential step is discerning their central point. Every parable, no matter how vivid its imagery or how detailed its narrative, is designed to press home a single, dominant truth. The inspired writers did not record parables to invite endless speculation about hidden symbols, but to convey one main message that strikes at the heart. To miss that focal point is to miss the meaning of the parable itself.

Exposition

The structure of parables consistently leads toward one controlling theme. The Parable of the Mustard Seed in Matthew 13, for instance, illustrates how the kingdom of God begins in small, unimpressive form but grows into something far greater than its humble beginnings. The imagery of the tiny seed becoming a tree is not meant to be dissected into dozens of speculative correspondences but to emphasize a single truth: God's kingdom advances with divine certainty from small beginnings to grand fulfillment.

Similarly, the Parable of the Lost Coin in Luke 15 communicates one central point: Jehovah's joy over the recovery of the lost. The details of the woman, the house, and the sweeping are not individual codes to unravel but elements of a picture that drives the hearer toward one truth—the immense rejoicing in heaven over a sinner who repents.

The inspired Gospel writers themselves underscore this principle. Often after presenting a parable, they record either Jesus' own explanation or the reaction of the audience that reveals the parable's focus. In Matthew 21:45, following the Parable of the Tenants, the religious leaders "perceived that he was speaking about them." The parable's details build toward the central message of judgment on those who reject God's Son.

This principle also accords with the parabolic teaching traditions in first-century Judaism. Teachers used parables (mashalim) as illustrative comparisons to highlight a moral or theological truth, not

204

as puzzles inviting multiple interpretations. Jesus' parables stand in continuity with this tradition, though He intensifies them to expose the heart and call for decisive response.

Application and Clarification

Recognizing the central point of a parable requires careful attention to context. The parable never floats in isolation but is always set within a dialogue, a challenge, or a teaching moment. For example, the Parable of the Good Samaritan arises from the lawyer's question, "Who is my neighbor?" (Luke 10:29). Every detail in the story supports the central point that true neighborly love is defined by mercy, not by boundaries of ethnicity or status. If one were to allegorize each detail, the message would be lost.

Another key to identifying the central point is observing the conclusion that Jesus or the Evangelist attaches to the parable. In Matthew 25:13, after the Parable of the Ten Virgins, Jesus declares, "Watch therefore, for you know neither the day nor the hour." The parable presses one truth—be watchful and ready for the coming of the Son of Man. The central point is stated clearly at the conclusion, guiding the hearer to the intended lesson.

Recognizing the central point also means exercising restraint. The human tendency is to press parables beyond their intended scope, drawing applications from every minor feature. Faithful interpretation requires humility, discipline, and submission to the inspired author's purpose. When we keep the central point in view, the parable remains sharp, convicting, and life-giving.

Why This Matters

Focusing on the central point of a parable preserves both the clarity of Scripture and the authority of Jesus' teaching. Parables are designed to confront the heart, not to invite speculative unraveling of symbols. By keeping to the main message, the interpreter avoids confusion, safeguards the authority of the inspired text, and delivers the truth with the same urgency with which Jesus first spoke it.

For the church today, this matters deeply. Parables are among the most familiar and most beloved portions of the Gospels. Yet when their central point is ignored, their convicting power is diluted, and their purpose is lost. To hear a parable rightly is to be struck by its main thrust, to have the conscience laid bare, and to be called into alignment with the will of God. Recognizing the central point ensures that parables do what they were given to do: confront, convict, and transform.

Contextual Clues for Proper Interpretation

No parable exists in isolation. Each one is spoken within a specific situation, to a particular audience, and for a clear purpose. Without recognizing the context in which a parable was delivered, the interpreter risks misidentifying its meaning. Contextual clues—found in the setting, the audience's reaction, and the surrounding discourse—are indispensable for grasping the author's intended message. Jesus' parables are not timeless riddles detached from their moment in history; they are divinely inspired lessons anchored in the realities of first-century life and ministry. Proper interpretation, therefore, must begin with careful attention to context.

Exposition

The Gospel writers consistently embed parables within a narrative frame that points the reader to their meaning. This framing is not incidental; it is essential. In Luke 15, the parables of the Lost Sheep, the Lost Coin, and the Prodigal Son are introduced by the statement: "Now the tax collectors and sinners were all drawing near to hear him. And the Pharisees and the scribes grumbled, saying, 'This man receives sinners and eats with them'" (Luke 15:1-2). This context makes plain that the parables are Jesus' response to the Pharisees' complaint. Their central theme is the joy of God in recovering the lost, a direct rebuttal to the hard-hearted self-righteousness of the religious leaders.

The same principle governs the Parable of the Two Debtors in Luke 7:41-43. Jesus speaks this parable not randomly, but in direct response to Simon the Pharisee's disdain toward the woman who anointed Jesus' feet. The contrast between the two debtors is calculated to expose Simon's lack of love and to highlight the woman's faith. Without the context, the parable might be abstracted into a general statement about forgiveness. With the context, it pierces with personal force, confronting Simon's unbelief.

Even when parables are grouped, the context governs their interpretation. The kingdom parables in Matthew 13 are delivered after mounting opposition to Jesus' ministry. His use of parables at this juncture both reveals and conceals—clarifying truth for disciples while hardening unbelievers who reject Him. The setting is thus critical to understanding both the purpose and the content of the parables.

Attention to audience is another contextual key. The Parable of the Rich Fool in Luke 12:16-21 was spoken after a man asked Jesus to settle an inheritance dispute. The parable addresses not abstract human greed but the specific request made before Him. The moral force rests on that context: life does not consist in the abundance of possessions.

Finally, the literary context of a parable—the verses before and after—often provides the clearest interpretive clues. In Matthew 18, the Parable of the Unforgiving Servant concludes a discourse on forgiveness. Jesus introduces the parable after Peter asks how often one must forgive. The story illustrates and drives home the teaching: the immeasurable forgiveness granted by God demands a spirit of forgiveness toward others. To sever the parable from this context would be to obscure its meaning.

Application and Clarification

For interpreters today, context provides both restraint and clarity. It restrains us from reading into parables ideas not present in the text. Allegorizing thrives when context is ignored, because the interpreter is free to invent symbolic meanings detached from the inspired setting. But context clarifies the authorial intent, guiding us to the main point Jesus sought to press upon His hearers.

When approaching any parable, the first question must be: *What prompted this parable?* Was it a question, a complaint, or a teaching moment? The second question must be: *Who is the audience?* Is Jesus addressing disciples, crowds, or hostile leaders? The third question must be: *How does the immediate and broader narrative frame the parable?* These questions, rooted in the historical-grammatical method, protect us from misinterpretation and keep us aligned with the inspired author's meaning.

Why This Matters

Ignoring context reduces parables to abstract moral tales or, worse, vehicles for speculative symbolism. But paying careful attention to contextual clues grounds interpretation in history, audience, and purpose. This ensures that the parables retain their sharp edge of conviction and their intended power to reveal the kingdom of God.

For the church today, contextual reading preserves both the clarity and authority of Jesus' teaching. When parables are interpreted in light of their setting, they remain what He intended them to be— penetrating comparisons that confront the conscience, challenge unbelief, and call for decisive obedience. Context keeps us from wandering into imagination and anchors us to the truth that God has spoken.

Avoiding Over-Interpretation of Details

Parables are designed to communicate a single dominant truth through familiar comparisons. Yet one of the most common errors in handling parables is pressing every feature into symbolic significance, as though each word were a code for some hidden reality. This practice, widespread in church history, distracts from the central point and clouds the clarity of Jesus' teaching. To interpret parables faithfully, the interpreter must resist the temptation to over-interpret details, recognizing that many of the narrative elements simply serve to make the story vivid, memorable, and realistic.

Exposition

Jesus' parables employ ordinary life scenes—farmers sowing seed, women baking bread, shepherds tending flocks, merchants seeking pearls. These details ground the stories in recognizable experience. Their purpose is often to provide realism, not symbolism. The Parable of the Sower in Matthew 13 illustrates this well. The sower's actions, the differing soils, the scorching sun, and the thorny ground all work together to portray responses to the Word. Yet Jesus' own explanation limits the symbolism to the seed as the Word and the soils as types of hearers. He does not invite speculation about the sower's bag, the method of scattering, or the type of thorns. To go beyond His explanation would be to impose meaning that the inspired text never intended.

The Parable of the Good Samaritan in Luke 10 offers another example. Some early interpreters allegorized every feature: the man who fell among robbers was said to represent Adam, Jerusalem stood for heaven, Jericho for the world, the robbers for demons, the Samaritan for Christ, the inn for the church, and the innkeeper for the apostle Paul. While creative, such interpretations obscure Jesus' plain point: true neighborly love is defined by mercy in action, even when it crosses social and ethnic boundaries. The details function to make the story gripping and relatable, not to provide a map of hidden theology.

The principle holds true across many parables. In the Parable of the Prodigal Son, the robe, the ring, and the shoes signify the father's lavish welcome, but they are not independent symbols to be dissected into theological minutiae. They reinforce the central point of undeserved grace, not a series of separate doctrines. In the Parable of the Ten Virgins, the oil and lamps must be understood in relation to the overarching lesson: the necessity of readiness for the coming of the Son of Man. To assign every feature a symbolic role is to turn the parable into a labyrinth of speculation, obscuring its urgent message.

Application and Clarification

Proper interpretation of parables requires disciplined focus on the main point and restraint in handling details. The interpreter must ask:

Do the details serve the central theme, or are they incidental to the story's realism? Only those details explicitly explained by Jesus or clearly essential to the parable's force should be treated as carrying symbolic weight. All others function as narrative scaffolding, supporting the story but not bearing interpretive meaning in themselves.

This discipline safeguards us from two dangers. First, it prevents subjectivity, where the interpreter projects personal ideas into the text. Second, it protects the authority of Scripture by allowing the inspired meaning—not the imagination of the reader—to govern interpretation. The parables lose their piercing clarity when every feature is loaded with independent symbolism. By contrast, when we focus on the central thrust, the parables strike with the convicting power Jesus intended.

Why This Matters

Avoiding over-interpretation of details preserves both the clarity and authority of Jesus' teaching. Parables are not puzzles waiting for clever interpreters to decode; they are Spirit-inspired comparisons that deliver truth with force and simplicity. When every detail is allegorized, the parables become distorted, their power weakened, and their meaning confused. When read with restraint and focus, they remain what Jesus intended—clear, direct confrontations with the conscience that call for repentance, faith, and obedience.

For the church today, this principle is critical. The parables are beloved portions of Scripture, often taught to children and cited in sermons. Their accessibility and simplicity are part of their power. To complicate them with speculative symbolism is to rob them of that very power. Faithful interpretation, rooted in the historical-grammatical method, keeps the parables sharp, clear, and transformative. They were given not to entertain the imagination, but to pierce the heart with truth.

The Place of Parables in Jesus' Teaching Ministry

Parables occupy a unique and deliberate place in the teaching ministry of Jesus Christ. They are not casual illustrations or entertaining stories, but purposeful comparisons designed to convey the truth of the kingdom of God in a way that both reveals and conceals. The inspired Gospel writers show that Jesus employed parables to press eternal realities upon His hearers, confronting unbelief while nurturing faith among those who were receptive to His Word. Understanding the place of parables within His ministry is essential for grasping both their design and their impact.

Exposition

From the very beginning of His public ministry, Jesus taught with authority, distinguishing Himself from the scribes and teachers of His day (Mark 1:22). While He employed many forms of teaching—direct proclamation, proverbial sayings, questions, and discourses—parables became one of His most characteristic methods. Matthew 13:34-35 records that "all these things Jesus said to the crowds in parables; indeed, he said nothing to them without a parable. This was to fulfill what was spoken by the prophet." Here, Matthew cites Psalm 78:2, showing that Jesus' parabolic method was not accidental but the fulfillment of God's redemptive plan.

Parables served two complementary purposes in His ministry. On one hand, they functioned to reveal the mysteries of the kingdom of heaven to those who were humble and believing. To His disciples, Jesus explained: "To you it has been given to know the secrets of the kingdom of heaven, but to them it has not been given" (Matthew 13:11). For the receptive, parables clarified profound truths with vivid imagery. On the other hand, parables concealed truth from the hard-hearted. Quoting Isaiah 6:9-10, Jesus explained that many would hear but not understand, see but not perceive, because their hearts were dull (Matthew 13:13-15). In this way, parables became both an instrument of revelation and of judgment.

This dual function is evident in many places. The Parable of the Wicked Tenants in Matthew 21 exposed the religious leaders' rejection of God's Son. They understood the parable's meaning and perceived that He was speaking against them, yet their hardened hearts only deepened in resistance. Conversely, when Jesus told the Parable of the Mustard Seed or the Leaven, His disciples were given insight into the nature of the kingdom—how it grows, often unseen, from the smallest beginnings into great fulfillment.

The use of parables also highlights the Christ-centered nature of Jesus' teaching ministry. Unlike other rabbis, who used parables primarily to illustrate moral lessons, Jesus' parables consistently pointed to the realities of the kingdom that He Himself was inaugurating. They were not abstract moral tales but kingdom confrontations, grounded in His identity as the Messiah and the Son of God.

Application and Clarification

Recognizing the place of parables in Jesus' ministry safeguards interpretation by reminding us of their function. They are not merely simple stories for children's instruction, nor are they mystical riddles open to endless speculation. They are kingdom instruments that divide hearers into two groups: those who hear with faith and those who harden themselves in unbelief. This distinction is critical. The clarity of parables depends not on clever decoding but on a heart receptive to the Word of God.

This also clarifies why Jesus often gave private explanations of parables to His disciples. The meaning was not hidden because it was mysterious in itself, but because unbelief blinded many from perceiving what was plain. Those who sought Him in faith received explanation and illumination, while those who rejected Him were left in their hardness. This pattern shows the seriousness of hearing the Word: parables demand response.

For modern interpreters, acknowledging the place of parables in Jesus' teaching ministry keeps us from reducing them to moral lessons detached from the kingdom. The parables cannot be rightly understood apart from the person of Christ, His kingdom mission, and His call to repentance and faith. They are not simply stories about how to live, but declarations of God's reign, confronting unbelief and inviting submission to Jesus as Lord.

Why This Matters

The place of parables in Jesus' teaching ministry highlights the urgency and seriousness of hearing the Word of God. Parables are not ornamental; they are central to the proclamation of the kingdom. They both reveal and conceal, depending on the posture of the hearer's heart. For the church today, this underscores the necessity of humble, receptive listening. Parables cannot be approached with detached curiosity or speculative imagination, but with a readiness to be confronted, corrected, and transformed by Christ.

Understanding their place in Jesus' ministry also guards us from reducing them to sentimental stories or allegorical puzzles. Instead, it directs us to hear them as kingdom proclamations—comparisons drawn from life to reveal the reality of God's reign through Christ. To receive them rightly is to receive Christ Himself; to reject them is to reject the very King they proclaim.

Conclusion: Interpreting Parables

Parables are among the most striking and memorable elements of Jesus' teaching ministry, yet they are also among the most misused when divorced from their intended function. This chapter has established several essential truths for interpreting them faithfully. First, parables are comparisons, not allegories. They are given to confront the conscience with one central truth, not to invite speculation about hidden codes. Second, every parable has a single main point, discerned by careful attention to its context and reinforced by Jesus' own explanations. Third, the details of a parable serve the narrative, lending realism and force, but they are not independent symbols to be pressed beyond their role. Fourth, parables must always be understood within the broader framework of Jesus' ministry. They are instruments of the kingdom—revealing truth to the humble while concealing it from the hard-hearted.

The interpreter who honors these principles remains safely within the bounds of the historical-grammatical method, protected from the distortions of allegorizing or over-interpretation. Such an approach safeguards both the authority of Scripture and the clarity of Jesus' teaching. The parables retain their God-given purpose: to expose unbelief, to call sinners to repentance, and to shape disciples into obedient followers of the King.

For the church today, the lesson is clear. Parables demand humility from the reader. They cannot be mastered by cleverness or decoded by imagination. They must be received with the same posture Jesus required from His original hearers—hearts open to truth, wills ready to obey, and faith eager to embrace the realities of the kingdom. Interpreted rightly, parables continue to confront, convict, and transform, just as they did when first spoken by the Master Teacher.

Review Questions – Chapter 12: Interpreting Parables

1. Why must parables be treated as comparisons rather than allegories?

2. How does the Parable of the Sower illustrate the importance of focusing on the central point rather than assigning meaning to every detail?

3. What dangers arise when interpreters attempt to find hidden meanings in every feature of a parable?

4. How does context (audience, setting, preceding and following verses) shape the meaning of parables?

5. Why is it significant that Jesus often explained parables privately to His disciples?

6. How does the Parable of the Good Samaritan expose the errors of allegorizing?

7. What is meant by the "dual function" of parables in revealing truth to the humble and concealing it from the hard-hearted?

8. Why is it dangerous to reduce parables to moral lessons detached from the kingdom of God?

9. How do parables demand a response from the hearer rather than passive reflection?

10. In what way does recognizing the place of parables in Jesus' ministry safeguard their interpretation for the church today?

Exercises in Interpretation – Chapter 12: Interpreting Parables

Exercise 1: Matthew 13:31-32 – The Mustard Seed

- What is the central truth conveyed through the growth of the seed into a tree?

- How should the details of the birds nesting be understood in light of the parable's main thrust?

- What lesson about the kingdom of God does this parable communicate?

Exercise 2: Luke 10:25-37 – The Good Samaritan

- What prompted Jesus to tell this parable?

- How do the details of the priest, Levite, and Samaritan support the central point?

- Why is it a misinterpretation to allegorize each character into hidden spiritual symbols?

Exercise 3: Matthew 25:1-13 – The Ten Virgins

- What does Jesus identify as the main point at the conclusion (v. 13)?

- How do the details of the lamps and oil serve the story rather than stand as separate symbols?
- What practical call to readiness does this parable place upon believers today?

CHAPTER 13 Interpreting Overstatement and Hyperbole

Hyperbole as a Rhetorical Device in Biblical Language

Among the many rhetorical tools used in Scripture, hyperbole occupies a prominent place. Hyperbole, or intentional exaggeration, is not a distortion of truth but a vivid device used to drive home a truth with force and clarity. In the ancient world, including the Jewish teaching tradition, exaggeration was a normal and accepted means of emphasizing seriousness, urgency, or importance. Jesus Himself frequently used hyperbole in His teaching ministry. To ignore or flatten hyperbolic language risks dulling its impact, while to press it literally risks misunderstanding the inspired author's intent. Recognizing hyperbole as a deliberate rhetorical device is therefore essential to proper biblical interpretation.

Exposition

Hyperbole appears throughout the Bible, both in the Old Testament and the New. For example, the spies sent into Canaan described the land's inhabitants as giants before whom "we seemed like grasshoppers" (Numbers 13:33). This was not a literal comparison but a rhetorical exaggeration highlighting their fear. Similarly, Job laments that his grief is heavier than the sand of the sea (Job 6:3). The point is not a measurable weight but the overwhelming nature of his suffering.

Jesus employed hyperbole often, particularly in His teaching on discipleship. In Matthew 5:29-30, He declared: "If your right eye causes you to sin, tear it out and throw it away... if your right hand causes you to sin, cut it off and throw it away." To read this literally would be to miss the point entirely. Jesus was not advocating physical mutilation but using hyperbole to stress the seriousness of sin and the radical measures necessary to avoid it. The shocking image presses the hearer to consider the eternal consequences of sin, making compromise unthinkable.

Another striking hyperbole appears in Luke 14:26: "If anyone comes to me and does not hate his own father and mother and wife and children and brothers and sisters, yes, and even his own life, he cannot be my disciple." Here, "hate" is hyperbolic. Jesus does not contradict the command to honor parents or to love one's neighbor. Rather, He employs exaggeration to demand that loyalty to Him surpass all other allegiances. The stark language jolts the hearer into grasping the supreme claim of discipleship.

Paul also employed hyperbole in his letters. In Galatians 4:15, he writes, "If possible, you would have gouged out your eyes and given them to me." The Galatians had not literally offered their eyes, but Paul's hyperbolic language conveyed their deep affection. Likewise, John closes his Gospel with an intentional overstatement: "Now there are also many other things that Jesus did. Were every one of them to be written, I suppose that the world itself could not contain the books that would be written" (John 21:25). The hyperbole magnifies the greatness of Christ's works without intending to describe a literal impossibility.

Application and Clarification

Recognizing hyperbole in biblical language safeguards interpretation in two ways. First, it prevents literalistic misreadings that would turn Jesus' words into absurd commands. No Christian is called to self-mutilation, nor is hatred of family a prerequisite for discipleship. When understood as hyperbole, such texts are seen as what they are— powerful rhetorical devices stressing the gravity of sin and the absolute demands of following Christ.

Second, it preserves the authority of Scripture. Critics often accuse the Bible of exaggeration or contradiction, failing to recognize the accepted rhetorical use of hyperbole in the ancient world. By acknowledging this device, interpreters uphold the integrity of God's Word and avoid false charges of error.

The practical application is clear: interpreters must learn to recognize when the biblical author uses hyperbole and interpret accordingly. The key is to discern the point of emphasis. Hyperbole does not obscure truth but sharpens it. It strips away indifference, compels attention, and forces a response. The exaggeration itself is not meant to be pressed literally but to highlight what is at stake.

Why This Matters

Hyperbole is one of Scripture's most effective rhetorical devices. When recognized and interpreted correctly, it awakens the conscience, clarifies the seriousness of God's demands, and magnifies the greatness of His promises. When misread, it either leads to distortion—where readers take extreme commands literally—or to dismissal—where readers assume the Bible is careless with truth. Neither response is faithful.

For the church today, understanding hyperbole as a deliberate device helps believers read Scripture as it was intended. Hyperbolic statements are not exaggerations born of error but purposeful overstatements to engrave truth upon the heart. They remind us that Jesus and the apostles did not aim to soothe the conscience with mild suggestions but to arrest the hearer with forceful truth. Hyperbole, rightly understood, remains a powerful instrument of divine revelation.

Identifying Intentional Exaggeration in Teaching

Because hyperbole was a common and deliberate rhetorical device in the biblical world, interpreters must learn how to recognize when exaggeration is being used intentionally. Failure to do so can lead to either harmful literalism or careless dismissal of inspired words. Hyperbole, rightly identified, strengthens the truth being taught by heightening its seriousness and urgency. Identifying intentional exaggeration, therefore, is an indispensable part of faithful biblical interpretation.

Exposition

The first step in identifying intentional exaggeration is to recognize the literary and cultural setting. In Semitic teaching styles, striking overstatement was not unusual but expected. Teachers in first-century Judaism often used bold, exaggerated contrasts to drive home a moral point. Jesus, as the Master Teacher, employed the same method with perfect authority.

Consider Jesus' words in Matthew 23:24: "You blind guides, straining out a gnat and swallowing a camel!" This is an intentional exaggeration. No Pharisee ever literally swallowed a camel. But the hyperbolic image exposes their hypocrisy: obsessing over minor ritual details while ignoring weightier matters of justice, mercy, and faithfulness. The extreme comparison magnifies the absurdity of their misplaced priorities.

Another clear example is in Matthew 19:24: "It is easier for a camel to go through the eye of a needle than for a rich person to enter the kingdom of God." Some interpreters have attempted to reduce this statement by suggesting that "the eye of the needle" referred to a small gate in Jerusalem, yet no such gate existed in the first century. Jesus is intentionally exaggerating. The image of a camel squeezing through the tiny opening of a needle is patently impossible. That is the point: apart from God's power, salvation is unattainable for anyone, including the rich.

Hyperbole also appears in the Sermon on the Mount. In Matthew 7:3-5, Jesus asks why someone sees the speck in his brother's eye but ignores the log in his own. The mental picture of a man walking around with a beam protruding from his eye is absurd, and that is precisely why it works. The exaggerated imagery drives home the point of hypocrisy more forcefully than a plain statement ever could.

The apostle Paul likewise used hyperbole to emphasize affection and hardship. In 2 Corinthians 11:23-28, his list of sufferings piles up one after another until the effect is overwhelming. Though every individual event was true, the cumulative presentation creates an intentionally exaggerated sense of relentless affliction, magnifying the cost of his ministry.

Application and Clarification

The interpreter must distinguish intentional exaggeration from literal instruction. The key lies in the overall sense of the passage and the impossibility or absurdity of a literal reading. For example, tearing out one's eye (Matthew 5:29) is impossible as a command meant for all disciples, yet it is perfectly fitting as hyperbole stressing the radical seriousness of dealing with sin.

Another guide is to observe how the author or immediate context clarifies the statement. When the disciples respond with astonishment to Jesus' words about the camel and the needle (Matthew 19:25-26), Jesus affirms that impossibility is exactly the point, for "with man this is impossible, but with God all things are possible." The exaggeration is not to be explained away but embraced as a deliberate device.

A third safeguard is to compare hyperbolic statements with the rest of Scripture. For example, Jesus' command to "hate" family members in Luke 14:26 cannot contradict His affirmation of the command to honor father and mother (Mark 7:9-13). Recognizing it as hyperbole resolves the tension: Jesus is demanding supreme loyalty, not literal hatred.

Why This Matters

Identifying intentional exaggeration in biblical teaching preserves the integrity of the inspired text. Without this recognition, interpreters risk either distorting God's Word into commands He never gave or dismissing its authority as careless overstatement. Hyperbole is neither error nor accident; it is a purposeful device used by inspired authors to engrave truth on the heart with unforgettable force.

For the church today, this recognition deepens both confidence and clarity in reading Scripture. Hyperbolic statements are not obstacles to be explained away but tools of divine persuasion. They remind us that God's Word is not bland or detached but confronts us with urgency, demanding a response. By learning to identify intentional exaggeration, we handle the Scriptures rightly, honoring both their form and their message.

Distinguishing Hyperbole From Literal Instruction

One of the greatest interpretive challenges with biblical hyperbole is knowing when a statement is intended as deliberate exaggeration and when it is to be taken literally. Because Scripture is the inspired, inerrant Word of God, we must never dismiss its language as careless. At the same time, we must recognize that Jesus and the biblical authors often used hyperbole as a normal rhetorical device. Proper interpretation, therefore, requires careful discernment to distinguish hyperbolic overstatement from straightforward instruction. This discernment protects both the clarity of God's Word and the obedience of His people.

Exposition

The Gospels provide several examples where hyperbolic language is unmistakable. In Matthew 5:29-30, Jesus declares: "If your right eye causes you to sin, tear it out and throw it away... if your right hand causes you to sin, cut it off and throw it away." To take this literally would be to contradict the rest of Scripture, which teaches that sin originates in the heart (Mark 7:21-23). Physical mutilation does not remove sinful desire. The hyperbole is deliberate: Jesus is stressing in the strongest possible terms the seriousness of sin and the radical steps required to avoid it.

Another case is Luke 14:26, where Jesus says: "If anyone comes to me and does not hate his own father and mother and wife and children and brothers and sisters, yes, and even his own life, he cannot be my disciple." Interpreted literally, this would contradict Jesus' own affirmation of the command to honor parents and His consistent teaching to love others. Recognized as hyperbole, however, the meaning becomes clear: loyalty to Jesus must surpass every other human tie, to the point that all other allegiances seem like hatred by comparison.

By contrast, some passages demand literal obedience. When Jesus commands in Matthew 28:19, "Go therefore and make disciples of all nations," there is no exaggeration. The imperative is plain and binding. Similarly, when Paul exhorts believers to "flee from sexual immorality" (1 Corinthians 6:18), the instruction is not overstatement but direct command.

The key lies in authorial intent and contextual sense. Hyperbole is used to shock, to exaggerate impossibility, or to create an absurd image that presses home a truth. Literal instruction, on the other hand, is given in direct commands or plain assertions without exaggeration.

Application and Clarification

Distinguishing hyperbole from literal instruction requires several interpretive safeguards. First, the broader teaching of Scripture must guide us. If a literal interpretation would contradict clear biblical commands, hyperbole is likely at work. For instance, Jesus' call to "hate" one's family cannot override His command to love one's neighbor; it must be understood as hyperbolic.

Second, the plausibility of literal obedience should be weighed. Commands to pluck out eyes or swallow camels (Matthew 23:24) are deliberately impossible or absurd. Commands to forgive others (Matthew 18:22) or to pray without ceasing (1 Thessalonians 5:17), while demanding, are realistic instructions that express divine expectations.

Third, the immediate context often provides clarification. When Jesus speaks of camels passing through the eye of a needle (Matthew 19:24), His disciples respond in astonishment, prompting His statement that salvation is impossible apart from God. The impossibility signals hyperbole, while the follow-up teaching clarifies the literal truth behind it.

Why This Matters

Failing to distinguish hyperbole from literal instruction either burdens believers with impossible misapplications or strips the text of its force. To take hyperbole literally can lead to distorted practices, while dismissing literal commands as exaggeration undermines obedience. Recognizing the difference allows the interpreter to honor both the rhetorical power of hyperbole and the binding authority of God's commands.

For the church today, this discernment is essential. Believers must not mutilate themselves in misguided attempts at holiness, nor should they dismiss Christ's demands for radical discipleship as mere overstatement. Hyperbole magnifies truth; literal commands direct obedience. Faithful interpretation means respecting both devices and responding rightly to each. Properly distinguished, the Scriptures confront us with both the seriousness of God's demands and the clarity of His will.

The Theological Purpose of Exaggeration in Scripture

Hyperbole in Scripture is not merely a stylistic flourish or a tool to capture attention; it serves profound theological purposes. By employing intentional exaggeration, the biblical writers, under inspiration, impress divine truth upon the human heart in a way that ordinary speech cannot. Exaggeration jolts the hearer, strips away complacency, and drives home the urgency of God's message. When properly understood, hyperbole reveals the seriousness of sin, the radical demands of discipleship, the surpassing greatness of God's promises, and the utter impossibility of salvation apart from divine grace. Recognizing these theological purposes safeguards us from trivializing hyperbolic statements or, conversely, from pressing them into wooden literalism.

Exposition

One primary theological purpose of exaggeration in Scripture is to **expose the seriousness of sin and the radical steps required to resist it**. In Matthew 5:29-30, Jesus commands His hearers to tear out an eye or cut off a hand if it causes sin. Taken literally, such actions would accomplish nothing, for sin springs from the heart (Mark 7:21-23). But as hyperbole, the command exposes the deadly seriousness of sin and the uncompromising demand that nothing be tolerated which leads to destruction. The exaggeration magnifies the absolute necessity of holiness in the life of a disciple.

Another theological purpose is to **highlight the absolute supremacy of loyalty to Christ**. In Luke 14:26, Jesus states that unless a disciple "hates" his father, mother, wife, children, brothers, sisters, and even his own life, he cannot follow Him. This exaggerated contrast presses home the reality that allegiance to Christ transcends every other human tie. The language is stark to awaken the conscience: discipleship requires undivided loyalty, even if it costs one's most precious relationships.

Hyperbole also serves to **demonstrate human inability and the necessity of divine grace**. When Jesus says that it is easier for a camel to pass through the eye of a needle than for a rich man to enter the kingdom (Matthew 19:24), the absurd impossibility communicates a theological truth. Salvation is impossible by human effort; it requires the intervention of God. The hyperbolic image makes the point unforgettable and underscores grace as the only foundation for eternal life.

In addition, exaggeration is employed to **magnify God's greatness and the abundance of His works**. John concludes his Gospel by writing that the world itself could not contain all the books if everything Jesus did were written down (John 21:25). This intentional overstatement magnifies the glory of Christ, impressing upon the reader the immeasurable nature of His deeds. Similarly, Paul speaks of a "weight of glory beyond all comparison" (2 Corinthians 4:17). The piling up of superlatives conveys that no earthly measure can capture the greatness of God's promises.

Application and Clarification

Recognizing the theological purposes of exaggeration in Scripture protects against misinterpretation. It prevents a literalistic reading that would burden believers with absurd practices, while also guarding against the opposite error of dismissing hyperbolic statements as unimportant. Hyperbole is not to be explained away but embraced for what it is: a divine tool to engrave truth with force.

For the interpreter, the task is to identify the theological thrust behind the exaggeration. Does it magnify the seriousness of sin? Does it demand absolute loyalty to Christ? Does it highlight human inability and God's sufficiency? Does it exalt the glory of God and His kingdom? These questions keep the focus on the inspired author's purpose, not on speculative or superficial explanations.

This understanding also strengthens proclamation. Preachers and teachers who grasp the theological function of hyperbole can communicate the piercing urgency of Jesus' words without falling into distortion. They can explain why the language is extreme, what truth it presses home, and how hearers must respond.

Why This Matters

Hyperbole in Scripture is not careless exaggeration but purposeful theology. It drives home truths that ordinary language could not carry with equal weight. By recognizing its theological purpose, the church honors both the form and the force of God's Word. Believers are reminded that Jesus did not speak to soothe the conscience with mild suggestions but to confront it with demands that require repentance, faith, and obedience.

For the church today, this recognition ensures that the radical edge of Jesus' teaching is not dulled. Hyperbolic statements expose the seriousness of sin, demand absolute loyalty, magnify God's greatness, and exalt His grace. They do not weaken truth but intensify it. To understand their purpose is to hear Scripture as it was intended: not as casual words but as the living voice of God pressing eternal realities upon the heart.

Safeguards Against Misreading Hyperbolic Sayings

Because hyperbole in Scripture is deliberate exaggeration meant to sharpen truth, it must be handled carefully. Without discernment, the interpreter may either press exaggerated sayings into literal commands or dismiss them as careless overstatement. Both errors distort the meaning of the inspired text. To interpret faithfully, safeguards must be applied that preserve the integrity of God's Word while recognizing the rhetorical function of hyperbole. These safeguards keep interpretation aligned with the historical-grammatical method, ensuring that truth is proclaimed as the biblical author intended.

Exposition

The first safeguard is **to read hyperbolic statements within their immediate context**. Scripture itself often clarifies the intended meaning. For example, when Jesus declares that it is easier for a camel to pass through the eye of a needle than for a rich person to enter the kingdom (Matthew 19:24), the disciples' astonishment confirms the impossibility being conveyed. Jesus' follow-up—"With man this is impossible, but with God all things are possible" (v. 26)—explains the theological thrust. Context makes clear that the statement is hyperbolic, stressing human inability apart from divine grace.

A second safeguard is **to compare hyperbolic statements with the rest of Scripture**. Jesus' command in Luke 14:26 to "hate" one's family cannot contradict the clear biblical command to honor parents and love one's neighbor. Recognizing hyperbole resolves the tension: loyalty to Christ must be supreme, not literal hatred of family. Scripture interprets Scripture, ensuring that exaggeration is rightly understood.

A third safeguard is **to test the plausibility of literal application**. Hyperbolic sayings often employ impossible or absurd imagery—swallowing camels (Matthew 23:24), carrying logs in the eye (Matthew 7:3-5), or cutting off body parts (Matthew 5:29-30). These images are intentionally extreme to expose hypocrisy or highlight urgency. Recognizing their impossibility protects against harmful misapplications, such as self-mutilation or needless guilt.

A fourth safeguard is **to identify the theological purpose behind the hyperbole**. Hyperbole always intensifies truth, not diminishes it. Whether it is exposing the seriousness of sin, demanding radical discipleship, or magnifying God's glory, exaggeration serves a theological function. Keeping that function in view prevents both literalism and dismissal.

Application and Clarification

For interpreters today, these safeguards provide a framework for responsible handling of hyperbolic sayings. Instead of stumbling over exaggeration, believers can appreciate the rhetorical force of Jesus' teaching. Proper safeguards allow hyperbole to pierce the conscience with its intended urgency while guarding against distortion.

Teachers and preachers, in particular, must explain to their hearers why hyperbolic statements sound extreme and how they function in biblical teaching. Doing so reassures believers that such language does not conflict with the rest of Scripture and that it is not intended to burden them with impossible commands. Instead, it magnifies the seriousness of sin, the supremacy of Christ, and the necessity of faith.

Why This Matters

Hyperbolic sayings, when misread, can lead to either error or unbelief. Taken literally, they create impossible or dangerous applications. Dismissed as exaggeration without purpose, they are stripped of their authority. But when interpreted with safeguards, hyperbole is understood as a deliberate rhetorical device that presses divine truth with striking clarity.

For the church today, these safeguards ensure that the radical force of Jesus' teaching is preserved without distortion. They remind us that hyperbole is not an obstacle to interpretation but a God-ordained means of communication, designed to confront the conscience and demand response. Safeguards against misreading keep the church faithful to both the meaning and the power of God's Word.

Conclusion: Interpreting Overstatement and Hyperbole

Hyperbole is woven deeply into the fabric of biblical communication, particularly in the teaching ministry of Jesus Christ. Far from being careless exaggeration, it is a purposeful rhetorical device chosen by the inspired authors to magnify truth, awaken the conscience, and press home divine realities with unforgettable force. In this chapter we have observed that hyperbole functions to expose the seriousness of sin, to demand supreme loyalty to Christ, to demonstrate the impossibility of salvation apart from God's grace, and to magnify the greatness of His promises.

We have also emphasized the importance of distinguishing exaggeration from literal instruction. Hyperbolic sayings must be recognized for what they are: deliberate overstatements that sharpen truth, not commands to be followed in a wooden or literalistic sense. At the same time, literal commands must not be weakened by treating them as mere exaggeration. The interpreter must exercise discernment, guided by context, the witness of the whole of Scripture, and the theological purpose of the passage.

Safeguards against misreading hyperbolic sayings keep us aligned with the historical-grammatical method of interpretation. They protect us from two errors: burdening the church with impossible or harmful applications on the one hand, and dismissing the sharp edge of Jesus' teaching on the other. By paying careful attention to context, comparing Scripture with Scripture, and discerning the theological thrust, the interpreter honors the form and force of the inspired Word.

For the church today, the recognition of hyperbole as a legitimate, Spirit-inspired device is crucial. Hyperbolic sayings remind us that Jesus was not a tame teacher offering gentle suggestions but the Son of God delivering urgent truth about sin, salvation, and the kingdom. His words strike with intentional severity, not to confuse or discourage, but to awaken faith, call for repentance, and demand full allegiance. Interpreted rightly, hyperbole does not weaken the clarity of Scripture but strengthens it, ensuring that God's Word confronts the conscience as it was intended.

Review Questions – Chapter 13: Interpreting Overstatement and Hyperbole

1. What is hyperbole, and how was it used in ancient Jewish and Greco-Roman teaching traditions?

2. Why is it important to recognize that hyperbole in Scripture is intentional exaggeration rather than error?

3. How do Old Testament examples such as Numbers 13:33 and Job 6:3 demonstrate the use of hyperbole?

4. How does Jesus' command in Matthew 5:29–30 illustrate the purpose of hyperbole in teaching about sin?

5. Why must Luke 14:26 ("hate father and mother") be read as hyperbole rather than literal instruction?

6. How did Paul and John use hyperbole in their writings to intensify their message?

7. What dangers arise from taking hyperbolic sayings literally? What dangers arise from dismissing them as careless exaggeration?

8. How does distinguishing between hyperbole and literal command safeguard the authority of Scripture?

9. What theological purposes does hyperbole serve in Scripture (e.g., seriousness of sin, supremacy of Christ, divine grace)?

10. How do interpretive safeguards protect the church from both misapplication and unbelief when reading hyperbolic statements?

Exercises in Interpretation – Chapter 13: Interpreting Overstatement and Hyperbole

Exercise 1: Matthew 7:3-5 - The Speck and the Log

- Identify the exaggerated image Jesus uses.

- What truth does this hyperbole expose about hypocrisy?

- Why would a literal reading distort His meaning?

Exercise 2: Luke 14:26 – Hating Father and Mother

- How does context clarify this hyperbolic statement?

- How does it align with Jesus' command to honor parents and love others?

- What is the main theological demand pressed by this exaggeration?

Exercise 3: Matthew 19:24 - Camel Through the Eye of a Needle

- Why is this a clear example of deliberate impossibility?

- How do the disciples' reaction and Jesus' explanation in verses 25–26 confirm the use of hyperbole?

- What does this exaggeration teach about salvation and divine grace?

CHAPTER 14 Interpreting Epistles and Letters

The Epistolary Form: Structure and Flow of Thought

Among the twenty-seven books of the New Testament, twenty-one take the form of epistles or letters. These writings, inspired by the Holy Spirit, are not abstract theological treatises but real correspondence shaped by the conventions of letter-writing in the first century. Recognizing the epistolary form—its structure, flow, and rhetorical features—is essential for understanding both the message and the method of these Spirit-breathed texts. Letters in the New Testament combine pastoral concern, theological instruction, moral exhortation, and practical application, all set within a framework that reflects both Greco-Roman literary practice and the unique authority of divine inspiration.

Exposition

The Common Structure of Ancient Letters

In the first-century Mediterranean world, letters followed a recognizable format. They typically opened with a greeting that identified the sender and recipient, followed by a word of thanksgiving or blessing. The body of the letter contained the main message, ranging from personal matters to formal instruction. Letters often concluded with final greetings, exhortations, and a benediction.

The New Testament epistles generally reflect this pattern, though often with theological depth that surpasses secular correspondence. For example, Paul's letters consistently begin with his name, a statement of his apostolic calling, and an address to the recipients (Romans 1:1–7; 1 Corinthians 1:1–3). The greetings are not empty formalities but theological affirmations, grounding the letter in the authority of Christ and the grace of God.

The Flow of Thought in Epistles

The inspired writers employed the letter form as a vehicle for sustained argument and exhortation. Paul, in particular, crafted his epistles with logical precision and theological depth. The letter to the Romans is a clear example. After the greeting (1:1–7) and thanksgiving (1:8–15), Paul unfolds the gospel systematically, moving from the universality of sin (1:18–3:20), to justification by faith (3:21–5:21), to sanctification and life in the Spirit (6:1–8:39), to God's plan for Israel (9:1–11:36), and finally to practical exhortations for Christian living (12:1–15:13). The epistolary form provides the structure through which this flow of thought develops naturally.

Other letters follow a similar progression. In Galatians, Paul begins with a sharp rebuke (1:6–9), then defends his apostleship (1:10–2:21), unfolds the doctrine of justification by faith (3:1–4:31), and concludes with exhortations to live by the Spirit (5:1–6:10). The logical movement from theology to application is consistent throughout the epistolary writings.

The Pastoral Character of the Epistles

Unlike abstract philosophical works, New Testament epistles are personal and situational. They are addressed to real congregations and individuals facing specific challenges, whether false teaching, persecution, or internal division. For instance, 1 Corinthians responds to reports of immorality and disorder within the church, while 1 Thessalonians offers encouragement in the face of suffering. Yet, because they are inspired Scripture, the letters transcend their immediate context and continue to instruct the church today.

The personal tone is often evident in closing sections. Paul sends greetings from companions, requests prayer, and names fellow workers (Romans 16; Colossians 4:7–18). These human touches remind us that the epistles were written to real believers living in real communities, not to abstract audiences.

Edward D. Andrews

Application and Clarification

For faithful interpretation, the epistolary form requires that readers trace the argument as it unfolds within the letter. Proof-texting—lifting isolated verses without regard to their context—violates the very nature of epistolary discourse. Instead, interpreters must follow the flow of thought, noting how the introduction sets the theme, how arguments build logically, and how practical exhortations arise from theological foundations.

Recognizing the epistolary form also guards against misinterpretation of greetings, benedictions, or personal remarks as if they were incidental. These features often carry theological weight. Paul's consistent invocation of "grace and peace" is not mere formality but a reminder of God's saving favor in Christ and the reconciled relationship believers enjoy with Him.

Finally, attention to structure and flow helps us see the balance in apostolic teaching. Doctrine is never presented in abstraction but always joined with exhortation. The letters are both theological and pastoral, grounding believers in the truth of the gospel and guiding them in obedience.

Why This Matters

Understanding the epistolary form is vital because it allows us to hear the letters as their first audiences did. The inspired authors did not write random collections of sayings but carefully structured correspondence designed to instruct, correct, encourage, and exhort. When we honor this form, we are better equipped to grasp their arguments, apply their exhortations, and live out their teaching.

For the church today, the epistles remain a primary source of doctrinal clarity and practical guidance. By recognizing their structure and flow of thought, believers can interpret them faithfully, avoiding misuse and drawing out their full pastoral and theological force. The epistolary form is not incidental but essential to understanding these Spirit-inspired letters as God intended.

The Relationship Between Doctrine and Exhortation

One of the defining features of the New Testament epistles is the inseparable union of doctrine and exhortation. The apostles never present theology as abstract speculation or mere intellectual exercise; instead, they consistently join doctrinal truth to practical commands for holy living. In the epistolary form, this relationship is deliberate and structural. Doctrine provides the foundation, and exhortation provides the outworking. To sever the two is to misread the letters, for the inspired authors intended that truth and obedience stand together as one unified message.

Exposition

Doctrine as the Foundation

The epistles regularly begin with rich theological instruction. Paul's letters, in particular, establish doctrine before moving to application. In Romans, the first eleven chapters unfold the depth of the gospel—universal sin (1:18–3:20), justification by faith (3:21–5:21), sanctification through union with Christ (6:1–8:39), and God's plan for Israel (9:1–11:36). Only after this doctrinal foundation does Paul write, "I appeal to you therefore, brothers, by the mercies of God, to present your bodies as a living sacrifice" (12:1). The exhortation rests upon the doctrinal "mercies of God."

Similarly, in Ephesians, Paul spends the first three chapters expounding God's eternal plan in Christ, the riches of redemption, and the unity of Jew and Gentile in the church. The final three chapters then exhort believers to walk worthy of this calling, to pursue holiness, and to stand firm in spiritual warfare. The shift from doctrine to exhortation is not incidental but intrinsic to the letter's design.

Exhortation as the Outworking

Exhortation in the epistles is never arbitrary. It always arises naturally from the doctrinal truths presented. Because believers are justified by faith, they must live in righteousness (Romans 6). Because they are new creations in Christ, they must put off the old self and put on the new (Ephesians 4:22–24). Because they belong to the body of Christ, they must exercise love and unity (1 Corinthians 12–13). The commands are practical, but they are rooted in theological reality.

This pattern reflects the biblical understanding that truth is transformative. Doctrine is not merely to be believed but to be lived. The indicative (what God has done) always grounds the imperative (what believers must do). For example, in Colossians 3:1-2, Paul writes: "If then you have been raised with Christ [doctrine], seek the things that are above... Set your minds on things that are above [exhortation]." The grammar of faith is always indicative first, imperative second.

Pastoral and Polemical Dimensions

The relationship between doctrine and exhortation also carries a pastoral dimension. False teachers often distorted doctrine, leading to immoral behavior. The apostolic letters confront error by reaffirming truth and commanding obedience. In Galatians, Paul defends justification by faith against Judaizers and then exhorts the believers to live by the Spirit rather than gratifying the flesh. In 1 Thessalonians, after clarifying the truth about Christ's return, he exhorts the church to remain steadfast and holy. Doctrine corrects error, while exhortation calls for faithfulness.

Application and Clarification

For interpreters today, recognizing the relationship between doctrine and exhortation guards against two distortions. First, it prevents the error of reducing epistles to mere theological treatises, as though their purpose were only to systematize doctrine. Second, it guards against the opposite error of treating them as lists of moral commands detached from theological foundation. Both distortions flatten the inspired message.

The proper approach is to follow the inspired structure. When Paul says "therefore," the interpreter must ask, *what truth is this command based on?* When the apostle issues commands, the interpreter must trace them back to the doctrinal foundation already laid. Conversely, when doctrine is expounded, the interpreter must anticipate the practical outworking that will inevitably follow.

This balance also informs application for the church. Doctrine must always lead to transformed living, and exhortation must always be grounded in revealed truth. Churches that emphasize one at the expense of the other risk imbalance—either cold orthodoxy without obedience or moralism without theological grounding. The apostolic pattern unites the two.

Why This Matters

The relationship between doctrine and exhortation is at the heart of the New Testament epistles. By design, the Spirit-inspired authors show that truth and life cannot be separated. What believers know about God must shape how they live before Him. Doctrine divorced from exhortation leaves the faith sterile; exhortation without doctrine leaves it rootless.

For the church today, this principle safeguards both clarity of belief and integrity of practice. By honoring the union of doctrine and exhortation, we interpret the epistles as they were intended and apply them with faithfulness. The letters remind us that the gospel is not merely to be understood but to be lived. Faith expresses itself through obedience, and obedience flows from faith grounded in the truth of God's Word.

Recognizing Argumentative Development in Epistles

The New Testament epistles are not random collections of sayings, nor are they disorganized streams of thought. They are carefully crafted letters in which the inspired authors develop arguments with logical progression and theological precision. To interpret these writings faithfully, one must recognize how the argument unfolds from beginning to end. Each epistle has a flow of thought that builds point upon point, so that doctrine leads naturally to exhortation and every section contributes to the author's central purpose. Failure to recognize this argumentative development often results in proof-texting, where isolated verses are removed from their context and misapplied. Understanding the structure of argument within the epistles safeguards against such distortions and enables us to hear the inspired reasoning as the first audience would have heard it.

Exposition

The Logical Flow of Pauline Epistles

Paul's letters, in particular, reveal the importance of argumentative development. His epistles often resemble speeches in their careful structure, though adapted to the epistolary form. Romans is the clearest example. After introducing himself and stating his theme—the gospel as the power of God for salvation (Romans 1:16-17)—Paul unfolds his argument step by step. He establishes universal human sinfulness (1:18–3:20), presents justification by faith as God's answer (3:21–5:21), develops the implications for sanctification (6:1–8:39), addresses God's purposes for Israel (9:1–11:36), and finally exhorts believers to live out the gospel (12:1–15:13). Each stage is carefully linked, moving the reader along the progression of his reasoning. To lift any single section from this development is to risk distorting the argument's intent.

The same can be seen in Galatians. Paul begins by defending his apostolic authority (1:1–2:21), then unfolds the doctrine of justification by faith apart from works of the law (3:1–4:31), before applying the truth in exhortations to walk by the Spirit (5:1–6:10). The argumentative development moves from defense, to doctrine, to application. Recognizing this flow clarifies both the urgency and coherence of the letter.

Argument in Other Epistles

Other New Testament letters follow similar patterns. Hebrews develops its argument by demonstrating the superiority of Christ—

over angels (1:1–2:18), over Moses (3:1–4:13), over the Levitical priesthood (4:14–7:28), and over the old covenant sacrifices (8:1–10:18). Each comparison builds toward the climactic exhortation: "Let us hold fast the confession of our hope without wavering" (10:23). The epistle's theological argument is inseparable from its pastoral aim.

James, though more proverbial in tone, still develops his letter with deliberate progression. From the opening command to count it all joy in difficulties (1:2), he moves through themes of hearing and doing the Word, controlling the tongue, practicing impartiality, and demonstrating faith through works. The development is not random but carefully ordered to confront the inconsistencies of a professing but inactive faith.

Rhetorical Markers of Development

The epistolary writers often employ rhetorical markers that signal shifts in argument. Transitional words like "therefore" (*oun*), "for" (*gar*), or "but" (*de*) often mark logical connections. For instance, in Romans 5:1, "Therefore, since we have been justified by faith" signals a conclusion drawn from the preceding argument and a transition to the benefits of justification. In Ephesians 4:1, "Therefore" marks the shift from doctrinal exposition to exhortation. Recognizing these markers helps the interpreter trace the flow of the author's reasoning rather than treating each verse in isolation.

Application and Clarification

For modern readers, recognizing argumentative development requires disciplined reading. It demands that we follow the flow of thought across chapters and not allow artificial chapter and verse divisions (which were added centuries later) to fragment the argument. When Paul's "therefore" introduces a section, the interpreter must ask, *What is this command or conclusion based upon?* When the writer shifts tone or theme, the interpreter must consider how the change fits within the overall structure of the letter.

This approach protects against proof-texting. A verse such as Philippians 4:13—"I can do all things through him who strengthens me"—is often quoted as a general motivational slogan. But in context, it belongs to Paul's argument about contentment in times of plenty or need (4:11–12). Recognizing the argumentative development restores the verse to its true meaning: strength in Christ to endure every circumstance.

Tracing the flow of thought also enhances application. When exhortations are seen as the natural outworking of doctrine, believers understand that obedience is not moralism but the fruit of faith. When arguments are traced step by step, the authority of the inspired reasoning is felt, not just the weight of isolated commands.

Why This Matters

Recognizing argumentative development in the epistles honors both the form and the message of these inspired writings. The apostles did not write random collections of advice but carefully reasoned letters designed to persuade, instruct, and exhort. When we follow their arguments from beginning to end, we are shaped by the Spirit's inspired logic rather than our own selective readings.

For the church today, this principle guards against distortion and deepens understanding. It keeps doctrine connected to exhortation, protects verses from being twisted into slogans, and allows the full force of the inspired reasoning to confront the conscience. The epistles, read in their argumentative flow, speak with coherence and power, calling the church to both believe rightly and live faithfully.

Historical Context and Occasion of Letters

Every New Testament epistle was written into a specific situation. The inspired writers did not compose abstract treatises meant to float above history. They wrote real letters to real people in real churches, addressing the needs, struggles, and questions of their time. Understanding the historical context and occasion of these letters is therefore vital for faithful interpretation. Occasion explains *why* the letter was written; context explains *how* the recipients would have understood it. By recovering these factors, we safeguard ourselves from imposing modern assumptions on the text and instead hear the message as the first audience would have heard it.

Exposition

The Occasional Nature of Epistles

The term "occasional" refers to the fact that each epistle was occasioned by specific circumstances. Paul's letter to the Galatians, for example, arose from the crisis of Judaizers persuading believers to add circumcision to faith in Christ. Without recognizing this, one might misinterpret Paul's passionate defense of justification by faith as an abstract theological debate rather than a pastoral intervention into a gospel crisis.

Similarly, 1 Corinthians was written in response to reports of division, immorality, lawsuits among believers, and disorder in worship. Paul also addressed specific questions raised by the congregation (1 Corinthians 7:1). Recognizing these occasions explains the variety of topics and the sharpness of Paul's tone. The letter is not a random assortment of teachings but a coherent response to concrete problems.

Other epistles reflect different occasions. Philippians is a warm letter of gratitude written from prison, acknowledging a gift the church had sent and encouraging perseverance in unity and joy. 1 Thessalonians addresses a young church facing persecution and confusion about the return of Christ. James writes to dispersed Jewish Christians, exhorting them to live out their faith in works and to resist favoritism and worldliness. Each letter is shaped by its historical situation.

The Historical Context of the First Century

The cultural, political, and religious context of the Greco-Roman world also shaped the epistles. Roman imperial authority, Jewish synagogue influence, pagan idol worship, and Greco-Roman philosophy all formed the background against which the apostles wrote. For instance, Paul's teaching on citizenship in Philippians 3:20 takes on greater force when one recalls that Philippi was a Roman colony where Roman citizenship was highly prized. His reminder that believers' true citizenship is in heaven confronts cultural pride with kingdom reality.

The same is true of household codes in letters like Ephesians and Colossians. Instructions to husbands, wives, children, and slaves reflect the household structure of the Roman world. By setting Christ at the center of these relationships, the apostles reoriented cultural norms under the lordship of Christ. Interpreters who ignore this context risk misreading the exhortations as either irrelevant or oppressive, rather than seeing their transformative intent within their original world.

The Inspired Balance

While occasion and context explain why the letters were written, we must remember that these writings are not bound to the first century alone. They are the inspired Word of God, profitable for teaching, reproof, correction, and training in righteousness (2 Timothy 3:16). The Spirit guided the authors to address immediate issues in ways that also provide timeless instruction for the church. The letters are both occasional and universal, bound to their context yet carrying divine authority for every generation.

Application and Clarification

Interpreters today must work to recover the historical context of each epistle before applying its teaching. This requires attention to the audience, setting, and presenting issues. Why was the letter written? What was happening in the church or community? What cultural realities shaped the situation? Only by answering these questions can we grasp the author's intent.

For example, reading Galatians without awareness of the Judaizer controversy could lead to a vague moral lesson about sincerity in faith, rather than the strong defense of justification by faith alone. Reading 1 Corinthians without understanding the background of Greco-

Roman idolatry and immorality could obscure Paul's radical call to holiness and unity. Context does not limit the letters; it illuminates them.

Why This Matters

Understanding the historical context and occasion of the epistles preserves both their clarity and authority. It prevents us from reading the letters as though they were written directly to us in the twenty-first century without first passing through their original setting. At the same time, it allows us to apply their timeless truths with integrity, recognizing how the Spirit inspired the apostles to address their situations in ways that continue to speak to the church today.

For the church, this means that every epistle is both a window into the life of the early Christians and a mirror held up to our own faith and practice. By honoring the context and occasion, we do not diminish the letters but hear them as they were first intended—real correspondence, with real urgency, speaking God's Word into real situations. Only then can we faithfully bridge the distance between their world and ours.

Applying Apostolic Teaching to the Church Today

The New Testament epistles were written nearly two thousand years ago to believers living in cultural, political, and religious contexts vastly different from our own. Yet because they are inspired by the Holy Spirit, their teaching remains authoritative and relevant for the church in every generation. The challenge for interpreters is to bridge the gap between the first-century setting and the contemporary church without distorting the apostolic message. This requires careful adherence to the historical-grammatical method, recognizing the original meaning of the text in its context, and then applying its timeless truths faithfully to the lives of believers today.

Exposition

The Timeless Authority of Apostolic Letters

The apostles wrote not as private correspondents but as Christ's appointed messengers, bearing divine authority. Paul reminded the Thessalonians that his instruction was "the word of God" and not merely human speech (1 Thessalonians 2:13). Peter acknowledged Paul's letters as Scripture, grouping them with "the other Scriptures" (2 Peter 3:16). Because these writings carry divine inspiration (2 Timothy 3:16), their teaching is binding on the church of every age. Their authority does not diminish with time, nor are they limited to their first-century audiences.

Principles Behind Particular Instructions

Many exhortations in the epistles are rooted in specific circumstances, but they carry underlying principles that remain applicable. For instance, Paul's instructions regarding meat sacrificed to idols (1 Corinthians 8–10) addressed a pressing issue in Corinth, where idolatry was pervasive. While most believers today do not face this precise situation, the principles remain relevant: the believer's freedom must be exercised in love, the conscience of weaker brothers must be respected, and all conduct must glorify God.

Similarly, Paul's teaching on head coverings in 1 Corinthians 11 was shaped by cultural expressions of modesty and order in Corinthian worship. While the cultural symbol may not carry the same meaning today, the principles of honoring God's design, upholding order in worship, and avoiding practices that bring shame or confusion remain binding.

The Unchanging Core of Apostolic Teaching

Not all instructions are cultural or situational. Many exhortations are universal and timeless, directly binding upon the church. Commands to pursue holiness (1 Peter 1:15-16), to love one another (Romans 13:8-10), to preach the Word (2 Timothy 4:2), and to hold fast to sound doctrine (Titus 1:9) are grounded in the unchanging nature of God and the gospel. These apply to believers in every place and age without qualification.

The apostolic pattern also shows that theology and practice are inseparable. For example, Paul's command in Ephesians 4:32—"Be kind to one another, tenderhearted, forgiving one another, as God in Christ forgave you"—is rooted in the theological reality of the believer's forgiveness in Christ. The application for the church today is not optional but obligatory: because we have been forgiven, we must forgive.

Application and Clarification

Applying apostolic teaching today requires three steps. First, interpreters must recover the original meaning: what did the apostle intend to communicate to the first audience? Second, they must discern whether the instruction was cultural and temporary or universal and timeless. This discernment is made by examining the context, theological grounding, and consistency of the teaching across Scripture. Third, they must apply the underlying principles and universal commands to the contemporary church.

This method guards against two extremes. On one side, some treat all instructions as cultural, dismissing the authority of Scripture whenever it conflicts with modern preferences. On the other, some press every instruction into rigid literalism, ignoring the cultural and situational elements. Both approaches distort the apostolic message. Faithful application honors both the immediate context and the enduring authority of God's Word.

Why This Matters

Applying apostolic teaching to the church today ensures that Scripture continues to shape belief, worship, and conduct according to God's will. The epistles are not relics of ancient correspondence but living words of divine authority, profitable for teaching, reproof, correction, and training in righteousness (2 Timothy 3:16). When the church applies their teaching faithfully, it remains anchored in the truth, guarded against error, and equipped for every good work.

Edward D. Andrews

For believers, this means that every passage of the epistles demands engagement. Whether addressing first-century controversies or laying down eternal principles, the letters confront the church with God's Word. Our task is to interpret them carefully, apply them faithfully, and submit to them obediently. In this way, the voice of the apostles continues to instruct and shepherd the people of God until the return of Christ.

The Authority and Inspiration of Apostolic Letters

The New Testament epistles are not ordinary correspondence, even though they follow the conventions of first-century letter writing. They are divinely inspired Scripture, carrying the full authority of God's Word. The apostles wrote not as private individuals offering personal reflections but as Christ's commissioned messengers, "carried along by the Holy Spirit" (2 Peter 1:21). For this reason, their letters possess enduring authority, binding the church of every age to the doctrines, exhortations, and instructions contained in them. Recognizing the authority and inspiration of apostolic letters is foundational for faithful interpretation and application.

Exposition

Apostolic Authority

The authority of the epistles rests on the divine commission of their authors. Jesus promised His apostles that the Holy Spirit would teach them all things and bring to remembrance everything He had said (John 14:26). He also promised that the Spirit would guide them into all truth (John 16:13). The apostles were not merely church leaders; they were uniquely chosen witnesses to Christ's resurrection, entrusted with His teaching, and given authority to lay the foundation of the church (Ephesians 2:20).

This apostolic authority is evident in the letters themselves. Paul begins many of his epistles by asserting his identity as "an apostle of Christ Jesus by the will of God" (1 Corinthians 1:1; 2 Corinthians 1:1;

246

Ephesians 1:1). His commands and teachings are not presented as suggestions but as binding instructions. In 1 Thessalonians 4:2, he reminds believers that they "received from us how you ought to walk and to please God." In 1 Corinthians 14:37, he declares, "The things I am writing to you are a command of the Lord."

Divine Inspiration

Beyond apostolic authority, the epistles are divinely inspired. Paul affirms that "all Scripture is breathed out by God" (2 Timothy 3:16), a statement that includes the very letters he and other apostles wrote. Peter acknowledges Paul's writings as Scripture, grouping them with "the other Scriptures" (2 Peter 3:16). Inspiration means that the Spirit superintended the writing of the epistles so that the final product is both fully human in expression and fully divine in authority.

The doctrine of inspiration ensures that the epistles are without error in all that they affirm and that their teaching carries God's authority for belief and practice. This is why the early church received these writings not merely as letters but as Scripture, to be read publicly, preserved, and obeyed (Colossians 4:16; 1 Thessalonians 5:27).

The Enduring Authority of the Epistles

Though written to specific churches and individuals in the first century, the epistles transcend their immediate contexts. Their instructions address timeless truths because they are grounded in the character of God, the work of Christ, and the presence of the Spirit. While cultural elements may shape the form of certain instructions, the authority of the underlying principles remains. Thus, the epistles continue to function as the voice of Christ to His church.

Application and Clarification

Recognizing the authority and inspiration of apostolic letters requires interpreters to approach them with submission, not suspicion. They are not optional guides, open to selective acceptance, but binding Scripture, "profitable for teaching, for reproof, for correction, and for training in righteousness" (2 Timothy 3:16). This means that even passages that address specific first-century issues carry relevance, for their inspired principles speak directly to the life of the church today.

It also means that doctrinal and moral exhortations in the epistles carry the same weight as the teachings of Jesus in the Gospels. There is no hierarchy of authority within the New Testament, as though Jesus' words were more inspired than Paul's or Peter's. All Scripture is equally God-breathed, equally authoritative, and equally binding.

For the church, the authority of the epistles demands both faith and obedience. To dismiss or downplay their teaching is to reject the authority of Christ Himself, who commissioned the apostles and inspired their writings. Faithful interpretation, therefore, must always begin with reverence for their inspired status.

Why This Matters

The authority and inspiration of the apostolic letters safeguard the church from error and ensure that its life and doctrine are anchored in God's Word rather than human opinion. Without this recognition, the epistles could be reduced to historical relics, valued for their antiquity but robbed of their binding force. By affirming their inspiration, the church confesses that the same Spirit who moved the apostles continues to speak through their words today.

For believers, this truth is profoundly reassuring. The epistles are not merely ancient correspondence but living Scripture, the very Word of God. They instruct, correct, encourage, and equip the people of God until the day of Christ's return. To honor their authority is to submit to Christ Himself, who speaks through His chosen apostles for the good of His church.

Practical Challenges in Applying Epistolary Teaching Today

The New Testament epistles are both ancient and living documents. They were written to specific churches and individuals in the first century, yet they continue to function as the Spirit-inspired

Word of God for the church today. The challenge for interpreters is not in affirming their authority but in faithfully applying their teaching across the centuries. Because cultural, linguistic, and situational differences exist between the original audience and modern readers, careful work must be done to bridge the gap without distorting the apostolic message. Recognizing these challenges equips the church to handle the epistles with both reverence and wisdom.

Exposition

Cultural Distance

One of the most obvious challenges is the cultural distance between the first century and today. The apostles addressed situations shaped by Greco-Roman culture, Jewish customs, and first-century social structures. For example, Paul's instructions to slaves and masters (Ephesians 6:5–9; Colossians 3:22–4:1) were written into a world where slavery was embedded in the economic system. While the principles of obedience, justice, and mutual accountability remain timeless, the direct social structure no longer exists in the same form today. Interpreters must discern how these principles apply in different contexts, such as the workplace, without distorting the inspired teaching.

Situational Specificity

Many letters were written to address particular crises or questions. For instance, 1 Corinthians responds to issues of division, immorality, lawsuits, and disorder in worship. While these exact circumstances may not exist today, the principles underlying Paul's counsel remain relevant. The challenge lies in distinguishing between what was specific to the Corinthian situation and what applies universally. Failure to do so may either limit the text's relevance or wrongly universalize cultural particulars.

Linguistic and Rhetorical Differences

Another challenge is linguistic. The epistles were written in Koine Greek, often employing rhetorical conventions unfamiliar to modern readers. For example, Paul's long sentences, filled with subordinate clauses (as in Ephesians 1:3–14), may feel overwhelming. Yet these were carefully crafted doxological statements in their original form. The challenge for interpreters is to grasp the rhetorical force without flattening the language into something foreign to the apostolic intent.

The Tension Between Doctrine and Practice

The epistles unite doctrine and exhortation, but modern readers often separate the two. Some churches emphasize doctrinal sections while neglecting practical exhortations; others stress moral application without grounding it in theology. The challenge is to preserve the unity of belief and practice that the apostles intended. To apply the epistles faithfully, doctrine must always be lived, and exhortation must always be rooted in revealed truth.

Application and Clarification

To address these challenges, interpreters must employ the historical-grammatical method with care and discipline. This involves asking: What did the apostle mean to communicate to his original audience? What principles are grounded in God's unchanging character, the gospel, and the life of the Spirit? How can those principles be applied today without distortion?

For example, when reading 1 Timothy 2:8–15, interpreters must acknowledge the specific setting of the Ephesian church, but also the theological reasons Paul provides for his instructions. The immediate occasion may shape the form of the command, but the theological foundation indicates its ongoing significance. Application today must carefully weigh both factors.

Similarly, when approaching exhortations about cultural practices, such as head coverings (1 Corinthians 11:2–16), interpreters must discern the underlying principle of order and propriety in worship, rather than binding modern believers to the exact cultural symbol. This allows the principle to remain authoritative without imposing a first-century cultural marker inappropriately.

Why This Matters

Recognizing the practical challenges in applying epistolary teaching ensures that the church neither dismisses difficult passages as irrelevant nor misapplies them through wooden literalism. The epistles are both ancient and timeless, occasional and universal. By honoring their historical setting while affirming their divine inspiration, the church remains faithful to the Word of God.

For believers today, this means that every epistle speaks directly to the life of the church. The task is not to strip them of their first-century context, nor to freeze them in that context, but to bridge the gap with integrity. When this is done, the epistles continue to guide doctrine, shape worship, correct error, and instruct believers in godly living, just as they did for their original recipients.

Conclusion: Interpreting Epistles and Letters

The New Testament epistles stand as Spirit-inspired correspondence, written into the life of the early church yet bearing enduring authority for all generations. In this chapter we have seen that their epistolary form is essential to interpretation. Each letter follows the recognizable patterns of first-century correspondence—greetings, thanksgiving, body, and conclusion—but carries theological weight in every part. These are not casual notes, but divinely guided writings that communicate doctrine, correction, exhortation, and encouragement in a unified flow of thought.

We have observed that the relationship between doctrine and exhortation is deliberate and inseparable. Apostolic teaching never presents truth as abstract speculation, nor does it issue commands without grounding them in God's saving work. The indicative of God's grace always precedes the imperative of obedience. Recognizing this unity preserves both clarity and balance in interpretation and application.

Furthermore, the argumentative development of the epistles demands that interpreters trace the author's reasoning from beginning to end. The inspired writers build their letters with logical progression, moving from theological foundation to practical outworking. Proof-texting, which isolates verses from this flow, undermines the Spirit's design and distorts meaning. Faithful interpretation follows the argument as it unfolds.

Equally vital is attention to historical context and occasion. Each epistle arose out of real circumstances in the early church—controversies, questions, encouragements, and corrections. These settings explain why the letters were written, yet the Spirit inspired them in such a way that their principles transcend their original situations. By recovering context, the church today hears the letters as the first recipients did and applies them with integrity.

The authority and inspiration of the epistles must never be questioned or diminished. The apostles wrote not on their own initiative but as Christ's commissioned messengers, moved along by the Holy Spirit. Their words are not optional counsel but binding Scripture, profitable for teaching, reproof, correction, and training in righteousness. The challenge of application across centuries does not lessen their authority; instead, it requires careful interpretation through the historical-grammatical method.

Finally, we acknowledged the practical challenges of applying epistolary teaching today. Cultural distance, situational specificity, and rhetorical differences require careful discernment. Yet when interpreted rightly, the epistles continue to equip the church for every good work. They confront error, strengthen faith, shape worship, and direct the life of God's people under the lordship of Christ.

For the church today, the epistles remain living words. They are the Spirit's inspired voice to the people of God, instructing both belief and practice, correcting where error intrudes, and encouraging perseverance until Christ returns. By honoring their structure, tracing their flow of thought, recognizing their context, and submitting to their authority, we receive them as the apostles intended—not as relics of the past but as God's Word for His church in every age.

Review Questions – Chapter 14: Interpreting Epistles and Letters

1. What distinguishes epistles from other forms of biblical literature?

2. How does recognizing the structure of ancient letters aid interpretation?

3. Why is the flow of thought essential in reading epistolary argumentation?

4. How do the greetings, thanksgivings, and conclusions in epistles carry theological significance?

5. Why must doctrine and exhortation be kept together when interpreting the letters?

6. How does separating belief from practice distort the apostolic message?

7. What is meant by the argumentative development of epistles, and why must readers trace it carefully?

8. How does historical context and occasion shape the meaning of each letter?

9. In what way do apostolic authority and divine inspiration guarantee the ongoing relevance of epistles?

10. How should modern interpreters apply the teaching of the epistles without either dismissing their cultural context or pressing it into rigid literalism?

Exercises in Interpretation – Chapter 14: Interpreting Epistles and Letters

Exercise 1: Romans 12:1-2 – From Doctrine to Exhortation

- How do these verses mark a transition in Paul's argument?
- In what way does the "therefore" connect back to the doctrinal foundation of chapters 1–11?
- How does this illustrate the inseparable link between belief and behavior?

Exercise 2: 1 Corinthians 7:1-16 – Occasion and Instruction

- What specific questions from the Corinthian church prompted Paul's teaching here?
- How does understanding the occasion protect against misapplying this chapter?
- What timeless principles can be drawn for the church today?

Exercise 3: Philippians 2:5-11 – The Flow of Thought and Christology

- How does this Christ-hymn fit into Paul's exhortation about humility and unity?
- Why must the interpreter trace the argumentative context rather than isolating the hymn?
- What doctrinal truth and practical exhortion flow together in this passage?

Glossary of Technical Terms

Allegory (as a Literary Device) – A figure of speech in which one thing is described in terms of another, such as Jesus calling Himself the Good Shepherd (John 10:11). Legitimate allegory in Scripture is always clear in context and inspired by God.

Allegorizing (as an Interpretive Method) – A faulty approach to Scripture that assigns hidden or symbolic meanings beyond what the inspired author intended. This method originated in Greek philosophy and was rejected by the Reformers for undermining authorial intent.

Authorial Intent – The meaning that the inspired biblical author consciously willed to communicate through his words in their historical, cultural, and literary context.

Context – The inspired framework in which meaning is embedded: words in sentences, sentences in discourses, discourses in books, and books within the canon. Context governs interpretation and guards against distortion.

Exegesis – The faithful process of drawing out the meaning intended by the author from the text, as opposed to imposing ideas onto the text.

Hermeneutics – The discipline of interpreting Scripture, derived from the Greek *hermēneuō* ("to interpret, translate"). In biblical studies, hermeneutics refers to the principles and methods by which one explains what the biblical text means.

Historical-Grammatical Method – The only valid method of interpretation for the church today. It seeks to uncover what the inspired author communicated by examining the grammar, vocabulary, literary form, and historical-cultural background of the text.

Implications – The principled extensions of an author's meaning into contexts not directly named in the text, yet consistent with what the author willed to communicate.

Interpretation – The act of expressing in words—spoken or written—the understanding one has gained of the text's meaning.

Literary Genre – The form of writing employed by the author (e.g., narrative, poetry, prophecy, parable, epistle), each with its own conventions that must be respected for correct interpretation.

Meaning – The single, fixed truth that the inspired author intended to communicate by his words. Meaning is public, shareable, and preserved in the text; it is never a matter of private imagination.

Mental Acts – The private, hidden experiences of the author while writing. These are inaccessible, unnecessary, and irrelevant to exegesis, unless disclosed in the text itself .

Semantic Range – The total set of possible meanings a word may bear in a language. Context selects the single meaning an author intends in each usage.

Significance – The varying importance or impact that an unchanging meaning has for different readers and situations across time .

Specific Meaning – The precise sense a word or phrase carries in its immediate context, chosen by the author from within its larger semantic range.

Subject Matter – The content or "stuff" a passage talks about (people, events, doctrines, realities). Subject matter is distinct from meaning, which is the author's communicative act about that subject .

Typology (Legitimate, Inspired Use) – A method used by inspired New Testament authors to identify certain Old Testament persons, events, or institutions as prophetic patterns fulfilled in Christ. Unlike allegorizing, legitimate typology is only valid where Scripture itself makes the connection (e.g., Adam as a type of Christ, Romans 5:14).

Understanding – The reader's correct mental grasp of the author's meaning. Understanding is distinct from significance and from personal impressions.

Bibliography

Adler, Mortimer J. *How to Read a Book*. New York: Simon & Schuster, 1940.

Andrews, Edward D. *UNDERSTANDING BIBLICAL WORDS: A Guide to Sound Interpretation*. Cambridge: Christian Publishing House, 2025.

Andrews, Edward D. *BIBLICAL WORDS AND THEIR MEANING: An Introduction to Lexical Semantics*. Cambridge: Christian Publishing House, 2025.

Andrews, Edward D. *LINGUISTICS AND THE BIBLICAL TEXT: Unlocking Scripture Through the Science of Language*. Cambridge: Christian Publishing House, 2025.

Andrews, Edward D. *BIBLICAL EXEGESIS: Biblical Criticism on Trial*. Cambridge: Christian Publishing House, 2025.

Andrews, Edward D., F. David Farnell *BIBLICAL CRITICISM: What are Some Outstanding Weaknesses of Modern Historical Criticism?*. Cambridge: Christian Publishing House, 2025.

Archer, G. L. *New International Encyclopedia of Bible Difficulties, Zondervan's Understand the Bible Reference Series*. Zondervan Publishing House: Grand Rapids, MI, 1982.

Brown, Jeannine K. *Scripture as Communication: Introducing Biblical Hermeneutics*. Grand Rapids: Baker Academic, 2007.

Caird, G. B. *The Language and Imagery of the Bible*. Philadelphia: Westminster, 1980.

Cotterell, Peter, and Max Turner. *Linguistics and Biblical Interpretation*. Downers Grove, IL: InterVarsity, 1989.

Fee, Gordon D., and Douglas Stuart. *How to Read the Bible for All Its Worth*. 3rd ed. Grand Rapids: Zondervan, 2003.

Green, Joel B., ed. *Hearing the New Testament: Strategies for Interpretation*. 2nd ed. Grand Rapids: Eerdmans, 2010.

Hirsch, E. D., Jr. *Validity in Interpretation*. New Haven: Yale, 1967.

Howe, T., & L., G. N. (1992). *Big Book of Bible Difficulties, The: Clear and Concise Answers from Genesis to Revelation.* Grand Rapids, MI: Baker Books, 1992.

Kaiser, Walter, and Moisés Silva. *An Introduction to Biblical Hermeneutics: The Search for Meaning.* Rev. and expanded ed. Grand Rapids: Zondervan, 2007.

Klein, William W., Craig L. Blomberg, and Robert L. Hubbard Jr. *Introduction to Biblical Interpretation.* Rev. and updated ed. Nashville: Nelson, 2004.

Lewis, C. S. "Fern-Seed and Elephants." In *Fern-Seed and Elephants: And Other Essays on Christianity.* Edited by Walter Hooper. Glasgow, Scotland: Fontana/Collins, 1975.

Osborne, Grant R. *The Hermeneutical Spiral: A Comprehensive Introduction to Biblical Interpretation.* Rev. and expanded ed. Downers Grove, IL: InterVarsity, 2006.

Pelikan, Jaroslav. *Interpreting the Bible and the Constitution.* New Haven: Yale, 2004.

Plummer, Robert L. *40 Questions about Interpreting the Bible.* Grand Rapids: Kregel, 2010.

Ramm, B. *Protestant Biblical Interpretation: A Textbook of Hermeneutics, 3rd rev. ed.* Grand Rapids, MI: Baker, 1999.

Ryken, Leland. *How to Read the Bible as Literature.* Grand Rapids: Zondervan, 1984.

Sandy, D. Brent. *Plowshares & Pruning Hooks.* Downers Grove, IL: InterVarsity, 2002.

Schreiner, Thomas R. *Interpreting the Pauline Epistles.* 2nd ed. Grand Rapids: Baker Academic, 2011.

Silva, Moisés. Biblical Words and Their Meaning: An Introduction to Lexical *Semantics.* Rev. and expanded ed. Grand Rapids: Zondervan, 1994.

Tate, W. Randolph. *Interpreting the Bible: A Handbook of Terms and Methods.* Peabody, MA: Hendrickson, 2006.

Terry, M. S. (1883). *Biblical Hermeneutics: A Treatise on the Interpretation of the Old and New Testaments.* Cambridge, OH: Christian Publishing House, 2022.

Thomas, R. L. *Evangelical Hermeneutics*. Grand Rapids: Kregel Publications, 2002.

Vanhoozer, Kevin J. *Is There a Meaning in This Text? The Bible, the Reader, and the Morality of Literary Knowledge*. Rev. ed. Grand Rapids: Zondervan, 2009.

Virkler, Henry A., and Karelynne Gerber Ayayo. *Hermeneutics: Principles and Processes of Biblical Interpretation*. 2nd ed. Grand Rapids: Baker Academic, 2007.

Zuck, R. B. *Basic Bible Interpretation: A Practical Guide to Discovering Biblical Truth*. Colorado Springs: David C. Cook, 1991.

9 781945 757075